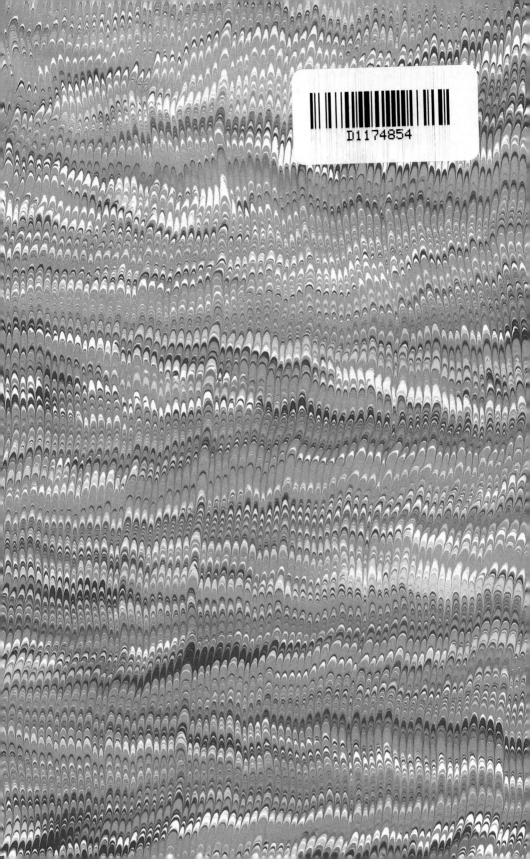

MEN OF HONOR

THIRTY-EIGHT HIGHLY DECORATED MARINES
OF WORLD WAR II, KOREA, AND VIETNAM

MEN OF HONOR

THIRTY-EIGHT HIGHLY DECORATED MARINES OF WORLD WAR II, KOREA, AND VIETNAM

Kenneth N. Jordan, Sr.

Schiffer Military History
Atglen, PA

DEDICATION

To all the men and women who have served in the United States Marine Corps.

AKNOWLEDGEMENTS

I would like to express my thanks to all those who helped me with this book. My wife Louise, my daughter Kathryn, with a special thanks to my daughter Diane and my son Ken Jr. for their help in the research and typing of this book. To Dan Crawford and Bob Aquilina at the Marine Corps Historical Center, John Ligato, and to Ms. Miller, Mr. Anthony, and Mr. Smith at the Marine Corps Military Awards Branch for their tremendous help. They all have my undying gratitude.

SOURCES

The Marine Corps Historical Center, Washington, D.C.
The Marine Corps Gazette, Quantico, Virginia.
U.S. Marine Corps, Military Awards Branch, Arlington, Virginia.
Leatherneck Magazine, Quantico, Virginia.

Book Design by Robert Biondi.
Marine Corps insignia courtesy of Ron L. Willis.

Printed in the United States of America.
ISBN: 0-7643-0247-7

We are interested in hearing from authors with book ideas on related topics.

Published by Schiffer Publishing Ltd.
77 Lower Valley Road
Atglen, PA 19310
Phone: (610) 593-1777
FAX: (610) 593-2002
Email: Schifferbk@aol.com.
Please write for a free catalog.
This book may be purchased from the publisher.
Please include $2.95 postage.
Try your bookstore first.

CONTENTS

INTRODUCTION

"First to fight for right and freedom and to keep our honor clean" are not just words to a song but have been a way of life for the United States Marine Corps for more than 200 years. During those years there have been many heroes. *Men of Honor* is about 38 such men of World War II, Korea, and Vietnam who proudly wear the title of "the Few, the Proud, the Marines."

From the Revolutionary War and our own Civil War to the killing fields of France the Marines have always had a prominent role. Sent on missions all over the world, to far off places like the jungles of Guadalcanal and Bougainville; the volcanic ash of Iwo Jima, and the hills and caves on Okinawa in World War II; the near impossible landings at Inchon, the mountains and bitter cold at Hagaru-ri, Koto-ri, and the Chosin Reservoir in Korea; and the mountains, jungles, and rice paddies of Da Nang, Quang Nam, Chu Lai, and Khe Sanh in Vietnam, the Marines have distinguished themselves with honor. They have always answered the call of duty. As one career Marine (1942 to 1962), who served in both World War II and Korea (he looked like he could still go into battle today) said to me "when the United States has trouble they just dial 911-MARINES and we go."

In *Men of Honor* you'll read the short biographies, many of the actual Medal of Honor, Silver Star, Legion of Merit, Distinguished Flying Cross, and Bronze Star citations for bravery, some eyewitness accounts, and a few newspaper articles about such highly decorated Marines as Colonel Merritt A. Edson who earned the Medal of Honor, Navy Cross, Silver Star, and 2 Legions of Merit in World War II; Colonel Raymond L. Murray who earned the Navy Cross, the Distinguished Service Cross, 2 Silver Stars, and Legion of Merit in Korea; and Captain Martin L. Brandtner who earned 2 Navy Crosses, in battles eight days apart, in Vietnam.

In these 38 men, to quote Admiral Chester A. Nimitz after the battle of Iwo Jima, in World War II, "uncommon valor was a common virtue."

You can have the fastest planes, the largest bombs, all the best equipment in the world but when it comes to fighting and winning battles, the one indispensable ingredient you need is *"Men of Honor."*

1

WORLD WAR II

THE PRESIDENT'S MESSAGE

Following is the text of President Roosevelt's war message to Congress, as recorded by The New York Times from a broadcast:

Mr. Vice President, Mr. Speaker, members of the Senate and the House of Representatives:

Yesterday, December 7, 1941 – a date which will live in infamy – the United States of America was suddenly and deliberately attacked by naval and air forces of the empire of Japan.

The United States was at peace with that nation, and, at the solicitation of Japan, was still in conversation with its government and its Emperor looking toward the maintenance of peace in the Pacific.

Indeed, one hour after Japanese air squadrons had commenced bombing in the American island of Oahu the Japanese Ambassador to the United States and his colleague delivered to our Secretary of State a formal reply to a recent American message. And, while this reply stated that it seemed useless to continue the existing diplomatic negotiations, it contained no threat or hint of war or of armed attack.

Attack Deliberately Planned

It will be recorded that the distance of Hawaii from Japan makes it obvious that the attack was deliberately planned many days or even weeks ago. During the intervening time the Japanese Government has deliberately sought to deceive the United States by false statements and expressions of hope for continued peace.

The attack yesterday on the Hawaiian Islands has caused severe damage to American naval and military forces. I regret to tell you that very many American lives have been lost. In addition, American ships have been reported torpedoed on the high seas between San Francisco and Honolulu.

Last night Japanese forces attacked Hong Kong.

Last night Japanese forces attacked Guam.

Last night Japanese forces attacked the Philippine Islands.

Last night the Japanese attacked Wake Island.

And this morning the Japanese attacked Midway Island.

Japan has therefor undertaken a surprise offensive extending throughout the Pacific area. The facts of yesterday and today speak for themselves. The people of the United States have already formed their opinions and well understand the implications to the very life and safety of our nation.

As Commander in Chief of the Army and Navy I have directed that all measures be taken for our defense, that always will our whole nation remember the character of the onslaught against us.

Victory Will Be Absolute

No matter how long it may take us to overcome this premeditated invasion, the American people, in their righteous might, will win through to absolute victory.

I believe that I interpret the will of the Congress and of the people when I assert that we will not only defend ourselves to the utmost but will make it very certain that this form of treachery shall never again endanger us.

Hostilities exist. There is no blinking at the fact that our people, our territory and our interests are in grave danger.

Chapter 1: World War II

With confidence in our armed forces, with the unbounding determination of our people, we will gain the inevitable triumph. So help us God.

I ask that the Congress declare that since the unprovoked and dastardly attack by Japan on Sunday, December 7, 1941, a state of war has existed between the United States and the Japanese Empire.

• • •

On August 7, 1942, the 1st Marine Raider Battalion along with some other members of the 1st Marine Division landed on Tulagi at the same time the rest of the 1st Marine Division was landing on Guadalcanal, Solomon Islands, in what was Americas first ground fighting in World War II.

When the Marines finished securing Tulagi, they moved to help in the Guadalcanal campaign.

The night of September 13-14, began some of the bloodiest fighting that would last another five months. The 2d Marine Division relieved the 1st Division in December, 1942, and Guadalcanal was finally secured on February 8, 1943.

On November 1, 1943, the Marines landed at Empress Augusta Bay on Bougainville, Solomon Islands and after almost five months of bitter fighting the Island was secured in March, 1944.

In November, 1943, the 2d Marine Division landed on Tarawa at Betio in the Gilbert Islands. Four days later, after some of the most violent fighting in the war, Betio fell, followed quickly by the rest of Tarawa.

On December 26, 1943, the 1st Marine Division landed at Cape Gloucester on New Britain.

Then came the landings, in the Marshall Islands, on Kwajalein followed, on February 17, 1944, by landings on Eniwetok Atoll by the 4th Marine Division.

On June 15, 1944, Marines landed on Saipan and on July 10, Saipan fell, quickly followed by the capture of Guam and Tinian on August 9, 1944.

On September 15, 1944, the 1st Marine Division landed on Peleliu in the Palau Group and, after killing approximately 11,000 Japanese soldiers, secured the island.

On February 19, 1945, the 3d, 4th, and 5th Marine Divisions landed on a small, seven square miles, volcanic ash covered island named Iwo Jima in the Volcano Islands.

After five days of bloody fighting, the 28th Marines, in what was the most famous picture of World War II, raised the flag on top of Mount Suribachi.

By February 28th, the Marines had taken the central section of Iwo, including the two airfields. Then the three divisions, the 5th on the left, the 3d in the middle, and the 4th on the right, started their push north to capture the final two miles of the island.

On March 26th, after 35 days of bitter fighting, Iwo Jima was secured. Its cost, in the bloodiest battle in Marine Corps history, was 6,821 Americans killed in action.

The capture of one more island was needed, for a staging area, before the Allies could begin the invasion of Japan.

On April 1, 1945, the 1st and 6th Marine Divisions took part in the landings on Okinawa in the Ryukyu Islands. After almost three months of heaving fighting, in what cost the Japanese 110,000 lives, Okinawa was secured on June 22, 1945.

On September 2, 1945, with the signing of the surrender aboard the *USS MISSOURI*, the war in the Pacific officially ended.

The Marine casualties in World War II were 19,733 killed and 67,207 wounded.

• • •

Name: Major Kenneth Dillon Bailey, USMC.

Biography - Written September, 1949:
Marine Major Kenneth D. Bailey was Posthumously awarded the Medal of Honor on March 24, 1943, by the late President Franklin D. Roosevelt during a special ceremony at the White House, for heroic conduct during action in the Solomon Islands.

The medal was presented to Major Bailey's wife, Mrs. Elizabeth S. Bailey. The major lost his life during the action on Guadalcanal for which he was cited and awarded the nation's highest military decoration.

Chapter 1: World War II

The citation praised his "extraordinary courage and heroic conduct as Commanding Officer of a Marine Raider Company during the Japanese attack on Henderson Field, Guadalcanal, on September 12-13. With great resourcefulness," the citation stated, "he stemmed a retreat against great odds, reorganized his troops, generally improved the position of our forces, and repeatedly led his troops in fierce hand-to-hand combat for a period of 10 hours despite a severe head wound."

His great personal valor," continued the citation, "while exposed to constant and merciless enemy fire, and his indomitable fighting spirit inspired his troops to heights of heroic endeavor which enabled them to repulse the enemy and hold Henderson Field. He gallantly gave up his life in the service of his country."

Major Bailey, who also won the Silver Star Medal during the initial landing on Tulagi in the Solomon Islands, was born in Pawnee, Oklahoma on October 21, 1910. He later moved to Danville, Illinois with his parents, Mr. and Mrs. Cyrus D. Bailey, who still reside there at 112 Michigan Avenue.

He spent three years with the 130th Infantry, Illinois National Guard, prior to receiving his Second Lieutenant's commission in the Marine Corps on July 1, 1935. He was ordered to the Marine Barracks, Philadelphia, where he completed a course of instruction in the Basic School.

Joining the Fifth Marines at Quantico, Virginia next, he participated in maneuvers in San Diego, and in the Caribbean. In June, 1938, he Joined the Marine Detachment, *USS PENNSYLVANIA* as Detachment and Battery Officer. He was advanced to First Lieutenant on January 19, 1939 while serving on board that vessel.

A short tour of duty at Quantico as Range Officer with the Rifle Range Detachment preceded his assignment to the Training Officer, Recruit Depot, at Parris Island, South Carolina. He then was ordered to Guantanamo Bay, Cuba, in December, 1940 where he Joined the First Marine Brigade. He later joined the Seventh Marines, then the First Marine Regiment, which returned to Parris Island not long after he reported for duty. He was promoted to Captain in March, 1941.

At Quantico in June, 1941, he joined the Fifth Marines as a company commander. In February, 1942, his unit was redesignated the First Marine Raider Battalion. The unit was ordered to San Diego, California in April,

1942, and on the last day of that month it reached Tutuila, Samoa. He was promoted to Major on May 8, 1942, prior to the assault on Tulagi.

Landing on Tulagi on August 7, 1942, he later moved with his unit to Guadalcanal, where he won the Medal of Honor. He was buried on Guadalcanal, and his remains were reinterred in Spring Hill Cemetery, Danville, Illinois in June, 1948.

In addition to the Medal of Honor and Silver Star Medal, Major Bailey was posthumously awarded the Purple Heart; Presidential Unit Citation; Asiatic-Pacific Campaign Medal; American Defense Service Medal with Fleet Clasp; and the World War II Victory Medal.

-USMC-

The following are Major Bailey's Medal of Honor and Silver Star Medal citations:

The President of the United States in the name of The Congress takes pleasure in presenting the MEDAL OF HONOR posthumously to:

MAJOR KENNETH D. BAILEY
UNITED STATES MARINE CORPS

for service as set forth in the following citation:

> *"For extraordinary courage and heroic conduct above and beyond the call of duty as Commanding Officer of Company C, First Marine Raider Battalion, during the enemy Japanese attack on Henderson Field, Guadalcanal, Solomon Islands, on September 12-13, 1942. Completely reorganized following the severe engagement of the night before, Major Bailey's company, within an hour after taking its assigned position as battalion reserve between the main line and the coveted airport, was threatened on the right flank by the penetration into a gap in the main line. In addition to repulsing this threat, while steadily improving his own desperately held position, he used every*

weapon at his command to cover the forced withdrawal of the main line before a hammering assault by superior enemy forces. After rendering invaluable service to the Battalion Commander in stemming the retreat, reorganizing the troops and extending the reserve position to the left, Major Bailey, despite a severe head wound, repeatedly led his troops in fierce hand-to-hand combat for a period of ten hours. His great personal valor while exposed to constant and merciless enemy fire, and his indomitable fighting spirit inspired his troops to heights of heroic endeavor which enabled them to repulse the enemy and hold Henderson Field. He gallantly gave up his life in the service of his country."

/S/ FRANKLIN D. ROOSEVELT

The President of the United States takes pleasure in presenting the SILVER STAR MEDAL to:

MAJOR KENNETH D. BAILEY
UNITED STATES MARINE CORPS

for service as set forth in the following citation:

"For conspicuous gallantry and intrepidity while attached to a Marine Raider Battalion during action against enemy Japanese forces on Tulagi, Solomon Islands, August 7, 1942. After the advance of his company had been stopped by concentrated machine-gun and rifle fire, Major Bailey worked his way, with great difficulty, to the side of a Japanese dugout and attempted to remove rocks from its wall in order to permit his men to attack it from the flank. With heroic and inspiring leadership, although severely wounded, he continued to direct the ensuing action of his company until he was forcibly evacuated, thereby contributing materially to the destruction of the machine-gun nest

*and enabling his men to successfully carry out their mis-
sion. His dauntless courage and complete disregard for
his own personal safety were in keeping with the highest
traditions of the United States Naval Service."*

/S/ SECRETARY OF THE NAVY

• • •

Name: Gunnery Sergeant John Basilone, USMC.

Biography - Written September, 1949.

The late Gunnery Sergeant John Basilone, USMC, of Raritan, New Jersey, was awarded the Medal of Honor in recognition of his outstanding heroism at Guadalcanal. Later, during the Iwo Jima campaign, he was killed in action on D-Day, February 19, 1945.

At Guadalcanal, where he was serving with the First Battalion, Seventh Marines, First Marine Division, he used a machine-gun and pistol to pile up 38 Japanese bodies in front of his emplacement and win his nation's highest military decoration.

At Iwo Jima, Sergeant Basilone again distinguished himself, single-handedly destroying a Japanese block-house while braving a smashing bombardment of enemy heavy caliber fire. For this exploit he was posthumously awarded the Navy Cross. While at Iwo Jima he was attached to the First Battalion, Twenty Seventh Marines, Fifth Marine Division.

Son of an Italian born father, Basilone had spent nearly six years in the U.S. Armed Forces, and is credited with playing a major part in the virtual annihilation of an entire Japanese regiment. He was a Sergeant at the time.

The citation that accompanied the Medal of Honor was signed by the late President Franklin D. Roosevelt.

The story about the 38 Japanese bodies comes from Private First Class Nash W. Phillips, of Fayetteville, North Carolina, who was in the same organization with the Sergeant on Guadalcanal.

"Basilone had a machine-gun on the go for three days and nights without sleep, rest, or food," Phillips recounted. "He was in a good emplacement, and was causing the Japs lots of trouble, not only firing his machine-gun but also using his pistol."

Basilone's buddies on Guadalcanal called him "Manila John" because he had served with the Army in the Philippines before enlisting in the Marine Corps.

John was one of a family of ten children. His father Salvatore Basilone, was born just outside Naples, Italy, and came to the United States at an early age, He operates a one-man tailor shop at 13 South Bridge Street, Somerville, New Jersey. The Marine hero's mother, Mrs. Dora Basilone, was born in Raritan, where the family now makes it home at 113 First Ave.

John has five brothers and four sisters. Two brothers followed John into the Marine Corps; George William and Donald Francis, another brother Alphonse, served with the Army in Iceland. Two married brothers, Angelo and Carlo, reside in New Jersey. The sisters are Mary, Katherine, Delores and Phyllis.

Sergeant Basilone was born in Buffalo, New York on November 4, 1916. He went to St. Bernard Parochial School in Raritan and enlisted in the Army at the age of 18. After completing his three-year enlistment he came home and went to work as a truck driver in Reistertown, Maryland.

In July, 1940 he enlisted in the Marine Corps at Baltimore. Before going to the Solomon Islands he saw service at Guantanamo Bay, Cuba, in addition to training at the Marine Barracks, Quantico, Virginia; Marine Barracks, Parris Island, South Carolina, and New River, North Carolina.

On July 10, 1944, Basilone and Sergeant Lena Riggi of Portland, Oregon, formerly a member of the Marine Corps Women's Reserve, were married. Mrs. Basilone was presented the posthumously awarded Navy Cross.

Following World War II, the Sergeant's remains were reinterred in Arlington National Cemetery, and in July, 1949, the *USS BASILONE*, a destroyer, was commissioned in his honor at the Boston Naval Shipyard.

In addition to the Medal of Honor and Navy Cross Sergeant Basilone was also awarded the Purple Heart, Presidential Unit Citation with one Bronze Star, American Defense service Medal with Base Clasp, American Campaign Medal, Asiatic-Pacific Campaign Medal with 2 Bronze Stars, and World War II Victory Medal.

Men of Honor

-USMC-

The following are Gunnery Sergeant Basilone's recommendation for Medal of Honor, the Medal of Honor citation, the recommendation for the Navy Cross, a witness statement, and the Navy Cross citation:

First Battalion, Seventh Marines,
First Marine Division, Fleet Marine Force,
In the Field.

31 October, 1942.

From: The Commanding Officer.
To: The Commanding General, First Marine Division, Fleet Marine Force.
Via: The Commanding Officer, Seventh Marines.
Subject: Recommendation for the award of a Medal of Honor to John Basilone, Sergeant, U.S. Marine Corps, serial number 287506.

1. In accordance with references (b) and (c), the following recommendation is submitted in connection with the distinguished conduct of the subject named during the engagement reported in reference (a):

In that he, on October 24 and 25, 1942, while attached to and serving with Company D, First battalion, Seventh Marines, First Marine Division, Fleet Marine Force, in the field, and while the noncommissioned officer in charge of two sections of heavy machine-guns on the main defense line, Sector #3, Lunga Area, Guadalcanal, Solomon Islands, during a mass frontal attack by Japanese Army forces. Perceiving that one section of his guns had been put out of action by enemy grenades and mortar fire, and that the personnel of both gun crews, with the exception of two men, had either been killed or wounded, did personally carry an extra machine-gun to the scene of the casualties under heavy fire of enemy machine-guns, mortars, and rifles, and did place said gun in action against the attacking forces, and did then repair one of the guns which had not been destroyed by fire and man it, delivering heavy effective fire against the enemy until a replacement arrived to relieve him at the gun. Later during the same action, when the ammunition supply route was cut off by the enemy, he made his way across the front of his company, in the face of heavy enemy fire and returned with an additional supply of ammunition for his guns. By his skill and daring, his courageous conduct under enemy fire, his conspicuous gallantry and intrepidity, at the repeated risk of his life above and beyond the call of duty and without detriment to the mission of the command to which he was attached, he distinguished himself in the line of his profession and contributed materially to the defeat and virtually the annihilation of a Japanese regiment.

2. Between 10:00 P.M., 24 October, 1942 and 3:30 A.M., 25 October, 1942, the First Battalion, Seventh Marines, repulsed repeated determined assaults by the Japanese Army along an extended front of 2300 yards in Sector #3 and virtually annihilated the 24th Regiment of the Imperial Japanese Army. At 3:30 A.M., on 25 October, 1942, the defending force was reinforced by the Third Battalion, 164th Infantry, U.S. Army. To date some 1000 Japanese dead have been buried in front of our lines and several hundreds yet remain unburied. Though the battalion was at only 75% of its authorized strength, due to casualties suffered in previous engagements and to sickness, and though it defended a frontage normally assigned to two battalions, throughout the attack the conduct of our officers and men was brilliant, determined, tenacious and, as evidenced by the enormous casualties inflicted upon the enemy in this action, decisive.

/S/ L. B. Puller

The President of the United States takes pleasure in presenting the CONGRESSIONAL MEDAL OF HONOR to:

SERGEANT JOHN BASILONE
UNITED STATES MARINE CORPS

for service as set forth in the following citation:

> *"For extraordinary heroism and conspicuous gallantry in action against enemy Japanese forces, above and beyond the call of duty, while serving with the First Battalion, Seventh Marines, First Marine Division, in the Lunga area, Guadalcanal, Solomon Islands, on October 24 and 25,*

1942. While the enemy was hammering at the Marines' defensive positions, Sergeant Basilone, in charge of two sections of heavy machine guns, fought valiantly to check the savage and determined assault. In a fierce frontal attack with the Japanese blasting his guns with grenades and mortar fire, one of Sergeant Basilone's sections, with its gun crews, was put out of action, leaving only two men to carry on. Moving an extra gun into position, he placed it in action, then, under continual fire, repaired another one and personally manned it, gallantly holding his line until replacements arrived. A little later, with ammunition critically low and the supply lines cut off, Sergeant Basilone, at great risk of his life and in the face of continued enemy attack, battled his way through hostile lines with urgently needed shells for his gunners, thereby contributing in large measure to the virtual annihilation of a Japanese regiment. His great personal valor and courageous initiative were in keeping with the highest traditions of the United States Naval Service."

/S/ FRANKLIN D. ROOSEVELT

Company C, 1st Battalion, 27th Marines,
5th Marine Division, c/o Fleet Post Office,
San Francisco, California.

24 April, 1945.

From: The Commanding Officer.
To: The Secretary of the Navy.
Via: (1) The Commanding Officer, 1st Battalion, 27th Marines.
(2) The Commanding Officer, 27th Marines.
(3) The Commanding Officer, 5th Marine Division.
(4) The Commanding General, Fleet Marine Force, Pacific.
(5) The Commander in Chief, United States Pacific Fleet.
(6) Commandant of the Marine Corps.

Subject: Navy Cross, recommendation for, case of Gunnery Sergeant John Basilone, USMC. (Deceased).

1. It is recommended that Gunnery Sergeant John Basilone be considered for the award of the Navy Cross.

2. On 19 February, 1945, Gunnery Sergeant Basilone was serving in combat with the 1st Battalion, 27th Marines, 5th Marine Division, on Iwo Jima, Volcano Islands.

3. On this date Gunnery Sergeant Basilone, moving forward in the face of heavy enemy artillery, mortar, and machine-gun fire, worked his way to the top of an enemy blockhouse which was holding up the advance of his company. Single-handedly, through the use of hand-grenades and demolitions, he completely destroyed the blockhouse and its occupants. Later, on the same day, Gunnery Sergeant Basilone calmly guided one of our tanks, which was trapped in an enemy mine field, to safety, through heavy mortar and artillery fire.

4. Gunnery Sergeant Basilone's courage and initiative did much to further the advance of his company at a time vital to the success of the operation. His expert tactical knowledge and daring aggressiveness were missed when he was killed at the edge of the airstrip by a mortar blast later the same day.

5. It is therefor recommended that for his extraordinary heroism in action, Gunnery Sergeant Basilone be awarded the Navy Cross.

/S/ Edward Kasky

STATEMENT OF WITNESS

I, George Migyanko, while serving with the 1st Battalion, 27th Marines, 5th Marine Division, saw Gunnery Sergeant John Basilone, (287506), USMC, single-handedly destroy an enemy blockhouse which was holding up the advance of his company. Later in the day he led one of our tanks from a trap in a mine field in the face of withering artillery and mortar fire.

/S/ George Migyanko
Private First Class, USMC.

Men of Honor

The President of the United States takes pride in presenting the NAVY CROSS posthumously to:

GUNNERY SERGEANT JOHN BASILONE
UNITED STATES MARINE CORPS

for service as set forth in the following citation:

"For extraordinary heroism while serving as a leader of a machine-gun section of Company C, First Battalion, Twenty-Seventh Marines, Fifth Marine Division, in action against enemy Japanese forces on Iwo Jima in the Volcano Islands, 19 February, 1945. Shrewdly gauging the tactical situation shortly after landing when his company's advance was held up by the concentrated fire of a heavily fortified Japanese blockhouse, Gunnery Sergeant Basilone boldly defied the smashing bombardment of heavy caliber fire to work his way around the flank and up to a position directly on top of the blockhouse and then, attacking with grenades and demolitions, single-handedly destroyed the entire hostile strong-point and its defending garrison. Consistently daring and aggressive as he fought his way over the battle-torn beach and up the sloping, gun-studded terraces toward Airfield Number One, he repeatedly exposed himself to the blasting fury of exploding shells and later in the day coolly proceeded to the aid of a friendly tank which had been trapped in an enemy mine field under intense mortar and artillery barrages, skillfully guiding the heavy vehicle over the hazardous terrain to safety, despite the overwhelming volume of hostile fire. In the forefront of the assault at all times, he pushed forward with dauntless courage and iron determination until, moving upon the edge of the airfield, he fell, instantly killed by a bursting mortar shell. Stouthearted and indomitable, Gunnery Sergeant Basilone, by his intrepid initiative, outstanding professional skill and valiant spirit of self-sacrifice in the face of fa-

natic opposition, contributed materially to the advance of his company during the early critical period of the assault, and his unwavering devotion to duty throughout the bitter conflict was an inspiration to his comrades and reflects the highest credit upon Gunnery Sergeant Basilone and the United States Naval Service. He gallantly gave his life in the service of his country."

/S/ For the President,
Secretary of the Navy.

• • •

Name: Lieutenant Colonel Gregory Boyington, USMC.

Biography: Written 1945.

Marine Lieutenant Colonel Gregory "Pappy" Boyington, most colorful of Marine fighter pilots, who spent twenty tortuous months in a Japanese prison camp after shooting down his 26th plane to tie the record then held jointly by Leatherneck Joe Foss and Army's Eddie Rickenbacker, started his flying young – "Pappy" got his first ride in a plane at the age of eight with Clyde Pangborn, who later flew the Pacific nonstop.

Boyington was born 32 years ago in Couer d'Alene, Idaho. His mother, Mrs. Ellworth J. Hallenbeck, is now living in Okanogan, Washington and with her are two of his three children: Janet, 7 and Bob, 10. A third child, Gloria, 5, lives with an aunt in Seattle.

He attended Lincoln High School, Tacoma, Washington and majored in aeronautical engineering at the University of Washington, graduating in 1934. He is a member of Lambda Chi Alpha fraternity. Always an athlete, Boyington was a member of the college wrestling and swimming teams and is a one-time holder of the Pacific Northwest Intercollegiate middle-weight wrestling title.

After graduating he worked one year as a draftsman for Boeing Aircraft. He entered Naval Aviation cadet training in 1935 and won his wings in 1937. His next four years as a Marine pilot were spent in advanced training and instruction at the Naval Air Station, Pensacola, Florida.

After the outbreak of World War II, he itched to get into action. Just a few months before the war with Japan, he resigned his First Lieutenant's commission to join Chennault's Flying Tigers in China.

Chennault recognized his combat leadership abilities then by appointing him division leader a short time after he joined the Tigers. He shot down at least 6 Jap planes, destroyed more than 30 on the ground, and was wounded during a fight above an enemy air base. Still he felt that the bitter air battles for Guadalcanal, then in their opening stages, might provide better hunting. He resigned from the Tigers. In November, 1942, he returned to the United States and the Marine Corps.

April, 1943, found him on Henderson Field, a Major and executive officer of Marine Fighter Squadron VMF-122. He had arrived just a little to late in the season. Enemy attacks were sporadic during his first tour in the combat zone. No Jap planes were in the skies while he was aloft.

In a rest area, he broke a leg and was told by doctors he would never fly in combat again. Hobbling about camp, raising hell at their decree and fearing a desk job, he demanded another chance. He found it with a restless group of pilots – spares from other squadrons and replacements fresh from the States, who also were awaiting assignments.

Preparations were underway for the aerial push against Bougainville when Boyington talked superiors into letting him organize the "misfits." He scraped together a few combat-scarred Corsairs, set up a night-and-day training program, and about a month later led VMF-214, better known as the "Black Sheep", into combat.

In their initial dogfight, September 16, Boyington drew his first blood in the South Pacific, established himself as an ace in the area, and had the best day of his career. Outnumbered by 50 Zeros, the "Black Sheep" got 11 confirmed kills and nine probables. Of these, five and one probable were Boyington's.

It was the beginning of a shooting spree that with each succeeding dogfight brought him closer to the 26-plane record. Enemy planes were not the only objective. There were plenty of strafing missions and shipping was also fair game.

Boyington led two flights a few days later which sank a Junk, a troop-laden barge, and a large steam launch.

Chapter 1: World War II

He got one more plane September 27th off southern Bougainville. In the same area October 4, during a long-odds battle, he made one spectacular firing run that lasted less than a minute, swung him in a complete circle and dropped three Zeros. A few days later he added another, bringing his total to 16.

Feeling the sting of Allied attacks, Jap fighter pilots grew reluctant to come off the ground. To decimate their ranks Boyington introduced the fighter sweep – a tactic which lured the Japs upstairs with radio insults and shot them down before they had a chance to organize. Leading two sweeps, October 17 and 18, "Pappy" got four Zeros and three probables. The two days action, in which another squadron participated, accounted for 40 Zeros with only one loss and broke the back of Jap air defense in the Northern Solomons.

As a parting shot before the "Black Sheep" left their New Georgia base for a rest, Boyington led a pre-dawn strafing mission through bad weather to Kahili. Separated from the flight, he hit Kahili alone, and exploded three bombers. On his way home he strafed a Destroyer and sank a barge.

On the second "Black Sheep" combat tour, Boyington led the first fighter sweep across the Solomon Sea to Rabaul, December 17 to establish an aerial beachhead for the forthcoming efforts of Solomons based bombers. It was springboarded from the newly completed Torokina fighter strip on Bougainville, to which the "Black Sheep" flew from their base on Vella Lavella for staging.

A typical Boyington anecdote grew out of this first Rabaul sweep, of which he was tactical commander. At the conclusion of the pilot's briefing another squadron skipper asked him what tactics he would use when they sighted Zeros.

"Tactics?" snorted "Pappy." "Hell, you don't need any tactics – when you see 'em, just shoot 'em down, that's all."

But Boyington himself made no contact that day.

December 23, on another sweep, he sent down four Zeros in flames, bringing his total to 24. He made it 25 four days later in the same arena.

December 28, he almost scored twice. Two Zeros he attacked were seen to smoke, but were not confirmed kills.

With the "Black Sheep" tour nearing an end, and with operations slowed down by bad weather, it was January 2 before "Pappy" got another chance at the record. By this time he was getting desperate. A faulty engine splashed oil on his windshield. While fellow pilots gaped, he stood up in his cockpit, pushed a rag into the airblast, and tried unsuccessfully to wipe off the oily film. There were plenty of Zeros around, but he scored nothing and went home disgusted.

The following day, leading a four-plane division, he dropped his record-tying 26th. A few seconds later, fellow "Black Sheep" saw Boyington and his wingman dive into a cloud bank on the tail of more enemy planes.

The two did not come back from that mission. Searches for days afterward failed to turn up a trace of them.

Boyington told on his release from a Honshu prison camp how he bagged two more before he was painfully wounded. His plane afire, he flipped it over 100 feet above the water and dropped out.

Suffering from a broken ankle he sustained when he hit the water, he finally managed to struggle into his rubber boat. Zeros strafed him while he drifted, half-unconscious. About an hour later an enemy submarine surfaced nearby. He was captured, taken to Rabaul and started on a long and tortuous road home.

-USMC-

The following are a newspaper article about Lieutenant Colonel Boyington, his Medal of Honor and Navy Cross citations:

ACE BOYINGTON TELLS
HOW JAPS TORTURED HIM

Aboard the Mercy Ship Reeves off Omori Prison Camp, Tokyo Bay, August 30, 1945. – Surviving 20 months of secret imprisonment and torture treatment with a baseball bat, Marine Major Gregory (Pappy) Boyington, Southwest Pacific flying ace, was rescued yesterday by an expedition commanded by Commodore Roger Simpson.

Boyington, reported dead when he was shot down over Rabaul, New Britain, had more than 20 Japanese planes and the Congressional Medal of Honor to his credit. His mother, Mrs. Grace Hallenback of Okanogan, Washington, never gave up hope of his return. She frequently expressed to newspapermen her belief that her son would come back, although she never heard from him directly or indirectly.

"I was shot down on the morning of January 3, 1944," the Marine ace said. "I had 20mm. wounds in my head, neck arms and an ear, and a broken ankle. My main gas tank blew up. I flipped the Corsair on her back, unfastened my safety belt and dropped 100 feet to the water, stunned."

"My Mae West lifebelt failed to inflate and investigation revealed 200 holes in it. I shucked my shoes and clothes and treaded water. Four Nips in Zeke fighters strafed me until they ran out of ammunition. I finally located my plane's rubber lifeboat and inflated it okay. After a few hours a Japanese submarine surfaced near me by coincidence and took me aboard off Cape St. George. The sub transported me to Rabaul."

"At Rabaul I was blindfolded and handcuffed and my medical equipment was taken away and I was questioned all night long."

"I had no medical treatment for 10 days, during which time my festering wounds smelled so foully that I wondered how the Japanese questioners could stand the stench. On the 11th day another internee was permitted to apply hot water bandages."

"I was held two months at Rabaul, during which time I was trucked into town daily from the camp for continuous grilling. There were 20 other airmen in the camp, but I was singled out as a special prisoner, with no prisoner of war privileges."

"On March 7, 1944, I was transferred to a secret navy camp in the country village of Una, Japan, for questioning."

"It was here that I was given the baseball-bat treatment. It consists of standing with your hands tied while a guard slugged my back and legs with the bat as hard as he could. My rump was so swollen I could see it over my shoulder. Then I got slugged in the jaw about 30 times. Similar beatings killed other prisoners in the camp."

"Even the Japanese civilians took part in administering the beatings. The barber who shaved our heads every two months, delighted in taking pokes at us."

"A Japanese pharmacist mate saw First Lieutenant Bill Harris, the son of Major General Phil Harris, who was captured on Corregidor, reading an item about Russian successes in Europe from a newspaper he had fished from a garbage can. The Jap called all prisoners into formation and then beat Harris for half an hour with a baseball bat, knocking him down 20 times. When Harris was finally knocked out, the Jap kicked him in the face and ribs with his heavy shoes. Fortunately Harris recovered."

"On April 5, this year, I was transferred to Omori where politeness was the order of the day."

"We were required to bow to the Emperor every morning and also to bow from the waist politely to the guard in asking the Japanese for permission to go to the toilet and then on returning we had to seek out the guard and bow again, thanking him. Since most of the prisoners were suffering from dysentery and could not conform to this rigmarole they were beaten and otherwise punished as a result."

"Our menu consisted of milo maize and rice in a combination tasting like chalk supplemented by soybean soup which was mostly water. As an occasional treat a fishhead or a seaweed was thrown in."

"My normal weight of 175 pounds fell off to 110 until I wangled a job for myself as a kitchen kobin (slave), whereupon the combination of my year-old hunger and the available food ballooned me up to 190."

The Marine ace, who still has boundless energy, but a jaundiced complexion, now weighs 160. The first news that the famed "Pappy" Boyington was still alive came last night when other prisoners, learning of the approach of Commodore Simpson's rescue party, painted his name in large letters in the toilet.

Note: The following is an article that appeared in the Marine Corps Gazette concerning Boyington's imprisonment at the hands of the Japanese:

"YUP, IT HURTS"
By Capt. Frank A. Tinker, USAF (Ret)

At first sight, there seemed little about him to distinguish this gent. Square-headed, chunky, dressed in the remnants of a blood-blackened tropical flying suit, he limped out into the pale Japanese sun one winter morning at the end of *I-ku*, or number one hut, in our POW camp at Ofuna. Huddling for warmth against one another on the opposite side of the compound, we noticed that the guard nervously shadowing him kept his bayonet fixed and ready.

Then, later in the day, the Australian camp interpreter hissed in the peculiar sidewise fashion common to prisoners of any stripe, "Have any of you heard of a chap named Boyington? These silly buggers are all agog – claim he's the top American pilot, supposed to have shot down a score of theirs..."

"And what does *he* say?" someone countered bitterly.

"Oh, he's quite jolly about it," marveled the Aussie. "Actually told them he'd lost count – put on an amazing performance."

"One thing we don't need in this camp is a prima donna," was the hard-bitten answer. Such resentment of one's own is more understandable when one remembers that reprisals for any offense in a POW camp usually comes in the form of slashed rations affecting all, notwithstanding any Geneva Convention. At Ofuna, later called an infamous torture camp, we were already down to a bowl of bean paste soup and a handful of seaweed a day.

Fortunately, our new companion in misfortune did not turn out to resemble anything theatrical. He had obviously been through some rough moments already and, to relieve the pressure, he smoked – whenever and whatever he could. He cadged tobacco from ashtrays in the interrogation room, ignoring his inquisitioners' embarrassment, and was not above rolling a stogie from roofing paper. It was inevitable that one particularly snoopy chief guard should apprehend him, and it happened when he was polishing off a butt during forbidden hours. Actually, it would have been difficult to ignore the cloud rising from the latrine cubicle in which "Pappy" was happily ensconced.

Ordinarily such an offense deserved a few angry shouts, a clout or two, and a period of standing at attention in the cold. But bad news from the war front had apparently arrived. The pharmacist's mate, or "Conga Joe", rushed out to deliver the punishment himself.

The camp was lined up at attention, with the still untried Boyington in front of us. The psychotic Conga Joe, beside himself with righteous rage, inarticulately tried to explain the prisoner's grave offense. Finally arriving at the apex of his fury, he instructed Boyington to raise his arms over his head. The Marine complied, deliberately and without subservience or defiance, the expression on his broad face saying only that he mildly regretted causing all the ruckus.

Conga Joe took a slim, new cut fence railing and reduced Boyington's butt to a purple pulp. At each blow, delivered full strength by the sturdy Japanese, Boyington's face twisted in pain. Yet he never seemed to lose control of the situation. When he finally collapsed from a blow to the small of his back he was in our eyes more of a man than the maniac wielding the bludgeon.

A pail of water revived Boyington. He shook his head and arose. As he stood upright again, Conga Joe shrieked at him: "What do you say, na? What do you say now Boyeenton?"

Inaudibly, but unmistakably, in such a quiet tone that nobody unfamiliar with Yankee slang could take offense, Boyington's mouth formed two words, which euphemistically translated suggested that Conga Joe "could go and have carnal knowledge of himself."

The camp held its collective breath; but Conga Joe's vanity would not let him admit he didn't understand.

"Yush!" he barked, dismissing us.

Ten minutes later the Aussie beckoned us to a window fronting on the compound – and the latrines.

"Can you really believe this?" he stammered.

Outside, the chief guard who had first apprehended Boyington was now standing watch by the same cubicle, while wisps of fragrant smoke curled from its open top.

"This boy seemed sorry for what had happened," Pappy explained later. "Offered me a smoke out of pity."

Close observers, however, believed that Boyington either had palmed the cigarette during the beating or conned the guard out of one. In any event, Boyington was seldom touched again by a guard in Ofuna – and there was no further mention of prima donnas.

As we came to know him better – and learned that he was, indeed, Maj. Gregory Boyington, then in command of the famous "Black Sheep" Squadron and with a personal score of 28 enemy aircraft – we found that he had a wry humor that was usually directed at himself. His starring role as an ace elicited no more than a jibe or smirk from him. In fact, most prisoners who served with him will remember Pappy not from his record aloft or the unfortunate publicity which dogged him after the war, but as a person who turned aside the worst that a vicious enemy could inflict, and this with a personal dignity that belied his reputation as a hell-raising, discipline-scorning rebel.

A case could easily be made for Maj. Boyington as a successful, if not model, POW – a distinction becoming more and more difficult as the profession of warfare deteriorates in its concern for the hapless prisoner. It may be worth examining those traits and abilities which served so admirably Boyington, his camp-mates, and their common mission.

First, *maturity*. Pappy would be the last to claim any mental wizardry, but he was shrewd and perceptive, traits acquired in a rough boyhood near Okanagan, Washington, which hastened his arrival at an early maturity. On his first trip to the Ofuna *benjo,* he was startled to hear questions hissed at him from the weathered planks.

"How's it going in the south?"

"Have we taken Rabaul yet?"

He didn't even stop scratching.

"I don't know you guys," he said, in effect. "When I can see you, I may talk to you. Meantime, we're winning, if that helps."

Tricks to make a POW talk were used, of course, in that war as in others, but Ofuna was not that sophisticated. The latrine questioners had been ourselves; later, squads of naval intelligence officials arrived from nearby Yokosuka to grill Boyington.

To survive these sessions demanded the second ingredient of success in this difficult role: *adaptability*. Greg made the same hard choice as most of us: To say as little as necessary to stay alive, but say something, thus admitting that the "name, rank, and serial number" routine no longer fitted that war.

One of the diversions of camp life was to compare notes on the absurdities and outdated information given so very reluctantly and sparsely to the interrogators. We hoped, in fact, that they would act on some of the information thus supplied, since it would mean catastrophe for them. But, admittedly, to do this convincingly required something more than a natural ability at lying, and this was *education.*

Pappy qualified. Not that he was devoutly studious by nature – we tried setting up a class in something or other to pass the time but he would rather limp around the compound pondering our sorry circumstances and what they might require of him. On the other hand, he was surprisingly well-informed, an engineering graduate (almost) of the University of Washington, where he was also a leading wrestler. He had learned not only numbers, but people, their history and nature; when he faced the interrogators, this knowledge provided much of his successful defense.

After hostilities ended we could read Pappy's book, *Baa Baa Black Sheep*, and understand better the pressures that had beset this Marine in the war's drama. Alighting from combat missions, in mess halls, or while grabbing naps from almost constant flying, Boyington was besieged by reporters for stories of daring-do-aloft – and were embittered when he answered with something less than pleasantry.

"Hell, I'm no plaster saint or Hollywood ace!"

Their bitterness may have been reflected in post-war stories, when Boyington proved his point again. Certainly some of the same pressures of fame followed him into the POW camp, where he received more attention than any other prisoner of the Japanese. But what showed through his natural gruffness was his concern for others in the camp, albeit this had to be made effective in devious ways. As soon as he was able, he ingratiated himself with some of the Japanese galley workers. One fat crone in particular took a personal fancy to the joshing Marine. Mama-san probably never realized – nor cared if she did – that Pappy put this affection to work for the POWs' benefit. After getting himself installed as a cook's helper, Greg stole (and here the word must be rinsed completely free of its natural taint) gloriously. While Mama-san looked elsewhere ladles of grain, extra *dai-kons*, huge pats of *miso-paste* – all went into the camp stew.

"I possess a natural talent for this sort of thing," Greg boasted, grinning.

He also possessed something else besides the *training* which made him not only proficient at his pilot's job, but so obviously responsive to the needs of the men under his command. This last, the *sine qua non* of a successful prison career, can be called guts, but it goes well beyond poetic bravery and brief heroics. After all, it is fairly easy to act the part of a hero once or twice on the spur of a moment; it takes much more to withstand a daily grind of tribulation and pain which seemingly may stretch into years.

The reason for Boyington's limp was simple – a finger-sized lump of shrapnel lodged deeply within his inner thigh near the groin. How it missed a vital femoral artery was a mystery. The deep infection had grown steadily worse until it was apparent even to Conga Joe that it must be removed. Accordingly, a cutting session was arranged, to which Greg, balancing the odds of deadly infection against those of maiming at the inexpert, sadistic hands of the pharmacist's mate, reluctantly but wisely agreed.

A small assembly of guards and hangers-on gathered in the makeshift dispensary. No anaesthetic was available – or at least it was not used. While Boyington gripped the table and looked aloft, the infected wound was opened with a whetted knife. A pair of scissors was then employed to snip through the flesh while the onlookers grimaced. Midway through this ordeal, obviously enjoying his position on center stage, Conga Joe stopped and looked up pleasantly at Pappy.

"Boyington! It hurts, da?"

Later the Navy seaman helping in the operation commented, "I don't know why the Major didn't kick out his teeth right then."

But he did not. Instead, he reflected a moment, then conceded in the same chatty tone, "Yup, it hurts..."

Conga Joe muttered and went back to work. A half hour later, stitched with a common needle, Boyington refused help, rose from the table, and made it back to his cubby-hole cell before collapsing on the *tatami*.

This same stoic acceptance of his fate characterized all of Pappy's POW career. Thus it came as no surprise to those who knew him, after the war, he refused to join the "sock-it-to-'em" home brigades who urged heavy penalties against Japan proper as well as its war criminals. Conga Joe was hanged, but for beating to death another prisoner.

"As far as I'm concerned, he was a bastard – but he probably saved my life with his butchery," said Greg, shortly after being awarded the Medal of Honor.

Boyington's behavior in Japan seemed about what the country should expect of its combat troops unlucky enough to wind up in the hands of the opposition. This, in addition to *adaptability, education, training, and guts* summarize the ingredients of his exceptional behavior as a POW. All of these remain the essential attributes of fighting men today.

As for courage, Certainly no one generation has a monopoly on this ingredient, but perhaps not every POW possesses the maturity to display it.

An example like Pappy's, however, is contagious enough to raise the guts level of an entire camp, and surely there are Boyingtons today scattered throughout the Corps.

It is intended as a compliment to Boyington that more than one compatriot of those trying days in Ofuna has carried the picture of his solid, unembittered defence of the enemy as a living guide for the intervening years. Despite a POW's natural despair at the time of his ordeal, it appears that life carries on well after that episode. There is still a long way to go, many friends to face, much time for reflection. All POW's, past, present, and future, should be able to face those years with the self-respect Pappy Boyington deserves.

Yup, it hurts, but surely those rewards are worth the pain.

• • •

The President of the United States takes pleasure in presenting the CONGRESSIONAL MEDAL OF HONOR to:

MAJOR GREGORY BOYINGTON
UNITED STATES MARINE CORPS RESERVE

for service as set forth in the following citation:

"For extraordinary heroism above and beyond the call of duty as Commanding Officer of Marine Fighting Squadron Two Fourteen in action against enemy Japanese forces in Central Solomons area from 12 September 1943 to 3 January 1944. Consistently outnumbered throughout successive hazardous flights over heavily defended hostile territory, Major Boyington struck at the enemy with daring and courageous persistence, leading his squadron into combat with devastating results to Japanese shipping, shore installations and aerial forces. Resolute in his efforts to inflict crippling damage on the enemy, Major Boyington led a formation of twenty-four fighters over Kahili on 17 October and, persistently circling the airdrome where sixty

hostile aircraft were grounded, boldly challenged the Japanese to send up planes. Under his brilliant command, our fighters shot down twenty enemy craft in the ensuing action without the loss of a single ship. A superb airman and determined fighter against overwhelming odds, Major Boyington personally destroyed twenty of the numerous Japanese planes shot down by his squadron and by his forceful leadership developed the combat readiness in his command which was a distinctive factor in the Allied aerial achievements in this vitally strategic area."

/S/ FRANKLIN D. ROOSEVELT

The President of the United States takes pride in presenting the NAVY CROSS to:

MAJOR GREGORY BOYINGTON
UNITED STATES MARINE CORPS

for service as set forth in the following citation:

"For extraordinary heroism as Commanding Officer of Marine Fighter Squadron TWO FOURTEEN during action against enemy aerial forces in the New Britain Island area, January 3, 1944. Climaxing a period of duty conspicuous for exceptional combat achievement, Major Boyington led a formation of Allied planes on a fighter sweep over Rabaul against a vastly superior number of hostile fighters. Diving in a steep run into the climbing Zeros, he made a daring attack, sending one Japanese fighter to destruction in flames. A tenacious and fearless airman under extremely hazardous conditions, Major Boyington succeeded in communicating to those who served with him, the brilliant and effective tactics developed through a careful study of enemy techniques, and led his men into combat with inspiring and courageous deter-

mination. His intrepid leadership and gallant fighting spirit reflect the highest credit upon the United States Naval Service."

/S/ Secretary of the Navy

• • •

Name: Brigadier General Evans F. Carlson, USMCR, (Deceased).

Biography: Written 4 February, 1954.

Brigadier General Evans F. Carlson, famed Marine leader of "Carlson's Raiders", was born February 26, 1896, at Sidney, New York. His father was a Congregationalist Minister.

His long and colorful military career began in 1912, when at the age of 16 he left high school and enlisted in the U.S. Army. When he finished his four-year enlistment he was a "Top Sergeant." He had served in the Philippines and in Hawaii. He stayed out of uniform less than one year and returned in time for the Mexican punitive expedition.

During World War I he saw action in France, and was awarded the Purple Heart for wounds received in action. He was commissioned a Second Lieutenant in May, 1917, and made Captain of field artillery in December, 1917. He served in Germany with the Army of Occupation.

His spectacular career as a Marine started in 1922 when he enlisted as a Private. In 1923 he was commissioned a Second Lieutenant.

After duty at Quantico, Virginia, he sailed for Culebra, Puerto Rico, in 1924 and remained there for five months before being ordered to the West Coast for duty with the Pacific Fleet. Applying for aviation in 1925, he went to Pensacola, Florida, for his instruction but subsequently returned to duty with ground units. He served another tour of foreign shore duty from 1927 to 1929 at Shanghai, China.

Carlson was ordered to Nicaragua in 1930 as an officer in the Guardia Nacional. A First Lieutenant at the time, he won his first Navy Cross for leading 12 Marines against 100 bandits. He also was commended for his actions following the earthquake at Managua in 1931, and for performance of duties as Chief of Police in 1932 and 1933.

Chapter 1: World War II

Returning to the United States in 1933, he was sent almost immediately to Shanghai again. Shortly afterward he was transferred to the Marine Detachment, American Legation, Peiping, China, where he served as Adjutant and studied the Chinese language. In 1936 he returned to the United States via Japan. At home he served at Quantico while attending Marine Corps Schools and studying International Law and Politics at George Washington University in Washington, D.C.

He went back to China for the third time, in 1937, as an official student of the Chinese language and as a military observer with Chinese forces. There he was afforded the opportunity to learn the tactics of the Japanese soldier.

Traveling thousands of miles through the interior of China, often on foot and horseback, over the most hazardous terrain, he lived under the primitive conditions of native troops. When he left China, in 1938, he was commended by the Commander in Chief of the Asiatic Fleet for his services.

He was so impressed with the danger of Japanese aggression in the Far East that in 1939 he resigned his commission as a Captain in order to be free to write and lecture on that subject. When the danger that he foresaw neared reality in 1941, he applied to be recommissioned in the Marine Corps and was accepted with the rank of Major. A year later he was placed in command of the Second Marine Raider Battalion with the rank of Lieutenant Colonel.

His leadership of that unit in the raid on Makin Island, August 17, 1942, won him a Gold Star in lieu of a second Navy Cross. A second Gold Star was awarded him for heroism and distinguished leadership on Guadalcanal in November and December of that year.

Colonel Carlson was ordered back to the United States for medical treatment in the Spring of 1943, and subsequently returned to Tarawa as an observer. In that engagement he was cited for volunteering to carry vital information through enemy fire from an advanced post to division headquarters.

He was wounded during the Saipan operation while attempting to rescue a wounded enlisted man from a front line observation Post, and was awarded a Gold Star in lieu of a second Purple Heart.

Physical disabilities resulting from the wounds received on Saipan caused the General's retirement on July 1, 1946. He was advanced to the rank of Brigadier General on the retired list at that time for having been specially commended for the performance of duty in actual combat.

On May 27, 1947, the 51-year-old veteran succumbed to heart illness at Emmanuel Hospital, Portland, Oregon. He had been living in Brightwood, Oregon, since his retirement. He was survived by his wife, Mrs. Peggy Tatum Carlson, and a son by a previous marriage, Evans C. Carlson.

In addition to the Navy Cross with two Gold Stars in lieu of a second and third Navy Cross and the Purple Heart with a Gold Star in lieu of a second Purple Heart, Brigadier General Carlson was awarded the Legion of Merit, Saipan 1944, Presidential Unit Citation with three Stars, Guadalcanal, Tarawa, and Saipan; Victory Medal with France Clasp, France 1918; World War II Victory Medal; China Service Medal, 1937; Yangtze Service Medal, 1927; Expeditionary Medal, China 1927; Italian Croix de Guerre, 1920; Asiatic-Pacific Campaign Medal with three Bronze Stars; and the American Defense Service Medal.

-USMC-

The following are a newspaper account of the battle on Makin Island for which Gen. Carlson was awarded the Navy Cross; his two Navy Cross, Silver Star, and Legion of Merit citations:

ONLY 2 JAPANESE OUT OF 350 ESCAPED AMERICAN MARINES IN MAKIN BLITZ

• • •

Super Mobile, Super Streamlined Force of U.S. Raiders Does Its Job Completely

• • •

By James F. Lowery
Star-Bulletin Staff Correspondent

Chapter 1: World War II

PEARL HARBOR, Aug. 28 – United States "Gung Ho" Marines – their memory of Wake Island still fresh – have completely leveled Makin Island.

There are but two Japanese left on that major island of the enemy-held Gilbert group to tell of the attack.

The other 348, there before the "super mobile, super streamlined" Marines struck August 17, are dead.

Attacking on a dark moonless night, the Marines destroyed all stores, three radio stations and two enemy planes and withdrew with "light losses."

That is the summary of that joint surprise attack by Navy and Marine forces as revealed today by the officers who directed it – Lt. Col. Evans F. Carlson, USMC Reserve, Plymouth, Conn., Commander of the Marines; Maj. James Roosevelt, USMC, Coronada, Cal., second in command of the Marines, and Cmdr. John M. Haines, USN, Coronada, Cal., who was in command of the expedition.

It was the first revelation of the use of "super mobile, super stream-lined" Marines in the Pacific.

(Makin is about 2,400 miles southwest of Honolulu and about 3,300 miles southeast of Tokyo.)

40 Hour Battle

It is a story of 40 hours of battle in which the Marines and Navy forces collaborated to completely eliminate a Japanese garrison of 200 men on the island, and destroy 150 more on two boats in the lagoon and withdraw with only "light losses" August 18.

It is the result of weeks of special training of men, personally interviewed and selected by Col. Carlson and Maj. Roosevelt. On the eve of their first battle the men were dubbed a "Gung Ho" outfit, meaning "work in harmony," by their commander, who learned the saying during the time he spent with the 8th Chinese Route Army.

Pointing out that his company was formed, as an answer to a directive from Admiral Nimitz, on the theory of being super mobile and super stream-lined and using the element of surprise to get in, strike hard, and get out, Col. Carlson, who acted as spokesman for the officers, began to relate the details of the attack.

"We got ashore undetected and started to move towards the vital area of the island. We came ashore on small boats on a dark, moonless night in

39

a heavy sea, but everyone got ashore safely."

"The Japanese were evidently on the alert, for they got news of our presence about 20 minutes after our arrival. Mobile reserves began coming up to meet us. They pushed up in American-made trucks and motorcycles using American-made gas."

The Marines discovered the presence of U.S. made gas when they destroyed some 1,000 gallons of it.

Lt. Wilfred S. Le Francois, Watertown, N.Y., an enlisted man who came up through the ranks and who was with Col. Carlson in Nicaragua, was in command of the advanced guard that first made contact on the island. According to the Marine commander the island is approximately seven miles long and from a mile to a mile and a half wide at various points.

Snipers Cause Trouble

"We began a flanking movement as the Japanese began arriving," Col. Carlson continued. "They had snipers in the trees wearing green uniforms and puttees that blended in beautifully with the foliage and it was the snipers that caused us more trouble than anything else."

"When resistance developed the Japanese appeared to have machineguns, several types of automatic weapons and flame throwers," Col. Carlson revealed.

"We had some trouble with grenade throwers," the Marine commander said, "but they only got off six salvos before we knocked them out. The snipers were strapped in the trees and when shot would merely hang there."

It was explained that Makin Island is almost completely bare of undergrowth and the trees mostly coconut.

Col. Carlson told of one sniper who continually tried to get Maj. Roosevelt. When asked if he succeeded, Jimmy said, "No, sir, we got him." The only sign of injury the President's son showed was a cut finger which became infected.

• • •

The President of the United States takes pleasure in presenting the GOLD STAR in lieu of a second NAVY CROSS to:

LIEUTENANT COLONEL EVANS F. CARLSON
UNITED STATES MARINE CORPS RESERVE

for action as set forth in the following citation:

> *"For extraordinary heroism and distinguished as Commanding Officer of the Second Marine Raider Battalion against enemy Japanese forces on Makin Island. In the first operation of this type ever conducted by United States forces, Lieutenant Colonel Carlson personally directed his forces in the face of intense fire from enemy ground troops and aerial bombing barrage, inflicting great personnel and material damage on the enemy. In the withdrawal of his forces under adverse sea conditions he displayed outstanding resourcefulness, initiative, and resolute purpose in evacuating all wounded and disabled men. His high courage and excellent leadership throughout the engagement were in keeping with the finest traditions of the United States Naval Service.*

> *For the President*
> */S/ FRANK KNOX*
> *Secretary of the Navy*

The President of the United States takes pleasure in presenting a GOLD STAR in lieu of a third NAVY CROSS to:

LIEUTENANT COLONEL EVANS F. CARLSON
UNITED STATES MARINE CORPS RESERVE

for service as set forth in the following citation:

> *"For extraordinary heroism and courage as leader of a Marine Combat Unit in action against enemy Japanese forces in the British Solomon Islands during the period from early November to early December, 1942. In the face*

Men of Honor

of most difficult conditions of tropical weather and heavy growth, Lieutenant Colonel Carlson led his men in a determined and aggressive search for threatening hostile forces, overcoming all opposition and completing their mission with small losses to our men while taking heavy toll of the enemy. His personal valor and inspiring fortitude reflect great credit upon Lieutenant Colonel Carlson, his command, and the United States Naval Service."

For the President,
/S/ FRANK KNOX
Secretary of the Navy

The President of the United States takes pleasure in presenting the LEGION OF MERIT to:

LIEUTENANT COLONEL EVANS F. CARLSON
UNITED STATES MARINE CORPS

for service as set forth in the following citation:

"Schooled by grim experience in the art of countering Japanese strategy, Lieutenant Colonel Carlson defined the most effective methods of attacking the objectives. Landing on D-day plus 1 under heavy mortar and artillery fire, he immediately volunteered to visit front line units in an effort to obtain information and, fearlessly moving into areas where the battle raged with savage fanaticism, he repeatedly risked his life during the critical days following the invasion. Consistently sound in his evaluation of enemy positions and strength, he continued his determined efforts persevering despite the mounting fury of hostile resistance and providing first hand information under increasingly difficult conditions, until he sustained serious wounds while engaged in a front-line reconnaissance on 22 June, 1944. A brilliant tactician and indomitable fighter,

Chapter 1: World War II

Lieutenant Colonel Carlson rendered services of inestimable value to his Commanding General prior to and during the assault and occupation of this fiercely defended Japanese base, and his dauntless initiative, outstanding professional skill and unwavering devotion to duty in the face of tremendous opposition were important factors in the ultimate seizure of the objective (Saipan)."

• • •

Name: Colonel Justice Marion Chambers, USMCR, Retired.

Biography: Written 1947.
"Jumping Joe" Chambers received the Medal of Honor, Silver Star Medal, Legion of Merit and three Purple Hearts – the winning of any one of which is no mean feat in any language. "Jumping Joe" is a Reserve officer, a "graduate" of Washington D.C.'s Fifth Reserve Battalion. He made good in a big way and proved that the Marine Corps' system of training civilians in peace for positions of prominence in time of war is a sound one.

Justice M. Chambers was born in Huntington, West Virginia on February 2, 1908, one of four children of Mr. and Mrs. Arthur F. Chambers. He obtained his primary education there and then entered Marshall College in Huntington. After three years of studying at Marshall, Chambers transferred to George Washington University in Washington, D.C. Two years later he moved over to National University also in Washington. It was from the latter university that he was graduated after one and one half more years of study. The degree of Bachelor of Law was conferred upon the West Virginian. In college his fraternity was Sigma Phi Epsilon, a national social fraternity.

Chambers enlisted in the Naval Reserve on May 21, 1928 and served for more than two years as an enlisted sailor before being honorably discharged on June 25, 1930 to enlist in the Marine Corps Reserve as a private on the following day.

At that time, Mr. Chambers was employed in the Office of Personnel and Business Administration in the Department of Agriculture.

He was assigned to Company F (442nd Company), 20th Reserve Marines, Sixth Marine Reserve Brigade in Washington and attended the 1930 summer camp with that unit. He missed the 1931 summer field training but applied for a commission in the Reserve early in 1932. Private Chambers was honorably discharged on July 17, 1932 and accepted a Second Lieutenant's commission on July 18.

Lieutenant Chambers started in on the correspondence courses which were recommended for all Reserve officers and continued his attendance at the weekly drill periods and the annual summer camps. By 1935 he was the Company Commander of Company C, Fifth Reserve Battalion, while in civilian life he held the position of Assistant to the Chief of the Planning Division, Procurement Division, Treasury Department. He was promoted to First Lieutenant on June 20, 1935.

In the Fifth Battalion, the annual field training periods were conducted on an inter-company competitive basis, there being 18 awards, trophies and medals in various lines of military endeavor. The winning of these awards counted "points" toward the General Efficiency Cup. The companies tried very hard for the honor of winning that cup and much of the Fifth Battalion's success was attributed to their system of awards. Lt. Chambers' Company C won the General Efficiency Cup in 1936. Summer camp was held at Camp Ritchie, Cascade, Maryland.

The next year, the Lieutenant was the Assistant Plans and Training Officer for the battalion as well as Battalion Athletic Officer and Battalion Publicity Officer. In civilian life he had moved once again and was now Chief of the Division of Administration, U.S. Maritime Commission. Promoted to Captain on February 9, 1938, the government worker requested active duty with the Fleet Marine Force in the latter part of that year but his request was turned down.

Again in 1940, Captain Chambers requested a period of active duty and again his request was denied because it was termed "impractical." Undaunted, the Captain immediately asked that his request be reconsidered. It was finally granted and he went on 15 days of active duty at Quantico, Virginia for instruction in infantry weapons. The summer camp for 1940 was held at the Marine Barracks, Naval Air Station, Lakehurst, New Jersey and here the Captain ran into a bit of trouble. He was hit by the discharge of a blank cartridge and had to be hospitalized.

Chapter 1: World War II

Scarcely out of the hospital, Captain Chambers and the whole Fifth Battalion were called to active duty and reported in at Reserve Training Center at Quantico. From there the Battalion went to Guantanamo Bay, Cuba, and was broken up. Captain Chambers was assigned to command Company F, Second Battalion, Fifth Marines, and when the First Marines was organized, he was assigned to command Company I, Third Battalion, First Marines. The Division returned to the United States in the Spring of 1941 and was based at Parris Island, South Carolina, for several months. During the summer, Captain Chambers was transferred to the Fifth Marines who were stationed at Quantico. When the First Raider Battalion was being formed in the Spring of 1942, the veteran Reserve Officer was transferred to it. He was promoted to Major on May 18, 1942 and went overseas that summer.

Landing on Tulagi with the Raiders on August 7, Major Chambers was wounded on the first day of the first American land offensive of World War II. With wounds in the left thigh and both arms, Major Chambers was taken to the battalion aid station. That night, while still a patient there, an enemy counter-attack threatened to envelope the station. The Major assumed control of the evacuation of the wounded to a less dangerous area and also directed the action of the detachment which had been left there to guard the aid station. He later received a Silver Star Medal for his bravery on that night of August 7-8.

Removed to a hospital in the rear area, Major Chambers was also a patient on the hospital ship, the *USS SOLACE*, and later was returned to the United States for further treatment. After hospitalization at Oakland and Treasure Island, California Naval Hospitals, the Major was transferred to the National Naval Medical Center at Bethesda, Maryland.

Following his discharge from Bethesda in January, 1943, Major Chambers was assigned to the Training Center at Camp Lejeune, North Carolina. He was promoted to Lieutenant Colonel on March 1, 1943, and assumed command of the 15th Replacement Battalion three days later. Subsequently, he commanded the Infantry Training Battalion at New River, which screened hundreds of Officer Candidates before they went to Quantico. When the 25th Marines were formed, the new Lieutenant Colonel was given command of the 3rd Battalion, 25th Marines, and went to Camp Pendleton, Oceanside, California, in August. The Division left the United States in

January, 1944, and made the first and only enemy landing from an American mainland base in the war. They swept through Roi and Namur in record time on the last day of January and the first few days of February. The 3rd Battalion participated in Phase 1, and then independently conducted Phase IV and Phase V, during which phases 49 additional islands were mopped up.

The next campaigns for Lieutenant Colonel Chambers and the Fourth Division were the Saipan and Tinian operations. During Saipan, "Jumping Joe" suffered blast concussion. However, he walked out of the hospital and returned to lead his battalion, time and again, against strongly held enemy positions and captured objective after objective in a conspicuously heroic manner. Many times during the operation he exposed himself to enemy fire in order to better control and direct the advance of his battalion. For that and his pre-invasion display of exceptional ability in the training of his troops, Colonel Chambers was subsequently awarded the Legion of Merit.

The Washingtonian's fifth blitz was the bloody Iwo Jima campaign. The 3rd Battalion, 25th Marines was picked to land on the critical right flank of the Fifth Amphibious Corps' landing force. The Colonel led his men ashore while mortars and machine-guns ripped his battalion wide open. Fearlessly exposing himself to the enemy's fire, he rallied and reorganized his command and led them in the assault and occupation of a strategically important and almost impregnable fortified cliff which was beyond his assigned objective. The heights dominated the landing beaches on the right flank and their neutralization brought a halt to the withering fire which was causing extremely high casualties among the Marines.

On February 23, Colonel Chambers was on the lines in an almost completely exposed forward observation post directing accurate harassing and interdicting artillery, mortar, and rocket fire on areas to the front. This fire was materially aiding the advance of the units on the left and prevented the enemy from organizing in that potentially dangerous sector. At the conclusion of the bombardment, the 3rd Battalion lashed out in a renewed attack against fanatical opposition. Colonel Chambers, leading his men in the attack, sudden fell severely wounded. This time it was an enemy bullet which plowed its way through his left lung during its course through the Colonel's body.

After treatment in a hospital in Hawaii, Colonel Chambers returned to the States once more as a patient. This time he went right from the Naval Receiving Hospital at San Francisco to Bethesda.

Originally recommended for the Medal of Honor, for his actions of February 19 and 23, the recommendation was approved by the regimental commander of the 25th Marines, the division commander of the 4th Division and the Commanding General of the V Amphibious Corps. However, when it reached the Board of Awards of the Fleet Marine Force, Pacific, they decided, after careful comparison with the accomplishments of comparable commanders in similar situations, that the Navy Cross represented a truer evaluation of the acts performed. The decision was concurred in by the Commanding General of FMF, Pacific.

The Navy Cross was pinned on Lieutenant Colonel Chambers by General Alexander A. Vandegrift, Commandant of the Marine Corps, at Marine Headquarters on August 31,1945. His case was later reviewed by the Navy Department's Board of Review for Decorations and Medals which recommended no change be made in the original award. (Later, after a third review by the board, Colonel Chambers was subsequently awarded the Medal of Honor).

Colonel Chambers went to Quantico following his discharge from Bethesda in June and entered the Ninth Command and Staff School. The war ended while he was a student there and under the point discharge system adopted by the Marine Corps, the Colonel had 168 discharge points.

Graduating from school in October, the veteran Marine Officer was assigned to duty at Quantico. As additional duty he became a member of the Marine Corps Reserve Policy Board at Headquarters Marine Corps.

The Colonel's medical case came before the Naval Retirement Board in the Fall of 1945 and their decision was that he was permanently incapacitated for further active duty with the Marine Corps due to his wounds received at Iwo Jima. Consequently, he was transferred to the retired list of officers of the Marine Corps Reserve on January 1, 1946 with the rank of Lieutenant Colonel.

Because he had been specially commended for his performance of duty in actual combat, Lieutenant Colonel Chambers was promoted to full Colonel on the retired list on May 8, 1946 with date of rank from January 1. At the time of his retirement, Colonel Chambers had 18 years, seven months, and ten days of continuous Navy and Marine Corps service.

In October, 1946, he was elected the first president of the newly formed Major Otho L. Rogers Chapter of the Marine Corps Reserve Officers Association.

-USMC-

The following are a newspaper article about Colonel Chamber, his Medal of Honor, and excerpts from his Silver Star and Legion of Merit citations:

JAPS LEARN MARINES ARE TOUGH, SAYS WOUNDED SOLOMONS OFFICER

Major J. M. Chambers Returns To Capital To Recuperate

Oct. 30 - Major Justice M. Chambers in Washington for treatment of a wound received in action with the United States Marines on Tulagi Island in the Solomons, said today that in fighting in the Pacific the Japanese have learned a "healthy respect" for the American Marines.

In a reply to a query as to whether the Japs were ferocious fighters, Major Chambers said they may be ferocious, but are no more so than the Marines, and "it didn't take them long to find this out."

"Our boys are just as tough as the Japs," Major Chambers said, "and after the intensive *raider* training received in the tropics before going into action, there wasn't a trick the Japs could pull that we couldn't go them one better."

Plenty of Grenades

Describing the action on Tulagi Island, which took place last August 7, Major Chambers said his Marine Raider Battalion, commanded by Colonel Merritt Edson, landed on Tulagi that morning stripped down to combat equipment, consisting of green dungarees, helmets, automatic rifles, Reising guns, knives, and "plenty" of grenades. He said that with faces "blacked out" and with the similarity in color of the uniforms worn by the Marines and Japs "we had to look sharp before shooting."

In the action that followed, Major Chambers was wounded in both wrists and the leg by a mortar shell which he said he could not be sure was a Jap shell or a premature explosion from the Marine's own gun.

"We were after a Jap machine-gun nest which I had spotted," he explained, "and were using our own mortars when a shell exploded in the air about 10 feet from us. The Japs were using mortars, so it could have been a shell from either."

Wounded Caught Between Lines

Major Chambers was removed to the rear, near the beach, and during the night said that Marines occupied the hill and the Japs occupied the beach, leaving the wounded in between the two forces.

"When morning came the firing started and we were right in between," he said. "My arms were in splints and I rolled to the ground to get out of the line of the firing. And then we managed to evacuate the wounded."

Declaring that the Marines have learned not to pull any of their punches on the Japs, Major Chambers said the Japanese soldiers will not hesitate to fire on their enemy's wounded. "I've seen them do it, and I suppose they logically believe that a wounded soldier, if left alive, will return to fight again."

"They are tough fighters and the only time I ever saw one attempt to surrender he was shot by his officer before he had gotten five steps from his own lines. They seem to fight, not with so much hate, as in desperation," he said.

Major Chambers, who expects to have his left wrist patched up while in Washington, is visiting his wife's parents, Mr. and Mrs. John Schmutzer, at 630 Quebec Place N.W.

• • •

The President of the United States takes pleasure in presenting the MEDAL OF HONOR to:

COLONEL JUSTICE M. CHAMBERS
UNITED STATES MARINE CORPS RESERVE

Men of Honor

for service as set forth in the following citation:

> *"For conspicuous gallantry and intrepidity at the risk of his life above and beyond the call of duty as Commanding Officer of the Third Assault Battalion Landing Team, Twenty-fifth Marines, Fourth Marine Division, in action against enemy Japanese forces on Iwo Jima, Volcano Islands, from 19 to 22 February 1945. Under a furious barrage of enemy machine-gun and small-arms fire from the commanding cliffs on the right, Colonel Chambers, then Lieutenant Colonel, landed immediately after the initial assault waves of his Battalion on D-Day to find the momentum of the assault threatened by heavy casualties from withering Japanese artillery, mortar, rocket, machine-gun and rifle fire. Exposed to relentless hostile fire, he coolly reorganized his battle-weary men, inspiring them to heroic efforts by his own valor and leading them in an attack on the critical, impregnable high ground from which the enemy was pouring an increasing volume directly onto troops ashore as well as amphibious craft in succeeding waves. Constantly in the front lines encouraging his men to push forward against the enemy's savage resistance, Colonel Chambers led the 8-hour battle to carry the flanking ridge top and reduce the enemy's fields of aimed fire, thus protecting the vital foothold gained. In constant defiance of hostile fire while reconnoitering the entire Regimental Combat Team zone of action, he maintained contact with adjacent units and forwarded vital information to the Regimental Commander. His zealous fighting spirit undiminished despite terrific casualties and the loss of most of his key officers, he again reorganized his troops for renewed attack against the enemy's main line of resistance and was directing the fire of the rocket platoon when he fell critically wounded. Evacuated under heavy Japanese fire, Colonel Chambers, by forceful leadership, courage and fortitude in the face of staggering odds, was directly*

50

instrumental in insuring the success of subsequent operations of the Fifth Amphibious Corps on Iwo Jima, thereby sustaining and enhancing the finest traditions of the United States Naval Service."

/S/ HARRY S. TRUMAN

(Silver Star)

"While a patient at a battalion aid station, suffering from multiple wounds inflicted by a mortar shell, Major Chambers personally assumed control of the evacuation of the wounded men when the hostile counter-attack threatened to penetrate to the station. With utter disregard for his own personal safety, he also directed the action of the Marine detachment covering the removal of the wounded to a less dangerous area" (Tulagi, Solomon Islands).

(Legion of Merit)

"Developing and maintaining a high state of combat efficiency,...(he) gallantly led his battalion against strongly fortified hostile positions to take one objective after another despite fierce enemy resistance. Dauntless in the face of grave danger, he repeatedly exposed himself to withering enemy fire throughout successive engagements. His forceful leadership, brilliant combat tactics and valiant fighting spirit served as an inspiration to the officers and men under his command" (Saipan and Tinian).

• • •

Men of Honor

Name: Major General Merritt A. Edson, USMC (Deceased).

Biography: Written December, 1955.
Major General Merritt Austin Edson, known as "Red Mike" of the Marine Corps, retired from the Corps on August 1, 1947, and died on August 14, 1955 in Washington, D.C. The World War II Medal of Honor winner was born in Rutland, Vermont, on April 25, 1897, and attended the University of Vermont. At the outbreak of World War I, he enlisted in the Marine Corps Reserve, and was commissioned a Second Lieutenant in the Regular Marine Corps on October 9, 1917. He served in France from September 1918 to December 1919.

Throughout his Marine Corps career, General Edson was closely associated with the development of small-arms marksmanship. In 1921, he was a firing member of the winning Marine Corps National Match Rifle Team at Camp Perry, Ohio. In 1927, 1930, and 1931, he was attached to the Marine Corps National Rifle and Pistol Teams as Assistant Team Coach. During the Regional Match years of 1932 and 1933, he acted as Team Coach and Team Captain respectively. Upon the resumption of the National Matches in 1935, he was Captain of the Marine Corps National Rifle and Pistol Teams of 1935 and 1936, successfully winning the national trophies in both years.

In June 1941, the General was assigned as Commanding Officer, 1st Battalion, 5th Marine Regiment. For the next six months, he was engaged in conducting experimental operations and training in close conjunction with Destroyer Transports, which led to the organization of the 1st Marine Raider Battalion one month after this country's entry into World War II. This Battalion was a prototype of every Marine Raider Battalion and Army Ranger Battalion formed throughout the war. On August 7, 1942, the 1st Marine Raider Battalion, commanded by General Edson, then Colonel, landed on Tulagi in the Solomon Islands, and captured that island after two days of severe fighting. After the airfield on Guadalcanal had been seized from the enemy, General Edson, with a force of 800 men, was assigned to the occupation and defense of a ridge dominating the jungle on either side of the airfield. He was awarded the Medal of Honor for this action.

In November 1943, General Edson participated as Chief of Staff of the 2d Marine Division in the battle of Tarawa. Shortly thereafter, he was promoted to the rank of Brigadier General. In 1944 he was appointed Chief of Staff, Fleet Marine Force, Pacific. After his return to the United States, having completed 44 months of continuous duty in the Pacific area, he was assigned to the Office of the Chief of Naval Operations, and later to Marine Corps Headquarters. Upon his retirement from the Corps, Major General Edson returned to his native state of Vermont, where he was appointed Commissioner of Public Safety. He also became President of the National Rifle Association. He returned to active duty for a short period in order to serve on a special commission to recommend standards of actions for prisoners of war.

The General's decorations, in addition to the Medal of Honor, include the Navy Cross with Gold Star in lieu of a second Navy Cross; the Legion of Merit with a Gold Star in lieu of a second award; the Silver Star Medal; and the Presidential Unit Citation with two Bronze Stars, Guadalcanal 1942, and Tarawa 1943; the Asiatic-Pacific Campaign Medal with five Bronze Stars; and the World War II Victory Medal.

-USMC-

The following are an article from the March 1944 issue of Leatherneck Magazine about General Edson, his Medal of Honor, Navy Cross, Silver Star, and 2 Legion of Merit citations:

RED MIKE
and his
"DO OR DIE" MEN

by Pfc. George Doying

"Red Mike" Edson's head pivoted up and down. He allowed a wry little smile to wrinkle his face. It was the same smile with which the First Raiders were to become very familiar – in the word of Platoon Sergeant "Red" Hills, "it got so when ever we saw that grin we knew that somebody was going to get killed, and soon."

On that hot mid-July morning of 1942 in New Caledonia, "Red Mike's" grin and approving nod showed that he knew his Raiders were ready for the real thing.

At that moment, the men of the First Raiders were springing up from their places of concealment and dog-trotting in from every direction to the center of the camp. They had landed from their rubber boats during the night and had honeycombed the bivouac area, unseen and unheard, just as they had said they would. Some of the Raiders had passed so near the restless sentries that they heard them muttering about being hoaxed.

Now the "hide and seek" with the guard company was over. Colonel Merritt A. Edson, commanding officer of the First Marine Raider Battalion, summoned his men around him.

"I'm ready to stack you men up alongside any other outfit in the world," Edson told them. "The next time we pull this operation it'll be for keeps."

There was more but "Red Mike's" words aren't recorded precisely and that's the gist of them. Anyway, the men of the First Raiders knew that they were ready.

"We were just beasts," said Gunnery Sergeant Robert Jernigan. "All we could think of or talk about was getting at the Japs." Jernigan is a pleasant enough fellow nowadays but he was a squad leader in C Company at that time and was fully deserving of his nickname, "The Wildcat."

On that July morning, the Raiders were just a little more than five months old. They were less than a month away from Tulagi.

Tulagi was supposed to be easy. It wasn't that they didn't have faith in the Raiders, just that somebody had to take the Japs off Tulagi if Guadalcanal was to be secured. And weren't the Raiders fretting for action?

There was no opposition to the landing. They waded ashore and started down the island – Raiders on the South side of the big ridge which cuts Tulagi in two, the Fifth Marines down the North side.

For fully an hour they moved along the beach. Then C Company, led by Major Kenneth D. Bailey, roused a Jap machine-gun nest pocketed in a cave. Major Bailey – "Ken Dill" to the Raiders who had two word nicknames to identify officers in the field – was a strapping big six-footer with a square chin and as rugged as they come even in the Marines, and it was the reckless manner in which he moved against those first Nips that set the pace for the Raiders. Gunnery Sergeant Jernigan told us about it.

"He hollers at us to give him a covering fire, that he's going in," Jernigan said. "Well, he made it to the edge of the nest, got in under the fire – how I'll never know – and let 'em have it with a BAR."

That was first blood for the Raiders; they felt better after that.

For most of the Raiders, Tulagi is remembered by some single incident, some of heroism, some of a lighter vein. The favorite is the story of little Eddie Ahrens of A Company. Eddie had joined the outfit only a short time before they shoved off from Quantico, a "boot" from Parris Island. He stood five feet seven and weighed 130 soaking wet, but he was a whiz with a BAR that seemed almost as big as himself.

Eddie was with a security patrol that first night on Tulagi when the Japs attacked. The patrol was ordered back but the Nips were coming fast so Ahrens stayed to cover the withdrawal of his buddies. They found him next morning, in his foxhole. His hands still throttled a Jap officer's throat and two more Japs lay dead just ahead beside their machine-gun.

There are stories about "Red Mike" on Tulagi, too. After several days of fighting, the Marines had the Nips bottled up at the South end of the island, but the enemy was well protected in coral caves.

"Lets go in an' blow 'em out," said "Red Mike." Dynamite and grenades will do the trick." And dynamite and grenades and Raider recklessness , did do the trick.

Another time, during the mopping up, Edson visited an advance post where Jap snipers were still at work. "Red Mike" strode up scorning protective trees and rocks. They warned him to be careful.

"They won't get me," Edson said. Just then a sniper's bullet clipped off a limb just above "Red Mike's" head. Deliberately, the Colonel put his finger up to feel the jagged limb stump. "Guess maybe it is time to move out of here," he grinned.

Tulagi was the first test of Marine Raiders and it proved they could run the Nips out of their own back yard.

Colonel Edson had conceived the Raiders during the months before Pearl Harbor as he worked with the men of the First Separate Battalion which had been detached from the Fifth Marines in 1941 to become specialists in rubber boat landings.

For the blueprint he drew on the vast experience of more than a score of years as a Marine officer. "Red Mike" was a second lieutenant in France during World War I, then, in succession, a Marine pilot, ordnance officer, company commander in Nicaragua – it was "Edson and his 40 thieves" there – captain of the Marine Rifle and Pistol Team, and observer of the Sino-Jap hostilities around Chapei.

The Raiders of Edson's blueprint were to be a hard hitting, fast moving outfit equally at home in an amphibious operation or in the jungle, steel-hard killers asking no quarter and giving none, fighting only with the weapons they could carry, and with their skill and cold nerve. They were to be specialists in four types of missions: Purely hit and run raids, secondary diversionary landings, covering force and participation as a regular unit in a campaign.

For equipment, Edson selected only the lightest types – light machine-guns instead of heavy, 60mm mortars but no 81's. The fire power they lacked in caliber, the Raiders more than made up by mobility and greater use of automatic weapons; one BAR for each two M1's.

For his men "Red Mike" insisted upon none but eager hands with un-flagging stamina. The prospective future of the Raiders was put up to the original muster of Fifth Marines vets individually, put up to them without any varnish. The training would be tough, the fighting tougher and the prospects of coming back in good shape none too good. Edson's only prom-ise was that those chosen would be in action.

Gaps in the ranks of the old First Separate as a result of this weeding out were filled with volunteer recruits – the final makeup was about one-half Old Salts from the Fifth Marines, one-half Young Salts, mostly from Parris Island.

These preliminaries over, the First Raiders went to work in earnest.

For two months at Quantico they took a preparatory course in the arts of physical endurance and deliberate mayhem. Basic requirement was that every man be able to use every weapon in the battalion.

That meant the M1 carbine, Reising machine-gun, and mortar, plus of course the more intimate tools for killing – knives, machetes and bayonets. Each man got schooling, also, in the versatile uses of grenades, dynamite and TNT.

"We spent so much time working with weapons that we actually felt naked without 'em," commented Gunnery Sergeant Jernigan.

Executive officer of the First Raiders was Major (later Lieutenant Colo-nel) Sam B. Griffith, who signed on fresh from a trip to England where he observed the training of British Commandos. Naturally quite a bit of what

Chapter 1: World War II

Griffith saw found its way into the curriculum of the First Raiders.

Officers trained alongside their men, with "Red Mike" himself setting the pace. During all of the time the battalion trained at Quantico, Edson maintained his residence in Washington, D.C., and drove home nightly, no matter how late the day's chores were finished. Yet no one recalls a day that he wasn't back at his office before reveille.

Edson devoted special attention during those days to the education of his runner, Corporal Walter J. Burak. A little fellow, with a shock of black hair, Burak was an efficient and tireless worker with an intense thirst for knowledge, and it was "Red Mike" who said that Burak was fearless.

Edson was like a father to Burak and many were the nights the two sat together in the battalion office after the day's work was done, the Colonel tutoring his runner in the art of compass and map reading.

Burak's death is the only recorded instance where Edson displayed emotion. Burak ran into a crossfire of Nip machine-guns at Matanikau. Those that were there say that Edson "cried like a baby" when they found Burak's body. More than a year later, "Red Mike's" own tribute to his runner was this sentence: "I don't think he can ever be replaced by anyone."

Edson had a way of inspiring his men; to each Raider it was something different.

"He could make you love him one minute and hate him the next," said Sergeant Louis Bunch, a lanky Georgian who was wounded on Guadalcanal.

"His men are simply tools which he uses to do a job," was the way Private First Class Bill Brown put it. "But he takes good care of his tools just like you take good care of your rifle."

Gunnery Sergeant Jernigan remembers that Edson never stormed or made a scene over a mistake. Typical were his admonishings during inspection. "He'd come to someone who'd maybe forgot to fill a canteen or whose pack was on crooked," said Jernigan. "He'd put his hand on the lad's shoulder and tell him "better get that fixed son, might be awful important to have it right out there.""

"That man could sure handle," the gunny concluded.

For two months after Quantico the Raiders trained overseas. That was the "finishing school," and after that came Tulagi. After Tulagi came Tasimboka and Savo, daring hit-and-run raids deep behind Jap lines to mess up enemy communications and supplies. Then came Bloody Ridge!

If Tulagi, Tasimboka and Savo proved the Raiders could run the Nips ragged, it was Bloody Ridge that proved the Japs couldn't budge the Raiders.

It was called Lunga Ridge before the Raiders bivouacked there, and that detail also was supposed to be easy. General Vandegrift sent Edson's men up on Lunga for a rest, after five weeks of blood and Hell.

They didn't get any rest on Lunga. The first night, patrols began bringing in to Edson's CP ominous reports of considerable Jap activity in the Jungle beyond. "Red Mike" called his haggard troops together and told them the bad news.

All told, "Red Mike" had 880 men with him that night, the 12th of September – all that was left of the First Raiders plus two companies of Paramarines who had been attached to them on the 'Canal.

The Paramarines were strung out along the easterly "fin" of the ridge. B Company of the Raiders held the westerly "fin" from the peak of the ridge to a lagoon, and C Company was stretched from the lagoon to the river. A Company was held on the reserve line – another "fin" some five hundred yards north of the defense line.

"Red Mike's" story of what followed is the precise account of the master tactician. He related it for us in that impersonal, unexcited monotone, for which he is noted when the going is toughest, and as he talked, he roughed out a map with red and black pencils on a sheet of scratch paper.

"The Japs began bombarding at 2300 on the 12th," he began. "It lasted until 0030. The attack came down the lagoon and the river and around both flanks of C Company by infiltration, dislodging C Company.

"We tried to re-establish our line during the morning but we couldn't do it, so we moved back to the reserve line in the afternoon.

"The paratroops simply moved back. A Company was shifted over to the river when B Company moved back, and C Company of the Engineers" – they had been rushed up from Henderson Field – "took the position between them. The Pioneers" – the demolition platoon of the Raiders – "were stationed farther down to cover a bridge over the river, C Company was moved back to the new reserve line.

"At 1845 the Nips struck at B Company, cutting out the end platoon. At 2200, the big attack came down the center of the ridge.

"From 2200 to 2400, B Company and the paratroops gave ground slowly, withdrawing to the reserve line in good order and inflicting heavy losses on the Nips. At that point our lines held fast and the enemy was forced to withdraw on the 14th."

There it is, the unadorned play-by-play account of the battle of Bloody Ridge which saved Henderson Field and probably Guadalcanal, in the words of the man who received the Congressional Medal of Honor and the British Distinguished Service Order for his masterly leadership.

But it isn't the way "Red Mike's" men tell the story!

You really get to know Edson, the man and the general, on Bloody Ridge. All through the terrible day of the 13th and all through the awful night that followed, Edson was in the thick of it. He made countless trips from the CP to the front lines. He strode up and down those lines time and again, encouraging, cajoling, correcting. He was continuously exposed to enemy fire, and why he wasn't hit is more than any Raider can tell you.

"He was just like maneuvers back in Samoa," one of them recalled. "When he saw someone in trouble he went over quietly and helped him get squared away."

Sergeant Bunch, the lean Georgian, can still see "Red Mike" put down his field telephone to go over to speak to a hard pressed group, and the Jap shell that plopped on the phone seconds later.

It was over the phone that Edson personally directed the Marine artillery fire from Henderson Field during the heaviest part of the battle, artillery fire which helped turn the tide in the final hours. The phone line was the achievement of Corporal Burak; it was the only communication the Raiders had with Headquarters.

"I don't know what it would take to scare that man," summed up Gunnery Sergeant Jernigan in an epitaph for the stories of "Red Mike" at Bloody Ridge. Then he added: "But it sure hasn't been built yet."

• • •

Bloody Ridge will always remain the shining spot in the saga of the First Raiders.

It's still the First Raider Battalion today, and the story won't be finished until the war is over. But only about 10 percent of the original Raiders are still out there. Both Edson, now a brigadier general, and Griffith, who succeeded him, have been given new tasks, as have many of the other officers and men who gave the outfit its sparkling flavor.

After Bloody Ridge, Edson's Raiders next appeared in the battles for the Matanikau River. It was there that they got their coveted nickname. When the Marines sent to storm the river had trouble getting across, General Vandegrift sent back word: "Send me the Do or Die Men."

After Matanikau, on the 13th of October, the Raiders were withdrawn from Guadalcanal. There were less than 500 of them who trudged down to the dock that day, and of these 267 had active cases of malaria.

They had a real rest before re-forming in April, 1943, in preparation for the New Georgia assignment. That story, of Enogai and Baikoro, is another story which should have its own telling.

• • •

The President of the United States takes pleasure in presenting the CONGRESSIONAL MEDAL OF HONOR to:

COLONEL MERRITT A. EDSON
UNITED STATES MARINE CORPS

for service as set forth in the following citation:

> *"For conspicuous gallantry and intrepidity at the risk of his life above and beyond the call of duty as Commanding Officer of the First Marine Raider Battalion, with the First Parachute Battalion attached, during action against enemy Japanese forces in the Solomon Islands on the night of September 13-14, 1942. After the airfield on Guadalcanal had been seized from the enemy on August 8, Colonel Edson, with a force of eight hundred men, was assigned to the occupation and defense of a ridge dominating the jungle on either side of the airport. facing a formidable Japanese attack which, augmented by infiltration, had crashed through our front lines, he by skillful handling of his troops, successfully withdrew his forward*

units to a reserve line with minimum casualties. When the enemy, in a subsequent series of violent assaults, engaged our force in desperate hand-to-hand combat with bayonets, rifles, pistols, grenades and knives, Colonel Edson, although continuously exposed to hostile fire throughout the night, personally directed defense of the reserve position against a fanatical foe of greatly superior numbers. By his astute leadership and gallant devotion to duty, he enabled his men, despite severe losses, to cling tenaciously to their position on the vital ridge, thereby retaining command, not only of the Guadalcanal airfield, but also of the First Division's entire offensive installations in the surrounding area."

/S/ FRANKLIN D. ROOSEVELT

The President of the United States takes pleasure in presenting the GOLD STAR in lieu of a second NAVY CROSS to:

COLONEL MERRITT A. EDSON
UNITED STATES MARINE CORPS

for service as set forth in the following citation:

"For extraordinary heroism as Commanding Officer of the Tulagi Combat Group during the landing assault on enemy Japanese-held Tulagi Island, British Solomon Islands, August 7 to 9, 1942. In personal command of the 1st Marine Raider Battalion during the initial operation, Colonel Edson advanced the attack of his battalion and its supporting units with such skill, courage, and aggressiveness that he was an inspiration to the entire Combat Group and was directly responsible for the capture of Tulagi Island. His gallant conduct throughout this hazardous action was in keeping with the highest traditions of the United States Naval Service."

Men of Honor

/S/ FRANK KNOX
Secretary of the Navy

The President of the United States takes pleasure in presenting the SIL-VER STAR MEDAL to:

BRIGADIER GENERAL MERRITT A. EDSON
UNITED STATES MARINE CORPS

for service as set forth in the following citation:

"For conspicuous gallantry and intrepidity as Assistant Division Commander of the Second Marine Division during operations against enemy Japanese forces on the island of Saipan and Tinian in the Marianas Group, from 15 June to 1 August, 1944. Responsible for the supervision and training of the Second Marine Division, Brigadier General Edson brought the regiments of his fighting organization to a high state of combat readiness in preparation for the Marianas Campaign. Landing at Saipan in the early afternoon of 15 June, he moved his men in under heavy enemy artillery and mortar fire, established communications with elements ashore and vigilantly maintained direct contact until the establishment of the Division Command Post ashore. Cool and courageous, he repeatedly risked his life to visit the front-line units, rallying his men and providing expert tactical advice during critical stages of the battle as the Second Division forces pushed relentlessly against fanatic Japanese resistance to render valiant service during the assault and aid in the ultimate capture of Saipan on 9 July. Participating in the invasion of Tinian on 24 July, Brigadier General Edson again demonstrated outstanding qualities of leadership, military acumen, and personal valor during the aggressive, sustained drive which resulted in the seizure of this second fiercely defended enemy base in the strategically important

Marianas Group on 1 August 1944. Stouthearted and indomitable, Brigadier General Edson contributed substantially to the success of our offensive operations in the Pacific Theater and, his brilliant combat skill, unfailing judgment and iron determination in the face of tremendous opposition reflect the highest credit upon himself and the United States Naval Service."

/S/ JAMES FORRESTAL
Secretary of the Navy

The President of the United States takes pleasure in presenting the LEGION OF MERIT to:

COLONEL MERRITT A. EDSON
UNITED STATES MARINE CORPS

for service as set forth in the following citation:

"For exceptionally meritorious in the performance of outstanding services to the Government of the United States as Chief of Staff of the Second Marine Division prior to and during operations against enemy Japanese forces on Tarawa, Gilbert Islands, from 20 to 28 November 1943. Schooled by grim experience in the art of countering Japanese strategies, Colonel Edson directed his division staff in a meticulous intelligence study of Tarawa Atoll, subsequently preparing a carefully evaluated estimate of the situation upon which the Commanding General based his decision to attack on the North Coast. Landing at Betio on D-Day plus-1, he quickly established an advance command post and, remaining ashore throughout the Tarawa Campaign, effected sound solutions to direct problems encountered during critical stages of the operation and prepared tactical plans for the final attack and for clearing the entire Atoll of Japanese positions when the area should be

secured. By his astute military acumen, brilliant profes-
sional skill and unwavering devotion to duty in the face of
fanatic opposition, Colonel Edson contributed essentially
to the assault and capture of this important Japanese base
and his conduct throughout upheld the highest traditions
of the United States Naval Service."

The President of the United States takes pleasure in presenting the GOLD
STAR in lieu of a second LEGION OF MERIT to:

BRIGADIER GENERAL MERRITT A. EDSON
UNITED STATES MARINE CORPS

for service as set forth in the following citation:

"For exceptionally meritorious conduct in the performance
of outstanding services from 26 August, 1944 to 30 June,
1945, as Deputy Chief of Staff and as Chief of Staff for the
Commanding General, Fleet Marine Force, Pacific. Briga-
dier General Edson performed outstanding service by as-
sisting the Commanding General in formulating all gen-
eral policies of the Fleet Marine Force, Pacific, Including
those relating to the amphibious forces, aircraft, supply
service, and those requiring cooperation with the United
States Army and Navy forces. His estimates of the situa-
tion, plans and orders for the Fleet Marine Force, Pacific,
and measures taken to assure the readiness of combat units
were of incalculable benefit in prompting the efficiency of
that organization. His coordination of the supply service
with combat units of the Fleet Marine Force was skillfully
and successfully accomplished. His constant studies of
matters pertaining to types of equipment, weapons, am-
munition, and organization raised the combat effective-
ness of the Fleet Marine Force Units. His untiring efforts
and thorough understanding of the strategic, tactical, and

logistical situations, and his energetic direction of all subordinate staff officers and unit commanders contributed substantially to the successful prosecution of the war against the Japanese enemy. His leadership and conduct throughout were in keeping with the highest traditions of the United States Naval Service."

• • •

Name: First Lieutenant Robert M. Hanson, USMC (Deceased)

Biography: Written October, 1949.

Marine First Lieutenant Robert M. Hanson, missing fighter pilot from Newtonville, Massachusetts, who shot down 25 Japanese planes from the South Pacific Skies, was Posthumously awarded the Medal of Honor, the highest award presented to the military of the United States for gallantry.

Lieutenant Hanson was one of the eleven Marine aviators awarded the Medal of Honor during World War II. In seven years he packed more adventure, excitement, and experience into his life than most people do in seventy years.

He was last seen February 3, 1944, when his plane crashed into the sea while he was flying an escort mission over Rabaul, New Britain.

Famous for one killing spree in which he downed 20 enemy planes in six consecutive flying days, First Lieutenant Hanson was commended in the citation accompanying the Medal of Honor for his bold attack against six enemy torpedo bombers November 1, 1943 over Bougainville Island, and for bringing down four Zeros while fighting them alone over New Britain January 24, 1944.

First Lieutenant Hanson arrived in the South Pacific in June, 1943 and his daring tactics and total disregard for death soon became well known. His fatal crash occurred just one day before his twenty-fourth birthday.

A member of the famed Fighting Corsairs Squadron, the ace was shot down only once before his final flight, when a Zero bagged him over Bougainville Island. Bringing his plane down on the ocean, he paddled for six hours in a rubber life raft before being rescued by a destroyer.

Men of Honor

First Lieutenant Hanson was a son of the Reverend and Mrs. Harry A. Hanson of 31 Brooks Avenue, Newtonville, Massachusetts, who were serving as Methodist missionaries in India at the time of his birth.

In Lucknow, India, his playmates were Hindu children. After attending junior high school in the United States, he returned to India to become light-heavyweight and heavyweight wrestling champion of the United Provinces.

In the spring of 1938, on his way back to the United States, to attend college, he bicycled his way through Europe and was in Vienna during the Anschluss. Though attending Hamline University, in St. Paul, Minnesota, at the time of the attack on Pearl Harbor, he enlisted for naval flight training in May, 1942, and won his wings and a Marine Corps commission as Second Lieutenant on February 19, 1943 at Corpus Christi, Texas.

The Medal of Honor which was awarded for services as a fighter pilot attached to Marine Squadron Two-Fifteen was presented to the Lieutenant's mother Mrs. Harry A. Hanson by General Lewis G. Merrit (now retired) on August 19, 1944 in Boston, Massachusetts.

-USMC-

The following are a newspaper article, written by Sergeant Marion D. Bailey, Atlanta, Georgia, a Marine Corps Combat Correspondent, about Lt. Hanson; his Medal of Honor, Navy Cross, and Air Medal citations:

MARINE PILOT DOWNS THREE JAP PLANES, BECOMING ACE, ON OPENING DAY OF BOUGAINVILLE OFFENSIVE

Vella Lavella, British Solomon Islands, November 7, 1943 – Shooting down three Jap planes, making himself an Ace, and crash-landing his plane in the ocean were one day's activities for First Lieutenant Robert M. Hanson, a Marine fighter pilot, on November 1 – the day the Marines invaded Bougainville.

Twenty-three year-old Lieutenant Hanson, 31 Brooke Avenue, Newtonville, Massachusetts, knocked down two Zeros and a dive bomber, which in addition to previous aerial victories, brought his total to five.

66

Chapter 1: World War II

The Marine Ace said he first saw the Zeros while patrolling over Empress Augusta Bay at 13,000 feet.

"There were six of them," he said. "At first my wingmen and I mistook them for P-40's, for the resemblance is very close. Then we realized our mistake and took out for them."

His intensive fire slowed up the first Zero so that Lieutenant Hanson zoomed right over him.

"Consequently he was able to get a few shots at me from below. When he went spinning" Lieutenant Hanson said, "I'd started after the second Zero. He was doing his best to get away, but I bore-sighted him and let go a long burst. He exploded like a gigantic firecracker."

By this time Lieutenant Hanson had lost his wingmen and started back to hunt for them.

"I never did find them," he said, "instead a group of some six Jap dive-bombers, evidently going to bomb the landing operations below."

"I opened up with everything I had on the closest one. He fell away from the formation, but I don't know if he crashed."

When he started after the second dive-bomber, Lieutenant Hanson said all the Jap planes dropped their bombs harmlessly in the water.

"I could tell what they were thinking: "To hell with the bombs, lets get out of here!" "Then I let go at the one I was chasing."

"I got a little smoke out of him and he started down. But I wanted to make sure he was a goner, so I followed him down to the water, firing short bursts at him all the way."

It was immediately after he saw the dive-bomber hit the ocean that his motor began to conk out.

Water-landing his plane as close as possible to an American Destroyer, the *USS SIGOURNEY*, in the Bay, he removed his life raft ... and began paddling like mad, because I knew the ships were due to pull out shortly."

"For four and a half hours I was a human speedboat," he said. "I didn't stop once – and reached the destroyer just five minutes before it left the Bay."

Even if I hadn't gotten any planes," Lieutenant Hanson declared, "all the steak and fresh eggs I ate while aboard that ship would have been worth the crash."

Men of Honor

-USMC-
Released by CINC PAC FLT for publication.

• • •

The President of the United States takes pleasure in presenting the MEDAL OF HONOR posthumously to:

FIRST LIEUTENANT ROBERT M. HANSON
UNITED STATES MARINE CORPS RESERVE

for as service set forth in the following citation:

"For gallantry and intrepidity at the risk of his life above and beyond the call of duty as a fighter pilot attached to Marine Fighting Squadron Two Fifteen in action against enemy Japanese forces at Bougainville Island, November 1, 1943, and New Britain Island, January 24, 1944. Undeterred by fierce opposition and fearless in the face of overwhelming odds, First Lieutenant Hanson fought the Japanese boldly and with daring aggressiveness. On November 1, while flying cover for our landing operations at Empress Augusta Bay, he dauntlessly attacked six enemy torpedo bombers, forcing them to jettison their bombs and destroying one Japanese plane during the action. Cut off from his division while deep in enemy territory during a high cover flight over Simpson Harbor on January 24, First Lieutenant Hanson waged a lone and gallant battle against hostile interceptors as they were orbiting to attack our bombers and, striking with devastating fury, brought down four Zeros and probably a fifth. Handling his plane superbly in both pursuit and attack measures, he was a master of individual air combat, accounting for a total of 25 Japanese aircraft in this theater of war. His great personal valor and invincible fighting spirit were in keeping with the highest traditions of the United States Naval Service."

Chapter 1: World War II

/S/ FRANKLIN D. ROOSEVELT

The President of the United States takes pleasure in presenting the NAVY CROSS to:

FIRST LIEUTENANT ROBERT M. HANSON
UNITED STATES MARINE CORPS RESERVE

for service as set forth in the following citation:

"For extraordinary heroism while serving as a pilot of a fighter plane attached to Marine Fighter Squadron TWO FIFTEEN in action against enemy Japanese forces in the Solomon Islands area from January 5 to February 3, 1944. Intercepted by a superior number of Japanese fighters while covering a flight of our bombers in a strike against enemy shipping in Simpson Harbor on January 14, First Lieutenant Hanson boldly engaged the hostile planes in fierce combat, pressing home repeated attacks with devastating force. Separated from his squadron during the intense action, he valiantly continued the engagement alone, successfully destroying five enemy Zeros before being forced by lack of ammunition and gasoline to return to his base. First Lieutenant Hanson's superb airmanship, brilliant initiative, and dauntless fighting spirit enabled our bombers to deliver a crushing blow to the Japanese in that sector and return safe to their base and his conduct throughout was in keeping with the highest traditions of the United States Naval Service."

For the President,
/S/ JAMES FORRESTAL
Secretary of the Navy

The President of the United States takes pleasure in presenting the AIR MEDAL to:

SECOND LIEUTENANT ROBERT M. HANSON, USMCR.,

for service as set forth in the following citation:

> *"For meritorious achievement as a pilot in Marine Fighting Squadron TWO FOURTEEN during action against enemy Japanese forces in the Solomon Islands area from July 22 to September 1, 1943. Intercepted by hostile fighters while covering a strafing mission, Second Lieutenant Hanson courageously ignored two Japanese flyers close on his tail in order to shoot down in flames a Zero which was menacing one of the members of his flight. Although his own plane was severely damaged in the course of the engagement, he nevertheless managed to return safely to his base. On escort for a flight of Liberators withdrawing from a bombing mission at Kahili, he was compelled to lag behind his three-plane division because of a defective operational blower. Despite this handicap, however, he intercepted and destroyed a Zero which was pressing his flight leader in a persistent stern run. His aggressive spirit and conscientious devotion to duty were in keeping with the highest traditions of the United States Naval Service."*

> *For the President,*
> */S/ FRANK KNOX*
> *Secretary of the Navy.*

• • •

Name: Major General Louis R. Jones, USMC (Retired)

Biography: Written 1950.

Retired Major General Louis R. Jones was Assistant Division Commander of the First Marine Division during the Okinawa operation in 1945 and was Commanding Officer of the Twenty-third Marine Regiment during the seizure of Kwajalein Atoll, Marshall Islands in February, 1944 and during

Chapter 1: World War II

the battles for Saipan and Tinian during June, July, and August of 1944.

For his outstanding services in the above capacities he was awarded a Legion of Merit, a Gold Star in lieu of a second Legion of Merit, and the Navy Cross.

General Jones was born on June 29, 1895, in Philadelphia, Pennsylvania. He enlisted in the Marine Corps on December 14, 1914. On July 10, 1917 he reported for active duty as a second lieutenant in the United States Marine Corps at the Marine Corps Rifle Range in Winthrop, Maryland.

He sailed for France in September, 1917, where as a member of the Sixth Marine Regiment he participated in the defense of the Verdun Sector where he was gassed. He also took part in the Aisne-Marne Defensive (Chateau Thierry), the Aisne- Marne Offensive (Soissons), and the St. Mihiel Offensive. He was a member of the Army of Occupation in Germany following the conclusion of the war, and sailed for the United States in April, 1919.

For outstanding services in the Aisne-Marne Offensive (Soissons) he was awarded the French Croix de Guerre. His citation reads in part, "Separated from his own organization in the action near Vierzy, July, 1918, he reported to the Commanding Officer of another Battalion and assisted in organizing a provisional unit on the advanced line, displaying the utmost coolness in the performance of his task."

He was also awarded the Silver Star with Oak Leaf Cluster in lieu of a second Silver Star, the Purple Heart Medal, and was cited both in the General Orders of the Second Division, AEF, and by the Commander-in-Chief, AEF. He is entitled to wear the French Fourragere. Following his return to this country he was assigned duty at the Naval Proving Ground, Indian Head, Maryland. In September, 1921, he joined the Marine Barracks, Quantico, Virginia, where he remained until October, 1922, when he was detached for duty with the Second Marine Brigade in the Dominican Republic.

The general returned to the United States in October, 1924, and was ordered to the Fourth Marine Regiment at the Marine Corps Base, San Diego, California, where he joined the First Battalion as Headquarters Company Commander. In September, 1925, he became Regimental Quartermaster and two years later in February, 1927, sailed with the Regiment for Shanghai, China.

In January, 1930, he was assigned to recruiting duty at Cleveland, Ohio, and in August of the same year he was ordered to the Marine Corps Schools, Quantico, Virginia, where he became a student at the Field Officers' Course.

Upon completion of the course in June, 1931, he went to sea duty as Commanding Officer of the Marine Detachment aboard the *USS TEXAS*.

He returned to shore duty in January, 1934, when he joined the Fifth Battalion, Fleet Marine Force, at the Marine Corps Base, San Diego. In August, he joined the Sixth Marine Regiment where he served as Regimental Executive Officer and Operations Officer. He was transferred to the East Coast in October, 1935, and was assigned to the Marine Corps Schools at Quantico, Virginia, as an instructor in the Correspondence School. In May, 1938 he was named Director of the School.

The General was ordered to the Marine Barracks at Parris Island, South Carolina, in June, 1939, where he became Commanding Officer of the Recruit Depot and Post Training Officer. In September, 1941, he was named Chief of Staff of the Post, in which capacity he was found upon this country's entry into World War II.

He took Command of the Twenty-third Marine Regiment in September, 1942, at Camp Lejeune and sailed for the Central Pacific in January, 1944, where he led the Regiment in battle for Roi Island, Kwajalein Atoll, Marshall Islands, February, 1944, and for which he received the Legion of Merit.

He continued as Commanding Officer of the Regiment during the Saipan and Tinian operations in the summer of 1944, where he was awarded the Navy Cross for his outstanding services.

He was named Assistant Division Commander of the First Marine Division in October, 1944, and participated in action against Japanese forces on Okinawa, Ryukyu Islands, from April 1 to June 21, 1945, where he received a Gold Star in lieu of a second Legion of Merit.

Following the conclusion he took part in the occupation of North China in September, 1945, where he was awarded an Oak Leaf Cluster in lieu of a third Legion of Merit.

He returned to the United States and in June, 1946, assumed duties as President of the Marine Corps Equipment Board at the Marine Corps Schools, Quantico, Virginia, in which capacity he was serving when he was retired on June 30, 1949.

Chapter 1: World War II

-USMC-

The following are General Jones' Navy Cross and two Legion of Merit citations:

The President of the United States takes pleasure in presenting the NAVY CROSS to:

GENERAL LOUIS R. JONES
UNITED STATES MARINE CORPS

for action as set forth in the following citation:

> "For distinguishing himself by extraordinary heroism while serving as Commanding Officer of a United States Marine Corps Regimental Combat Team in the assault on the Japanese held islands of Saipan and Tinian, Marianas Islands, from 15 June to 2 August, 1944. Landing on both islands in the initial assault on a vital sector, the Regiment under his inspiring and determined leadership seized a beachhead in the face of heavy artillery, mortar, and machinegun fire and held the beaches against repeated counterattacks until the full force of the supporting elements could be landed. By his outstanding professional ability, resourcefulness in meeting battle exigencies and keen analysis of enemy tactics, he coordinated the efforts of the units under his command and led his Regiment in constant attack against a fanatical and tenacious enemy, Seizing successively assigned objectives daily and destroying thousands of the enemy. With complete disregard for his own personal safety he was constantly in the field throughout the operation, visiting his front-line units and coordinating their efforts. His brilliant leadership and personal example were inspiring and were in keeping with the highest traditions of the United States Naval Service."

/S/ JAMES FORRESTAL
Secretary of the Navy

The President of the United States takes pleasure in presenting the LEGION OF MERIT to:

GENERAL LOUIS R. JONES
UNITED STATES MARINE CORPS

for service as set forth in the following citation:

> *"For exceptionally meritorious conduct in the performance of outstanding service to the Government of the United States while serving as Commanding Officer of a regimental combat team in the attack on the enemy airfield and defenses on Roi Island, Kwajalein Atoll, on 1 and 2 February, 1944. Under his leadership his combat team attacked with speed and determination and secured control of this important objective in a matter of six hours. The efficient manner in which enemy resistance was overcome resulted in the capture of the objective with minimum casualties. His initiative and leadership were in keeping with the highest traditions of the United States Naval Service."*

The President of the United States takes pleasure in presenting the GOLD STAR in lieu of a second LEGION OF MERIT to:

GENERAL LOUIS R. JONES
UNITED STATES MARINE CORPS

for service as set forth in the following citation:

> *"For exceptionally meritorious conduct in the performance of outstanding services while serving as Assistant Division Commander of a Marine Division prior to and in the course of operations on Okinawa Shima, Ryukyu Islands,*

during the period 7 November, 1944 to 22 June, 1945. It being necessary to divide the reinforced division to ensure adequate training prior to the operation, Brigadier General Jones displayed his high professional achievements in commendable manner, and was chiefly responsible for the high state of combat efficiency they attained. Throughout the eighty-three day campaign, the tactical skill he had developed in the Marshalls and Marianas was an important factor in carrying the attack to the enemy. His presence among the assault forces unified to a marked degree and contributed materially to the success of a most difficult operation. His personal courage, determination, and abundant energy were in keeping with the highest traditions of the United States Naval Service."

• • •

Name: Brigadier General Harry B. Liversedge, USMC, (Deceased).

Biography: 1951
Brigadier General Harry Bluett Liversedge, whose regiment figured in the historic Iwo Jima flag raising, died in 1951 after almost 25 years of Marine Corps service. His last assignment was as director of the Marine Corps Reserve.

The former Olympic track star was awarded his second Navy Cross for extraordinary heroism as commander of the 28th Marines at "Iwo." He had won his first while leading the crack 1st Marine Raider Regiment in the tough jungle fighting on New Georgia.

Two decades ago the name Liversedge was a familiar one in sports page headlines, when as a member of the Navy track squads, he participated in the 1920 and the 1924 Olympic Games. He also figured prominently in football as a member of the championship Marine football teams of the early 1920s.

Born in Volcano, California on September 21, 1894, he attended the University of California at Berkeley. While a student at the school from 1914-17, he set an inter-collegiate mark with the 16-pound shot. It was in that event that he participated in the 1920 Olympics at Antwerp, winning third place in the international competition.

General Liversedge began his career as a Leatherneck in May, 1917, when he enlisted as a private, and was commissioned a second lieutenant in September, 1918. He was promoted to first lieutenant in July, 1919 while serving with the Fifth Brigade in France.

Following his return to the United States in August, 1919, he was ordered to the Marine Barracks, Quantico, Virginia, but shortly thereafter was assigned to the Second Provisional Marine Brigade at Santo Domingo, arriving in October of that year. In April of the following year he was returned to the United States and played football in the Army-Marine Corps game at Baltimore, Maryland.

Upon return from the Olympic Games in 1920 and after a tour at the Naval Academy at Annapolis, he was ordered to the Marine Barracks at Quantico in March, 1922. As aide to Brigadier General John H. Russell, he later sailed to Port au Prince, Haiti, but was ordered back to Quantico in August of the same year. He returned to Haiti in December of that year for duty as aide to the American High Commissioner.

In July, 1923, he reported for duty again at Quantico, and in the early part of the following year was transferred to the Naval Academy for participation in the 1924 Olympics. He returned to Quantico in August of that year, this time to attend the Company Officers' Course at the Marine Corps Schools. Upon completion of his course he was transferred to Mare Island, California.

He served at Quantico from September, 1926 to February, 1927 when he was detached for duty in China. Following his arrival in the Orient he was temporarily detached to the Third Brigade at Tientsin to act as boxing coach, and while in Shanghai, participated in the International Track and Field Meets.

In August, 1929, he was transferred to Quantico and in November of the same year was ordered to the Marine Corps Base at San Diego, California. Following his promotion to the rank of captain in January, 1930, he was ordered to Headquarters, Department of the Pacific, San Francisco, in May,1932. There he served as Aide-de-Camp to the Commanding General.

He served aboard the *USS CALIFORNIA*, from June,1933 to June, 1935, when he returned to Quantico. He completed the Senior Course at the Marine Corps Schools and in June 1936, was transferred to serve on the Staff of the Basic School, Marine Barracks, Navy Yard, Philadelphia. He was appointed a major in July of that year.

Early in 1938 he was again ordered to Quantico, this time to serve with the First Marine Brigade. In May, 1940 another transfer saw the General on the West Coast. There he was assigned duty as the Inspector-Instructor, Fourteenth Battalion, Marine Corps Reserve at Spokane, Washington.

Following his promotion to the rank of lieutenant colonel in August, 1940, he was ordered to the Marine Corps Base, San Diego, and was subsequently assigned to the Eighth Marines, Second Marine Division.

In January, 1942, General Liversedge departed from the United States for American Samoa, in command of the Second Battalion, Eighth Marines. He was promoted to colonel in May of that same year and in August he assumed command of the Third Marine Raider Battalion. He led this unit ashore at Pavuvu in the unopposed occupation of the Russell Island. He commanded the battalion until March, 1943 when he was given command of the newly-organized First Marine Raider Regiment.

In January, 1944, he was transferred to the Fifth Marine Division and assumed command of the 28th Marines. He gallantly led the 28th ashore in the Iwo Jima campaign, for which he was awarded a Gold Star in lieu of a second Navy Cross. Following a brief tour of duty with the occupation forces in Japan, he was ordered to the Marine Corps Base in San Diego in March, 1946. In July, 1946 he was assigned duties as Director of the Twelfth Marine Reserve District and District Marine Officer, Twelfth Naval District, San Francisco.

He served in that capacity until he was named Assistant Commander of the 1st Marine Division, Camp Pendleton, California, in February, 1948. In May of that year he was promoted to Brigadier General, and the following May, he took command of Fleet Marine Force, Guam, where he remained until April, 1950. He then served briefly as Deputy Commander, Marine Barracks, Camp Pendleton, before becoming Director of the Marine Corps Reserve in June, 1950. He died at the Navy Medical Center, Bethesda, Maryland, on November 25, 1951, survived by a sister, Mrs. Ruette Fessel of Pine Grove, California.

The following are General Liversedge's two Navy Cross citations:

The President of the United States takes pleasure in presenting the NAVY CROSS to:

COLONEL HARRY B. LIVERSEDGE
UNITED STATES MARINE CORPS

for action as set forth in the following citation:

> *"For extraordinary heroism as the Commanding Officer of Marine Corps and Army forces during operations on New Georgia Island, Solomon Islands, during the period from July 5 to August 29, 1943. Colonel Liversedge gallantly led his troops against a fanatic and savage enemy, well versed in jungle warfare and entrenched in strong, previously prepared positions, with such relentless courage and heroic determination that the Japanese were forced to withdraw and their ultimate defeat accomplished. His complete disregard for his own safety during exposure to enemy fire while leading advance elements of his forces and his daring and brilliant tactics were an inspiration to his command and were in keeping with the highest traditions of the United States Naval Service."*

> */S/ WILLIAM F. HALSEY, JR.*
> *Admiral, United States Navy*

The President of the United States takes pleasure in presenting a GOLD STAR in lieu of a second NAVY CROSS to:

COLONEL HARRY B. LIVERSEDGE
UNITED STATES MARINE CORPS

for service as set forth in the following citation:

"For extraordinary heroism in action against the enemy while serving as Commanding Officer of a Marine Regimental Combat Team on Iwo Jima, Volcano Islands, from 19 February to 27 March, 1945. Colonel Liversedge, by landing on the fire-swept beaches twenty-two minutes after H-hour in order to personally direct the assault of his regiment on the ground, inspired his officers and men by his gallant conduct and brilliant leadership, to advance across the island and execute the turn to the south, prepared to assault Mount Suribachi. Attacking Mount Suribachi on 21 February, his regiment had effected a partial seizure of a formidable enemy position consisting of caves, pill boxes, and blockhouses, but because of intense enemy resistance, it was receiving severe casualties causing the advance to be checked. Fully aware of his own peril, He fearlessly went forward and in spite of the heavy enemy fire, traversed the front lines and by his heroism and brilliant leadership, encouraged his troops and reorganized them. By nightfall they advanced four-hundred yards, over-running the enemy stronghold. This advance led to the vital seizure of Mount Suribachi. His indomitable fighting spirit, conspicuous gallantry, and superb leadership were an inspiration to all, and were in keeping with the highest traditions of the United States Naval Service."

/S/ H.M. SMITH
Lt. General, USMC

• • •

Men of Honor

Name: Lieutenant Colonel Joseph J. McCarthy, USMCR.

Biography: Written 1945.

Lieutenant Colonel Joseph Jeremiah McCarthy, USMCR, earned the Medal of Honor for gallantry in action while commanding a rifle company on Iwo Jima.

Colonel McCarthy was borne in Chicago, Illinois, August 10, 1911. He first enlisted in the Marine Corps on February 20, 1937 at Chicago and served for four years. Following the attack on Pearl Harbor, he reenlisted and returned to active duty in February, 1942. In June of that year he was discharged with the rank of First Sergeant in order to accept a commission in the Marine Corps Reserve.

He joined the Fourth Marine Division shortly thereafter, and went overseas in January, 1944. Overseas, he took part in the Roi-Namur, Saipan-Tinian, and Iwo Jima campaigns. For heroism as a rifle company commander on Saipan in 1944, he was awarded the Silver Star Medal. The Purple Heart with Gold Star was awarded him for wounds received on Saipan and Iwo Jima.

On February 21, 1945, as a captain, he earned the Medal of Honor on Iwo Jima, while leading an assault team across exposed ground to wipe out positions holding up the advance of his company. The Medal was presented to him by President Truman in ceremonies at the White House, October 5, 1945.

Released from active duty following the war, he holds the grade of Lieutenant Colonel in the Marine Corps Reserve.

-USMC-

The following are Lt. Colonel McCarthy's Medal of Honor and Silver Star citations:

The President of the United States takes pride in presenting the MEDAL OF HONOR to:

CAPTAIN JOSEPH J. McCARTHY
UNITED STATES MARINE CORPS RESERVE

for service as set forth in the following citation:

"For conspicuous gallantry and intrepidity at the risk of his life above and beyond the call of duty as Commanding Officer of Company G, Second Battalion, Twenty Fourth Marines, Fourth Marine Division, in action against enemy Japanese forces during the seizure of Iwo Jima, Volcano Islands, on 21 February 1945. Determined to break through the enemy's cross-island defenses, Captain McCarthy acted on his own initiative when his company's advance was held up by uninterrupted Japanese rifle, machine-gun and high velocity 47-mm. fire during the approach to Motoyamo Airfield Number Two. Quickly organizing a demolitions and flamethrower team to accompany his picked rifle squad, he fearlessly led the way across seventy-five yards of fire-swept ground, charged a heavily fortified pillbox on the ridge to the front and, personally hurling hand grenades into the emplacement as he directed the combined operations of his small assault group, completely destroyed the hostile installation. Spotting two Japanese soldiers attempting an escape from the shattered pillbox, he boldly stood upright in full view of the enemy and dispatched both troops before advancing to a second emplacement under greatly intensified fire and blasted the strong fortifications with a well-planned demolitions attack. Subsequently entering the ruins, he found a Japanese taking aim at one of his men and with alert presence of mind jumped the enemy, disarmed and shot him with his own weapon. Then, intent on smashing through the narrow breach, he rallied the remainder of his company and pressed a full attack with furious aggressiveness until he had neutralized all resistance and captured the ridge. An inspiring leader and indomitable fighter, Captain McCarthy consistently disregarded all personal danger during the fierce conflict and by his brilliant professional skill, daring tactics and tenacious perseverance in the face

81

of overwhelming odds, contributed materially to the success of his division's operations against this savagely defended outpost of the Japanese Empire. His cool decision and outstanding valor reflect the highest credit upon Captain McCarthy and enhance the finest traditions of the United States Naval Service."

/S/ HARRY S. TRUMAN

The President of the United States takes pleasure in presenting the SILVER STAR MEDAL to:

CAPTAIN JOSEPH J. McCARTHY
UNITED STATES MARINE CORPS RESERVE

for service as set forth in the following citation:

"For conspicuous gallantry and intrepidity as Commanding Officer of Company G, Second Battalion, Twenty Fourth Marines, Fourth Marine Division, in action against enemy Japanese forces on Saipan, Marianas Islands, 4 July 1944. With his company in a defensive position and receiving intense and accurate enemy rifle and machine-gun fire, Captain McCarthy gallantly left cover to answer the cries of the wounded after two hospital corpsmen had been shot in quick succession while attempting to aid a wounded officer. Finding one of the men still alive, he attempted to remove him to safety despite the withering enemy fire, but during this endeavor the wounded man was shot through the head and died in Captain McCarthy's arms. His outstanding courage, unselfish efforts, and gallant devotion to duty were in keeping with the highest traditions of the United States Naval Service."

For the President,
/S/ JOHN L. SULLIVAN
Secretary of the Navy

Chapter 1: World War II

• • •

Name: Lieutenant General Lewis B. Puller, USMC (Deceased).

Biography: Revised October, 1970.

Lieutenant General Lewis Burwell Puller, colorful veteran of the Korean fighting, four World War II campaigns and expeditionary service in China, Nicaragua and Haiti, was one of the most decorated Marines in the Corps and the only Leatherneck ever to win the Navy Cross five times for heroism and gallantry in action. Promoted to his present rank and placed on the temporary disability retired list November 1, 1955, he now makes his home in Saluda, Virginia.

The general's last active duty station was Camp Lejeune, North Carolina, where he was commanding the 2nd Marine Division when he became seriously ill in August, 1954. After that he served as Deputy Camp Commander until his illness forced him to retire.

A Marine officer and enlisted man for 37 years, General Puller served at sea or overseas for all but ten of those years, including a hitch as commander of the "Horse Marines" in China. Excluding medals from foreign governments, he won a total of 14 personal decorations in combat, plus a long list of campaign medals, unit citation ribbons and other awards. In addition to his Navy Crosses (the next-highest decoration to the Medal of Honor for Naval personnel), he holds its Army equivalent, the Distinguished Service Cross.

He was awarded the Distinguished Service Cross and his fifth Navy Cross for heroism in action as commander of the 1st Marines, 1st Marine Division, during the bitter fight to break out of Korea's Chosin reservoir area. The latter citation, covering the period from December 5, to 10, 1950, states in part:

"Fighting continuously in sub-zero weather against a vastly outnumbering hostile force, (the then) Colonel Puller drove off repeated and fanatical enemy attacks upon his Regimental defense sector and supply points. Although the area was frequently covered by grazing machine gun fire and intense artillery and mortar fire, he coolly moved among his troops to insure their correct tactical employment, reinforced the lines as the situation demanded and successfully defended his perimeter, keeping open the main supply routes for the movement of the Division.

"During the attack from Koto-ri to Hungnam, he expertly utilized his Regiment as the Division rear guard, repelling two fierce enemy assaults which severely threatened the security of the unit, and personally supervised the care and prompt evacuation of all casualties.

"By his unflagging determination, he served to inspire his men to heroic efforts in defense of their positions and assured the safety of much valuable equipment which would otherwise have been lost to the enemy. His skilled leadership, superb courage and valiant devotion to duty in the face of overwhelming odds reflect the highest credit upon Colonel Puller and the United States Naval Service."

Serving in Korea from September, 1950, to April, 1951, the general also earned the Army Silver Star Medal in the Inchon landing, his second Legion of Merit with Combat "V" in the Inchon-Seoul fighting and the early phases of the Chosin reservoir campaign, and three Air Medals for reconnaissance and liaison flights over enemy territory.

General Puller also fought with the 1st Marine Division in the World War II campaigns on Guadalcanal, Eastern New Guinea, Camp Gloucester and Peleliu, earning his third Navy Cross and the Bronze Star and Purple Heart Medals at Guadalcanal, his fourth Navy Cross at Cape Gloucester and his first Legion of Merit with Combat "V" at Peleliu. He won his first Navy Cross in November, 1930, and his second in September and October, 1932, while fighting bandits in Nicaragua.

Born June 26, 1898, at West Point, Virginia, the general attended Virginia Military Institute until enlisting in the Marine Corps in August, 1918. He was appointed a Marine reserve second lieutenant June 16, 1919, but due to the reduction of the Marine Corps after World War I, was placed on inactive duty ten days later. He rejoined the Marines as an enlisted man on the 30th of that month, to serve as an officer in the Gendarmerie d'Haiti, a military force set up in that country under a treaty with the United States. Most of its officers were U.S. Marines, while its enlisted personnel were Haitians.

After almost five years in Haiti, where he saw frequent action against the Caco rebels, General Puller returned to the United States in March, 1924. He was commissioned a Marine second lieutenant that same month, and during the next two years, served at the Marine Barracks, Norfolk,

Virginia, completed the Basic School at Philadelphia, Pennsylvania, and served with the 10th Marine Regiment at Quantico, Virginia. He was then detailed to duty as a student naval aviator at Pensacola, Florida, in February, 1926.

In July, of that year, the general embarked for a two-year tour of duty at the Marine Barracks, Pearl Harbor. Returning in June, 1928, he served at San Diego, California, until he joined the Nicaraguan National Guard Detachment that December. After winning his first Navy Cross in Nicaragua he returned to the United States in July, 1931, to enter the Company Officers Course at the Army Infantry School, Fort Benning, Georgia. He completed the course in June, 1932, and returned to Nicaragua the following month to begin the tour of duty which brought him his second Navy Cross.

In January, 1933, General Puller left Nicaragua for the west coast of the United States. A month later he sailed from San Francisco to join the Marine Detachment of the American Legation at Peiping, China. There, in addition to other duties, he commanded the famed "Horse Marines." Without coming back to the United States he began a tour of sea duty in September, 1934, as commanding officer of the Marine Detachment aboard the USS Augusta of the Asiatic Fleet. In June, 1936, he returned to the United States to become an instructor in the Basic School at Philadelphia. He left there in May, 1939, to serve another year as commander of the Augusta's Marine detachment, and from that ship, joined the 4th Marine Regiment at Shanghai, China, in May, 1940.

After serving as a battalion executive and commanding officer with the 4th Marines, General Puller sailed for the United States in August, 1941, just four months before the attack on Pearl Harbor. In September he took command of the 1st Battalion, 7th Marines, 1st Marine Division, at Camp Lejeune. That regiment was detached from the 1st Division in March, 1942, and the following month, as part of the 3rd Marine Brigade, it sailed for the Pacific theater. The 7th Regiment rejoined the 1st Marine Division in September, 1942, and General Puller, still commanding its 1st Battalion, went on to win his third Navy Cross at Guadalcanal.

The action which brought him that medal occurred on the night of October 24-25, 1942. For a desperate three hours his battalion, stretched over a mile-long front, was the only defense between vital Henderson Airfield and a regiment of seasoned Japanese troops. In pouring jungle rain, the Japanese smashed repeatedly at his thin line, as General Puller moved up and down its length to encourage his men and direct the defense. After reinforcements arrived he commanded the augmented force until late the next afternoon. The defending Marines suffered less than 70 casualties in the engagement, while 1400 of the enemy were killed and 17 truckloads of Japanese equipment were recovered by the Americans.

After Guadalcanal, the general became executive officer of the 7th Marines. He was fighting in that capacity when he won his fourth Navy Cross at Cape Gloucester in January, 1944. There, when the commanders of two battalions were wounded, he took over their units and moved through heavy machine gun and mortar fire to reorganize them for attack, then led them in taking a strongly-fortified enemy position.

In February, 1944, General Puller took command of the 1st Marines at Cape Gloucester. After leading that regiment for the remainder of the campaign, he sailed with it for the Russell Islands in April, 1944, and went on from there to command it at Peleliu in September and October, 1944. He returned to the United States in November, 1944, was named executive officer of the Infantry Training Regiment at Camp Lejeune in January, 1945, and took command of that regiment the next month.

In August, 1946, General Puller became Director of the 8th Marine Corps Reserve District, with headquarters at New Orleans, Louisiana. After that assignment he commanded the Marine Barracks at Pearl Harbor until August, 1950, when he arrived at Camp Pendleton, California, to re-establish and take command of the 1st Marines, the same regiment he had led at Cape Gloucester and Peleliu.

Landing with the 1st Marines at Inchon, Korea, in September, 1950, he continued to head that regiment until January, 1951, when he was promoted to brigadier general and named Assistant Commander of the 1st Marine Division. That May he returned to Camp Pendleton to command the newly reactivated 3rd Marine Brigade, which was redesignated the 3rd Marine Division in January, 1952. After that, he was assistant division commander until he took over the Troop Training Unit, Pacific, at Coronado, California, that June. He was promoted to major general in September, 1953, and in July, 1954, assumed command of the 2nd Marine Division at Camp Lejeune. Despite his illness he retained that command until February, 1955, when he was appointed Deputy Camp Commander. He served in that capacity until August, when he entered the U.S. Naval Hospital at Camp Lejeune prior to retirement.

As already mentioned, the general holds the Navy Cross with Gold Stars in lieu of four additional awards; the Army Distinguished Service Cross, the Army Silver Star Medal;the Legion of Merit with Combat "V" and Gold Star in lieu of a second; the Bronze Star Medal; the Air Medal with Gold Stars in lieu of second and third awards; and the Purple Heart Medal. His other medals and decorations include the Presidential Unit Citation Ribbon with four bronze stars; the Marine Corps Good Conduct Medal with one bronze star; the World War I Victory Medal with West Indies clasp; the Haitian Campaign Medal; the Second Nicaraguan Campaign Medal; the Marine Corps Expeditionary Medal with one bronze star; the China Service Medal; the American Defense Service Medal with Base clasp; the American Area Campaign Medal; the Asiatic-Pacific Area Campaign Medal with four bronze stars; the World War II Victory Medal; the National Defense Service Medal; the Korean Service Medal with one silver star in lieu of five bronze stars; the United Nations Service Medal; the Haitian Medaille Militaire; the Nicaraguan Presidential Medal of Merit with Diploma; the Nicaraguan Cross of Valor with Diploma; the Republic of Korea's Ulchi Medal with Gold Star; and the Korean Presidential Unit Citation with Oak Leaf Cluster.

General Puller died on October 11, 1971, in Hampton, Virginia., after a long illness. He was buried in a family plot at the Christ's Church Cemetery, Middlesex County, Virginia.

-USMC-

The following are a news paper article, that appeared in *THE DAYTON DAILY NEWS*, about Lt. General Puller, his two Navy Cross, Bronze Star, and Legion of Merit citations:

Gen. Puller, Marine Boss, To Retire

WASHINGTON, Oct. 1, 1955 - Major General Lewis B. "Chesty" Puller, a living legend of the Marine Corps, will retire November 1.

The Marines announced yesterday that Puller - holder of seven Purple

Hearts, five Navy Crosses and the Army's Distinguished Service Medal - has been ordered retired for physical disability. Puller is 57.

Many are the vivid stories told by Marine veterans who saw the two-fisted Puller in action in World War II and Korea.

At the Chosin Reservoir in Korea an Army battalion commander asked Puller for a route of retreat. Puller just picked up a field telephone and told his tank commander to shoot if the Army battalion moved. Then he barked at the Army officer: "that answer your question?"

On Guadalcanal where he led the First Battalion, Seventh Marines, Puller earned a Navy Cross for holding vital Henderson Field against the Japanese.

After the fight that night, Puller was severely wounded helping repair a vital communications line. When a hospital corpsman put a casualty tag on him, Puller snarled, "take that damn tag and label a bottle with it." He remained in the line and to this day carries a hunk of lead in his thigh.

On Cape Gloucester Puller always found it easier on inspection trips to walk outside the barbed wire with his back to the enemy.

Probably his toughest fight was on Peleliu where his First Marine Regiment lost 1672 men in 197 hours of fighting. Many a Marine will remember Puller there, stripped to the waist in the broiling heat, a pipe clipped in his teeth as he barked orders.

Born at West Point, Va., on June 26, 1898, Puller quit the Virginia Military Institute in 1918 to join the Marines as an enlisted man. He will retire to Saluda in his native Virginia.

• • •

The President of the United States takes pleasure in presenting the GOLD STAR in lieu of a third NAVY CROSS to:

LIEUTENANT COLONEL LEWIS B. PULLER
UNITED STATES MARINE CORPS

for service as set forth in the following citation:

"For extraordinary heroism as Commanding Officer of the First Battalion, Seventh Marines, First Marine Division, during action against enemy Japanese forces on Guadalcanal, Solomon Islands, on the night of October 24-25, 1942. While Lieutenant Colonel Puller's battalion was holding a mile-long front in a heavy downpour of rain, a Japanese force, superior in number, launched a vigorous assault against that portion of the line which passed through a dense jungle. Courageously withstanding the enemy's desperate and determined attacks, Lieutenant Colonel Puller not only held his battalion to its position until reinforcements arrived three hours later, but also effectively commanded the augmented force until late in the afternoon of the next day. By his tireless devotion to duty and cool judgment under fire, he prevented a hostile penetration of our lines and was largely responsible for the successful defense of the sector assigned to his troops."

For the President
/S/ FRANK KNOX
Secretary of the Navy

The President of the United States takes pleasure in presenting the GOLD STAR in lieu of a fourth NAVY CROSS to:

LIEUTENANT COLONEL LEWIS B. PULLER
UNITED STATES MARINE CORPS

for service as set forth in the following citation:

"For extraordinary heroism as Executive Officer of the Seventh Marines, First Marine Division, serving with the Sixth United States Army, in combat against enemy Japanese forces at Cape Gloucester, New Britain, from December 26, 1943, to January 19, 1944. Assigned temporary command of the Third Battalion, Seventh Marines, from

January 4 to 9, Lieutenant Colonel Puller quickly reorganized and advanced this unit, effecting the seizure of the objective without delay. Assuming additional duty in command of the Third Battalion, Fifth Marines, from January 7 to 8, after the commanding officer and executive officer had been wounded, Lieutenant Colonel Puller unhesitatingly exposed himself to rifle, machine-gun and mortar fire from strongly entrenched Japanese positions to move from company to company in his front lines, reorganizing and maintaining a critical position along a fire-swept ridge. His forceful leadership and gallant fighting spirit under the most hazardous conditions were contributing factors in the defeat of the enemy during this campaign and in keeping with the highest traditions of the United States Naval Service."

For the President,
/S/ JAMES FORRESTAL
Secretary of the Navy

The President of the United States takes pleasure in presenting the BRONZE STAR MEDAL to:

LIEUTENANT COLONEL LEWIS B. PULLER
UNITED STATES MARINE CORPS

for service as set forth in the following citation:

"For heroic achievement as Commanding Officer of the First Battalion, Seventh Marines, First Marine Division, in action against enemy Japanese forces on Guadalcanal, British Solomon Islands, 8 and 9 November, 1942. After leading his battalion in an arduous three-day advance through treacherous jungle and swamp, Lieutenant Colonel Puller skillfully deployed his men and launched a vigorous, coordinated attack against unusually strong enemy

positions supported by at least two field guns, and, although wounded while directing the assault, valiantly remained in command of his intrepid battalion until the following morning. By his aggressive leadership, indomitable fighting spirit and devotion to duty, Lieutenant Colonel Puller served as an inspiration to his officers and men, thereby reflecting great credit upon himself and the United States Naval Service."

For the President,
/S/ JAMES FORRESTAL
Secretary of the Navy

In the name of the President of the United States, the Commanding General, Fleet Marine Force, Pacific, takes pleasure in awarding the LEGION OF MERIT to:

COLONEL LEWIS B. PULLER
UNITED STATES MARINE CORPS

for service as set forth in the following citation:

"For exceptionally meritorious conduct in the performance of outstanding services to the Government of the United States as a Marine infantry regimental commander in a Marine Division, prior to and during the action against Japanese forces on PELELIU and NGESEBUS, PALAU GROUP, 15 September to 2 October, 1944. Landing with the assault battalions of his regiment on a strongly fortified and heavily mined beach, Colonel PULLER, with skillful leadership, effectively reorganized his attacking force and under intense enemy gunfire, promptly seized the initial objective. When the enemy counterattacked, by skillful use of his combined arms, including tanks, Colonel PULLER coolly coordinated his defensive fires and repulsed all attacks, inflicting heavy losses upon the enemy.

With resolute determination he masterfully maneuvered his assault elements into positions where the enemy was blasted out of an intricate system of caves inter-connected in the coral-lime terrain. The combat efficiency and bold tenacity displayed by his regiment resulted directly from his leadership and high example. His exceptionally meritorious conduct materially aided in the success of the operation and was at all times in keeping with the highest traditions of the United States Naval Service."

/S/ H.M. SMITH
Lieutenant General, U.S. Marine Corps.

• • •

Name: First Lieutenant Carlton R. Rouh, USMCR.

Biography: Circa 1945.
Lieutenant Rouh, 26, was awarded the Medal of Honor for gallantry in risking his life to save two comrades from a Jap grenade on Peleliu Island, September 15, 1944, during the first few hours of the assault on the key enemy island in the Palau group.

Rouh had been moving his mortar platoon near the top of a small coral ridge preparatory to digging in for the night, according to a field dispatch from Staff Sergeant James F. Woser Jr., of Culpeper, Va., a Marine Corps Combat Correspondent. Rouh decided to inspect an apparently empty Jap dugout before permitting his men to utilize it.

A few minutes before, a flame-throwing squad had blasted fire into the position. Near the entrance two Japs lay dead, still burning. Rouh could hear nothing. He stepped over the pair, and into the dark interior, his carbine ready. Creeping along the wall, he could see stores of supplies. He saw no life.

Suddenly a shot rang out, hitting the lieutenant in the left side. He stumbled back to his men outside. Japs followed, throwing grenades. Fragments filled the air. One grenade landed close to the Lieutenant and two of his men. There was no escape, for the Jap had held it too long to be thrown back.

Despite his weakened condition, Rouh shoved his two comrades to the ground to save them from flying fragments. He dropped his carbine and dove for the grenade. He was down on his elbows and one knee when the grenade exploded. His abdomen and chest caught the blast, and he sank to the ground. None of his men was hit.

Still conscious, Rouh could half hear and see the rest of the fight. Tommy guns spurted death at the Japs. One of his men stood over him. Soon it was all over – and Rouh's Marines had their cover for the night.

Rouh's body was pock-marked by the grenade blast. One steel fragment had passed through his left lung and lodged near his heart. Other fragments sprayed his chest, left side and left arm.

Still under enemy artillery and mortar fire, Rouh was given first aid by a passing doctor, and was carried back to an evacuation point. "That was a miserable trip back," he said. "I thought they would get all the men with me. But somehow we made it."

The exploit occurred near the same coral beach on Peleliu and within a few hours of a similar incident involving the late Marine Corporal Lewis K. Baussell of Washington, D.C. Baussell was leading a charge on a pillbox when a Jap grenade fell amid his men. He leaped on it, sacrificing his own life to save his fellows. Baussell's parents received his Congressional Medal of Honor, awarded posthumously on June 11.

Lieutenant Rouh enlisted as a private one month after Pearl Harbor, and has fought in three Pacific campaigns. At Guadalcanal, then a private, Rouh won the Silver Star Medal "for carrying wounded out under fire until wounded himself." Moreover, "for outstanding leadership and initiative in combat" he was given a field commission as a second lieutenant while at a rest camp in Australia. He commanded a machine gun platoon during the New Britain campaign.

He is the son of Mrs. Adelheith Rouh of Maple and Carlton Avenues, Lindenwold, N.J. He attended the Haddon Heights High School at Haddon Heights, N.J., where he won his letter in football. During recent months Rouh has been at the Naval Hospital in Philadelphia.

-USMC-

The following are Lieutenant Rouh's Medal of Honor and Silver Star Medal citations:

The President of the United States takes pleasure in presenting the MEDAL OF HONOR to:

FIRST LIEUTENANT CARLTON R. ROUH
UNITED STATES MARINE CORPS RESERVE

for service as set forth in the following citation:

> *"For conspicuous gallantry and intrepidity at the risk of his life above and beyond the call of duty while attached to the First Battalion, Fifth Marines, First Marine Division, during action against enemy Japanese forces on Peleliu Island, Palau Group, 15 September 1944. Before permitting his men to use an enemy dugout as a position for an 81-mm. mortar observation post, First Lieutenant Rouh made a personal reconnaissance of the pillbox and, upon entering, was severely wounded by Japanese rifle fire from within. Emerging from the dugout, he was immediately assisted by two Marines to a less exposed area, but while receiving first-aid, was further endangered by an enemy grenade which was thrown into their midst. Quick to act in spite of his weakened condition, he lurched to a crouching position and thrust both men aside, placing his own body between them and the grenade and taking the full blast of the explosion himself. His exceptional spirit of loyalty and self-sacrifice in the face of almost certain death reflects the highest credit upon First Lieutenant Rouh and the United States Naval Service."*

> */S/ FRANKLIN D. ROOSEVELT*

Chapter 1: World War II

The President of the United States takes pleasure in presenting the SIL-VER STAR MEDAL to:

PRIVATE FIRST CLASS CARLTON R. ROUH
UNITED STATES MARINE CORPS

for service as set forth in the following citation:

> *"For conspicuous gallantry and intrepidity while a member of Company M, Third Battalion, Fifth Marines, First Marine Division, during action against enemy Japanese forces on Guadalcanal, Solomon Islands, October 9, 1942. While under tremendous hostile fire, Private First Class Rouh, with cool courage and utter disregard for his own personal safety, unhesitatingly volunteered time after time to act as a stretcher bearer, tirelessly assisting in the transportation of injured personnel to the company aid station until he, himself, was wounded by enemy fire. His heroic conduct, maintained at great risk in the face of grave danger, was in keeping with the highest traditions of the United States Naval Service."*

For the President,
/S/ FRANK KNOX
Secretary of the Navy

• • •

Name: Captain James V. Shanley, USMCR (Deceased).

Biography: Written 1963.
Captain James Vincent Shanley, who was awarded two Navy Crosses – one at Cape Gloucester and the second, posthumously, at Peleliu – was killed in action October 4, 1944.

Captain Shanley was born May 31, 1919 in New York City, the son of Mr. and Mrs. James G. Shanley of 63 Longridge Road, Plandome, Long

Island, New York, and was graduated from James Madison High School in Brooklyn in 1937. He entered the United States Marine Corps immediately after graduation from Columbia University, and was assigned to Officer Candidates' School, Quantico, Virginia. Upon graduation from OCS, he was commissioned a Marine Reserve Second Lieutenant, November 1, 1941.

During college, he was manager of the tennis team, president of Phi Kappa Psi Fraternity, president of the Dolphins (swimming and diving team), a class officer, chairman of the senior prom, and a cheerleader.

After being commissioned, he completed Reserve Officers' School and departed Quantico in February, 1942 for New River (later Camp Lejeune), North Carolina, where he joined the 3rd Battalion, 7th Marines, 1st Marine Division. He served with that organization until his death.

Captain Shanley embarked with his unit for the Pacific area April, 1942, and served consecutively as Battalion Athletic and Recreation Officer, Company Executive Officer, and Company Commander. He was stationed first at Tutuila, Samoa, and later moved to Guadalcanal where he was promoted to Captain.

From September, 1942 to January, 1943, he took part in the assault and seizure of Guadalcanal. He was later stationed at Camp Mt. Martha, Victoria, Australia, for training and combat exercises. In November, 1943, he again went into combat at Papua, New Guinea. In the months that followed, from December, 1943 through April, 1944, he participated in the Cape Gloucester campaign, during which he earned the Navy Cross.

Major General Henry W. Buse, Jr. (then a Lieutenant Colonel), now Commanding General of the 3d Marine Division on Okinawa, was Captain Shanley's Battalion Commander at the time, and referred to him as: "An outstanding officer in combat. One of the best company commanders I have ever seen."

From May, 1944 through April, 1944, Captain Shanley was stationed at Pavuvu, Russell Islands. That September he disembarked from the *USS ORMSBY* and participated in the landing, assault, and occupation of Peleliu Island, and continued in combat until he was killed in action, leading his company, October 4, 1944. He was recommended for his second Navy Cross by his battalion commander, Colonel Edward H. Hurst (then Major). Colonel Hurst described him at that time as: "A natural and inspiring leader in combat, this officer performed the duties of a company commander in an outstanding manner."

Captain Shanley was buried at the United States Armed Forces Cemetery at Peleliu, October 5, 1944, and later reinterred in the Philippines, prior to being returned to the United States following the war for burial in Calvary Cemetery, Queens County, New York, at the request of his parents.

A Gold Star in lieu of his second Navy Cross was presented to Captain Shanley's parents, August 18, 1945, by the Commander, United States Naval Reserve Officer Training Center.

-USMC-

The following are Captain Shanley's two Navy Cross citations:

The President of the United States takes pleasure in presenting the NAVY CROSS to:

CAPTAIN JAMES V. SHANLEY
UNITED STATES MARINE CORPS RESERVE

for service as set forth in the following citation:

> *"For extraordinary heroism while attached to the Third Battalion, Seventh Marines, First Marine Division, during action against enemy Japanese forces at Cape Gloucester, New Britain, on January 14, 1944. With assault elements disorganized and suffering heavy casualties under the vicious concentration of enemy artillery, machine-gun and mortar fire after making a determined struggle up the steep slopes of "Hill 660" to its crest, Captain Shanley, alert to the grim necessity of capturing the hill before nightfall, unhesitatingly made his way to the front where, as senior officer initially present, he assumed command of the elements of three different companies. Continually exposing himself to enemy fire and narrowly escaping serious injury several times as he personally led*

*his men to strategic points, Captain Shanley skillfully or-
ganized them for a frontal assault which overwhelmed the
enemy and swept them from the hill with heavy losses. His
splendid leadership, unrelenting aggressiveness, and
staunch devotion to duty inspired the valiant officers and
men of his command to supreme effort and were in keeping with the highest traditions of the United States Naval
Service."*

/S/ SECRETARY OF THE NAVY

The President of the United States takes pleasure in presenting the GOLD
STAR in lieu of a second NAVY CROSS to:

CAPTAIN JAMES V. SHANLEY
UNITED STATES MARINE CORPS

for service as set forth in the following citation:

*"For extraordinary heroism as Commanding Officer of
Company L, Third Battalion, Seventh Marines, First Marine Division, during action against enemy Japanese forces
at Peleliu Island, Palau Islands, on 4 October, 1944.
Steadily pressing forward over the extremely difficult terrain, Captain Shanley's Company assaulted and captured
three successive coral ridges against fanatic Japanese resistance. With the leading assault platoon pinned down at
the base of the ravine by Japanese fire emanating from
two higher peaks during an advance against the fourth
ridge and the route of supply and reinforcement entirely
severed, he valiantly exposed himself to the withering barrage to direct the withdrawal. Seeing the forward platoon
leader killed and many of the men wounded immediately
thereafter, Captain Shanley left his post and, risking his
life in the face of the unceasing barrage, proceeded to the
aid of the fallen Marines and personally carried two men*

to safety. Struck twice by bursting shellfire while rescuing a third, he refused evacuation and continued directing the withdrawal of the helpless platoon until succumbing to his wounds. By his brilliant leadership, great personal valor, and self-sacrificing devotion to his men, Captain Shanley contributed to the saving of many lives and upheld the highest traditions of the United States Naval Service. He gallantly gave his life for his country."

/S/ SECRETARY OF THE NAVY

• • •

Name: Lieutenant General Alan Shapley, USMC (Deceased).

Biography: Revised May 1973.

Retired Lieutenant General Alan Shapley, who earned both the Navy Cross and the Silver Star during combat action in World War II, died May 13, 1973, at the national Naval Medical Center, Bethesda, Maryland, after prolonged illness. He was 70 years old.

The Silver Star was awarded to him for heroism in action as commander of the Marine Detachment aboard the *USS Arizona* when that ship was sunk at Pearl Harbor, December 7, 1941. He was awarded the Navy Cross for extraordinary heroism as a Lieutenant Colonel, commanding the Fourth Marines (Reinforced) on Guam from July 21 to August 10, 1944.

The general, who competed in football, basketball and track at the Naval Academy, had been active in athletics throughout his career. He coached and played on the All-Marine Corps football teams of 1927 and '28, refereed U.S. Fleet boxing events for three years, and coached or participated in football, basketball, baseball and boxing at most of his duty stations prior to World War II.

General Shapley was born February 9, 1903, in New York City. His early schooling was received at Vallejo, California, and he was graduated from the Peddie School at Hightstown, New Jersey, in 1922. He then entered the United States Naval Academy, graduating June 2, 1927, with his commission as a Marine second lieutenant.

After further training at the Academy, duty at Quantico, Virginia, and completion of the Marine Officer's Basic School at the Philadelphia Navy Yard, he sailed for Hawaii in January 1929 to begin almost three years of duty at the Marine Barracks, Pearl Harbor. He returned to the United States in October 1931, and served in various capacities at San Diego, California, prior to taking command of the Marine Detachment aboard the *USS San Francisco* in January 1934. Detached from the *San Francisco* in June 1936, he returned to Quantico where he served as Aide-de-Camp to the Commanding General of the Marine Barracks.

In June 1937, he entered the Junior Course, Marine Corps Schools, Quantico. He completed the course in May 1938, and was ordered to San Francisco, California, as Aide-de-Camp to the Commanding General, Department of the Pacific. After serving in that capacity until July 1939, he served as Operations, Training and Intelligence Officer of the Department of the Pacific until May 1940. A month later he departed for Hawaii, where he took command of the Marine Detachment on the *USS Arizona*.

He was awarded the Silver Star Medal for heroism on December 7, 1941, when the *Arizona* was sunk at Pearl Harbor. There, in the water after the ship had been bombed and set afire by the Japanese, he disregarded his own exhaustion and the enemy's bombing and strafing to rescue one of his men from drowning.

Two days after the attack on Pearl Harbor, he sailed for San Diego to become personnel officer of the Amphibious Corps, Pacific Fleet.

Shapley assumed a similar post with the 1st Amphibious Corps in October 1942, and that same month he sailed with that unit for the Pacific area. There he commanded the 2d Raider Battalion, First Marine Raider Regiment from March to September 1943. Later, he led the crack Second Marine Raider Regiment in the fighting at Bougainville, earning the Legion of Merit with Combat "V" for outstanding service in November 1943.

After the Bougainville campaign, the general was given command of the First and Second Marine Raider Regiments from which he organized the Fourth Marines, that he commanded at Emirau, Guam and Okinawa. In addition to the Navy Cross for heroism on Guam, he was also awarded a second Legion of Merit with Combat "V" for outstanding service on Okinawa from April to June 1945.

Chapter 1: World War II

Following the Okinawa campaign, he returned to the United States in July 1945 to become Assistant Inspector in the Inspection Division at Marine Corps Headquarters, Washington, D. C. In that capacity he accompanied Admiral William F. Halsey on an official goodwill tour of Central and South America from June to August 1946, receiving decorations from Chile and Peru during that assignment. In September he entered the National War College in Washington, D. C.

After graduation from the War College in June 1947, he served for two years in Norfolk, Virginia, as Assistant Chief of Staff, G-3 (Operations and Training), Fleet Marine Force, Atlantic. Subsequently, he was ordered to the Marine Corps Recruit Depot, San Diego, in June 1949, and after serving as personnel officer of the depot, became its chief of staff in September 1949.

In January 1951, Shapley was ordered again to Washington, D. C., where he served on the International Planning Staff of the Standing Group, North Atlantic Treaty Organization, until June 1953. Ordered to Korea, he served as Chief of Staff, 1st Marine Division, earning the Bronze Star Medal with Combat "V" for meritorious achievement during this period. For subsequent service as Senior Advisor to the Korean Marine Corps, he was awarded the Republic of Korea's Ulchi Medal with silver star.

From Korea, he was ordered to Japan in May 1954 for duty as Commanding Officer and, subsequently, Commanding General, Troop Training Team, Amphibious Group, Western Pacific.

In July 1955, on his return to the United States, the general became Assistant Commander of the 1st Marine Division, Camp Pendleton, California. Following his detachment from the 1st Marine Division in May 1956, he commanded the Recruit Training Command at the Marine Corps Recruit Depot, San Diego, briefly, prior to being ordered to the Far East. Upon his promotion to Major General in September 1956, he assumed duties on Okinawa as Commanding General, 3d Marine Division, Fleet Marine Force.

General Shapley returned to the United States in July 1957, reporting to Headquarters Marine Corps, Washington, D. C., as Director of the Marine Corps Reserve. After holding this post for over two years, he returned to the west coast in November 1959, and served as Commanding General, Marine Corps Base, Camp Pendleton, until March 1961. He was promoted to the rank of lieutenant general in April 1961 upon assuming duties Commanding General, Fleet Marine Force, Pacific, headquartered at Camp H. M. Smith, Hawaii, and served in this capacity until he retired from active duty, July 1, 1962. He was awarded the Distinguished Service Medal on retirement.

The general's other promotions were as follows: first lieutenant, January 1934, captain, July 1936, major, August 1941, lieutenant colonel, August 1942, colonel, November 1944, and brigadier general, July 1954.

A list of the general's medals and decorations included: the Navy Cross, the Distinguished Service Medal, the Silver Star Medal, the Legion of Merit with Combat "V" and gold star in lieu of second award, the Bronze Star Medal with Combat "V", the Presidential Unit Citation, the Navy Unit Citation, the Navy Unit Commendation with two bronze stars indicative of second and third awards, the American Defense Service Medal with Fleet clasp, the American Campaign Medal, the Asiatic Pacific Campaign Medal with one silver star, the World War II Victory Medal, the National Defense Service Medal, the Korean Service Medal with one bronze star, and the United Nations Service Medal.

-USMC-

The following are an eyewitness account of General Shapley's actions for his Silver Star, his Navy Cross, Silver Star, and Legion of Merit citations:

STATEMENT OF WITNESS

"At approximately eight o'clock on the morning of December 7, 1941, I was leaving the breakfast table when the ship's siren for air defense sounded. Having no anti-aircraft battle station, I paid little attention to it. Suddenly I hear an explosion, I ran to the Port door leading to the quarterdeck and saw a bomb strike a barge of some sort along side the NEVADA, or in that vicinity. The Marine Color Guard came in at this point saying we were being attacked. I could distinctly hear machine-gun fire. I believe at this point our anti-aircraft battery opened up. We stood around awaiting orders of some kind. General quarters sounded and I started for my battle station in Secondary Aft. As I passed through casemate Nine I noted that it was manned and being trained out. The men seemed extremely calm and collected. I reached the boat deck and our anti-aircraft guns were in full action firing very rapidly. I was about three quarters of the way to the first platform on the mast when it seemed as though a bomb struck our quarter-deck. I could hear shrapnel or fragments whistling past me. As soon as I reached the first platform, I saw Second Lieutenant Simonsen laying on his back with blood on his shirt front. I Bent over him and taking him by the shoulders asked if there was anything I could do. He was dead, or so nearly so that speech was impossible. Seeing there was nothing I could do for the Lieutenant, I continued to my battle station. When I arrived in Secondary Aft I reported to Major Shapley that Mr. Simonsen had been hit and there was nothing that could be done for him. There was a lot of talk going on and I shouted for silence, which came immediately. I had been there a short time when a terrible explosion caused the ship to shake violently. I looked at the boat deck and everything seemed aflame forward of the main mast, I reported to the Major that the ship was aflame, which was rather needless, and after looking about, the Major ordered us to leave. I was the last man to leave Secondary Aft because I looked around and there was no one left. I followed the Major down the port side of the tripod mast. The railings, as we ascended, were very hot and as we reached the boat deck I noted that it was torn up and burned. The bodies of the dead were thick, and badly burned men were heading for the quarterdeck, only to fall apparently dead or badly wounded. The Major and I went between No. 3 and No. 4 turret to the starboard side and found Lieutenant Commander Fuqua ordered the men over the side, and assisting the wounded. He seemed exceptionally calm and the Major stopped and they talked for a moment. Charred bodies were everywhere. I made my way to the quay and started to remove my shoes, when I suddenly found myself in the water. I think the concussion of a bomb threw me in. I started swimming for the pipeline which was about one hundred and fifty feet away. I was about half way when my strength gave out entirely, my wet clothes and shocked condition sapped my strength and I was about to go under when Major Shapley started to swim by, and seeing my distress, he grasped my shirt and told me to hang onto his shoulders while he swam in. We were perhaps twenty-five feet from the pipeline when the Major's strength gave out and I saw he was floundering, so I loosed my grip on him and told him to make it alone. He stopped and grabbed me by the shirt and refused to let go. I would have drowned but for the Major. We finally reached the beach where a Marine directed us to a bomb shelter, where I was given dry clothes and a place to rest.

/S/ Earl C. Nightingale
Corporal, United States Marine Corps

The President of the United States takes pleasure in presenting the NAVY CROSS to:

LIEUTENANT COLONEL ALAN SHAPLEY
UNITED STATES MARINE CORPS

for service as set forth in the following citation:

"For extraordinary heroism as Commanding Officer of the Fourth Marine (Reinforced), First Provisional Marine Brigade, during action against enemy Japanese forces on Guam, Marianas Islands, from 21 July to 10 August, 1944. Courageously leading his regiment in an assault landing against strong enemy beach defenses, Lieutenant Colonel Shapley rapidly seized the assigned beachhead and defended the area against fanatical hostile counterattacks. Upon relief of the force beachhead line, he valiantly led his troops in a determined assault up the left half of the Orote Peninsula and, despite the difficult terrain and strong enemy defenses, seized an important airfield and annihilated the Japanese in that area. Vigorously patrolling in the southern half of the island to eliminate hostile elements there, he then directed his men in the final attack on the northern half of the island. His leadership, daring combat tactics and great personal valor reflect the highest credit upon Lieutenant Colonel Shapley and the United States Naval Service."

The President of the United States takes pleasure in presenting the SIL-VER STAR MEDAL to:

MAJOR ALAN SHAPLEY
UNITED STATES MARINE CORPS

for service as set forth in the following citation:

> *"For gallant and courageous conduct during the attack on the United States Pacific Fleet by enemy Japanese forces at Pearl Harbor, Territory of Hawaii, December 7, 1941. While swimming toward Ford Island after his ship had been bombed and set afire by the enemy, Major Shapley noticed a shipmate in distress in the water and about to go under. With no thought for his own safety, he braved the hazards of continuous enemy strafing and bombing to swim to the assistance of his helpless shipmate and, although exhausted himself, persisted in his efforts until he finally succeeded in bringing him safely ashore. His heroic action, performed at great peril to his own life, was in keeping with the highest traditions of the United States Naval Service."*

For the President,
/S/ FRANK KNOX
Secretary of the Navy

The President of the United States takes pleasure in presenting the GOLD STAR in lieu of a second LEGION OF MERIT to:

LIEUTENANT COLONEL ALAN SHAPLEY
UNITED STATES MARINE CORPS

for service as set forth in the following citation:

> *"For exceptionally meritorious conduct in the performance of outstanding services to the Government of the United States as Commanding Officer of the Second Marine Raider Regiment, in connection with the operations of the Third Marine Division, Reinforced, against enemy Japanese forces on Bougainville, Solomon Islands, 1 November 1943. From the date of the division's initial attack until his regiment was withdrawn from the Island, Lieutenant Colonel Shapley capably directed and coordinated operations of his regiment in furtherance of the seizure of a beachhead from Japanese forces. By his brilliant tactics and matchless leadership, he contributed materially to his regiment's success in defeating and inflicting heavy casualties upon the enemy at every encounter. His skill, sound judgment, and unwavering devotion to duty were in keeping with the highest traditions of the United States Naval Service."* Lieutenant Colonel Shapley is authorized to wear the Combat *"V."*

> *For the President,*
> */S/ JAMES FORRESTAL*
> *Secretary of the Navy*

• • •

Name: General David M. Shoup, USMC (Retired).

Biography: Revised January 1, 1964.
General David Monroe Shoup served as the 22d Commandant of the Marine Corps from January 1, 1960 until his retirement from active service, December 31, 1963.

As a colonel in World War II, General Shoup earned the Nation's highest award, the Medal of Honor, while commanding the Second Marines, Second Marine Division, at Betio, a bitterly contested island of the Tarawa

Atoll. The British Distinguished Service Order was also awarded him for this action.

General Shoup was the 25th Marine to receive the Medal of Honor in World War II. It was presented to him on January 22, 1945 by the late James V. Forrestal, then Secretary of the Navy.

The general was born December 30, 1904, at Battle Ground, Indiana. A 1926 graduate of DePauw University, Greencastle, Indiana, he was a member of the Reserve Officers Training Corps at the University. He served for a month as a second lieutenant in the Army Infantry Reserve before he was commissioned a Marine second lieutenant on July 20, 1926.

Ordered to Marine Officers Basic School at the Philadelphia Navy Yard, Lieutenant Shoup's instruction was interrupted twice by temporary duty elsewhere in the United States, and by expeditionary duty with the Sixth Marines in Tientsin, China. After serving in China during most of 1927, he completed Basic School in 1928. He then served at Quantico, Virginia; Pensacola, Florida; and San Diego, California.

From June 1929 to September 1931, Lieutenant Shoup was assigned to the Marine Detachment aboard the *USS MARYLAND*. By coincidence, the *USS MARYLAND* was the flag ship for the assault on Tarawa 12 years later – providing emergency Naval gunfire support with her 16-inch guns early on D-day. On his return from sea duty, he served as a company officer at the Marine Corps Base (later Marine Corps Recruit Depot), San Diego, until May 1932 when he was ordered to the Puget Sound Navy Yard, Bremerton, Washington. He was promoted to first lieutenant in June 1932.

Lieutenant Shoup later served on temporary duty with the Civilian Conservation Corps in Idaho and New Jersey from June 1932 to May 1933. Following duty in Seattle, Washington, he was again ordered to China in November 1934, serving briefly with the Fourth Marines in Shanghai, and, subsequently, at the American Legation in Peiping. He returned to the United States, via Japan, early in June 1936 and was again stationed at Puget Sound Navy Yard. He was promoted to captain in October 1936.

Captain Shoup entered the Junior Course, Marine Corps Schools, Quantico, in July 1937. On completing the course in May 1938, he served as an instructor for two years. In June 1940, he joined the Sixth Marines in San Diego. He was promoted to major in April 1941.

One month later, Major Shoup was ordered to Iceland with the Sixth

Marines and, after serving as Regimental Operations Officer, became Operations Officer of the 1st Marine Brigade in Iceland in October 1941. For his service in Iceland during the first three months after the United States entered World War II, he was awarded the Letter of Commendation with Commendation Ribbon. He assumed command of the Second Battalion, Sixth Marines, in February 1942. On returning to the States in March, the 1st Marine Brigade was disbanded and he returned with his battalion to San Diego. In July 1942, he became Assistant Operations and Training Officer of the 2d Marine Division. He was promoted to lieutenant colonel in August 1942.

Sailing from San Diego aboard the *USS MATSONIA* in September 1942, Lieutenant Colonel Shoup arrived at Wellington, New Zealand, later that month. From then until November 1943, he served as G-3, Operations and Training Officer of the 2d Marine Division during its training period in New Zealand. His service in this capacity during the planning of the assault on Tarawa earned him his first Legion of Merit with Combat "V." During this period he also served briefly as an observer with the 1st Marine Division on Guadalcanal in October 1942, and with the 43d Army Division on Rendova, New Georgia, in the summer of 1943, earning a Purple Heart in the latter operation.

Promoted to colonel November 9, 1943, Colonel Shoup was placed in command of the Second Marines (Reinforced), the spearhead of the assault on Tarawa. During this action he earned the Medal of Honor as well as a second Purple Heart. In December 1943, he became Chief of Staff of the 2d Marine Division. For outstanding service in this capacity from June to August 1944, during the battles for Saipan and Tinian, he was again awarded the Legion of Merit with Combat "V." He returned to the United States in October 1944.

On his return to the United States Colonel Shoup served as Logistics Officer, Division of Plans and Policies, Headquarters Marine Corps. He was again ordered overseas in June 1947. Two months later he became Commanding Officer, Service Command, Fleet Marine Force, Pacific. In June 1949, he joined the 1st Marine Division at Camp Pendleton as Division Chief of Staff. A year later he was transferred to Quantico where he served as Commanding Officer of the Basic School from July 1950 until April 1952. He was then assigned to the Office of the Fiscal Director, Headquarters Marine Corps, serving as Assistant Fiscal Director. He was promoted to brigadier general in April 1953.

In July 1953, General Shoup was named Fiscal Director of the Marine Corps. While serving in this capacity, he was promoted to major general in September 1955. Subsequently, in May 1956, he began a brief assignment as Inspector General for Recruit Training. Following this, he served as Inspector General of the Marine Corps from September 1956 until May 1957. He returned to Camp Pendleton in June 1957 to become Commanding General of the 1st Marine Division.

General Shoup joined the 3d Marine Division on Okinawa in March 1958 as Commanding General. Following his return to the States, he served as the Commanding General of the Marine Corps Recruit Depot, Parris Island, from May to October 1959. On November 2, 1959, he was promoted to lieutenant general and assigned duties as Chief of Staff, Headquarters Marine Corps.

General Shoup was nominated by President Dwight D. Eisenhower on August 12, 1959 to be the 22d Commandant of the Marine Corps, and his nomination for a four-year term was confirmed by the Senate. Upon assuming his post as Commandant of the Marine Corps on January 1, 1960, he was promoted to four-star rank.

On December 23, 1963, shortly before his retirement, General Shoup was awarded the Distinguished Service Medal by President Lyndon B. Johnson in a White House ceremony.

A list of the general's medals and decorations include: the Medal of Honor, the Distinguished Service Medal, the Legion of Merit with Combat "V" and Gold Star in lieu of a second award, the Letter of Commendation with Commendation Ribbon, the Purple Heart with Gold Star in lieu of second award, the Presidential Unit Citation, the World War II Victory Medal, and the British Distinguished Service Order.

-USMC-

The following are General Shoup's Medal of Honor, two Legion of Merit, and Presidential Unit citations:

Men of Honor

The President of the United States takes pleasure in presenting the MEDAL OF HONOR to:

COLONEL DAVID M. SHOUP
UNITED STATES MARINE CORPS

for service as set forth in the following citation:

"For conspicuous gallantry and intrepidity at the risk of his own life above and beyond the call of duty as commanding officer of all Marine Corps troops in action against enemy Japanese forces on Betio Island, Tarawa Atoll, Gilbert Islands, from November 20 to 22, 1943. Although severely shocked by an exploding shell soon after landing at the pier, and suffering from a serious painful leg wound which had become infected, Colonel Shoup fearlessly exposed himself to the terrific relentless artillery, machine-gun, and rifle fire from hostile shore emplacements and rallying his hesitant troops by his own inspiring heroism, gallantly led then across the fringing reefs to charge the heavily fortified island and reinforced our hardpressed thinly-held lines. Upon arrival on the shore, he assumed command of all landed troops and, working without rest under constant withering enemy fire during the next two days conducted smashing attacks against unbelievably strong and fanatically defended Japanese positions despite innumerable obstacles and heavy casualties. By his brilliant leadership, daring tactics, and selfless devotion to duty, Colonel Shoup was largely responsible for the final, decisive defeat of the enemy and his indomitable fighting spirit reflects great credit upon the United States Naval Service."

For the President,
/S/ JAMES V. FORRESTAL
Secretary of the Navy

Chapter 1: World War II

The President of the United States takes pleasure in presenting the LEGION OF MERIT to:

COLONEL DAVID M. SHOUP
UNITED STATES MARINE CORPS

for service as set forth in the following citation:

"For exceptionally meritorious conduct in the performance of outstanding services to the Government of the United States as Chief of Staff of the Second Marine Division, prior to and during operations against enemy Japanese forces on Saipan and Tinian, Marianas Islands, from 15 June to 1 August 1944. Skilled and tireless in the performance of his duty, Colonel Shoup welded the various units of the division into a highly cooperative organization and thereby contributed materially to its outstanding combat record. With his post frequently under intense enemy fire during this critical period, he continued to direct personnel under his command with outstanding ability and, by his forceful initiative and thorough knowledge of the tactical situation, was in large measure responsible for the smooth functioning of the numerous and varied activities of the Second Marine Division. His resourceful leadership and unwavering devotion to duty were in keeping with the highest traditions of the United States Naval Service." Colonel Shoup is authorized to wear the Combat "V."

For the President,
/S/ JAMES FORRESTAL
Secretary of the Navy

The President of the United States takes pleasure in presenting the GOLD STAR in lieu of a second LEGION OF MERIT to:

Men of Honor

LIEUTENANT COLONEL DAVID M. SHOUP
UNITED STATES MARINE CORPS

for service as set forth in the following citation:

"For exceptionally meritorious conduct in the performance of outstanding services to the Government of the United States as Operations and Training Officer of the Second Marine Division, during the planning and the assault on Tarawa, from 15 September 1942 to 7 November 1943. Exercising a thorough knowledge of the tactics and logistics of both land and amphibious operations, Lieutenant Colonel Shoup effectively planned and coordinated the training of the units of the division. As head of the Operations Section of the Division Staff, he prepared and submitted plans for the attack on Betio. By his initiative, organizing ability and untiring efforts to procure the best weapons and equipment available, he contributed materially to the high state of training and efficiency of the Second Marine Division and its decisive victory at Tarawa. Lieutenant Colonel Shoup's leadership throughout this period reflects great credit upon himself and the United States Naval Service."

For the President,
/S/ JAMES FORRESTAL
Secretary of the Navy

The President of the United States takes pleasure in presenting the PRESIDENTIAL UNIT CITATION to:

SECOND MARINE DIVISION (REINFORCED)

consisting of Division Headquarters, Special Troops (including Company C, 1st Corps Medium Tank Battalion), Service Troops, 2nd, 6th, 8th, 10th, and 18th Marine Regiments in the battle of Tarawa, as set forth in the following citation:

> *"For outstanding performance in combat during the seizure and occupation of the Japanese-held Atoll of Tarawa, Gilbert Islands, November 20 to 24, 1943. Forced by treacherous coral reefs to disembark from the landing craft hundreds of yards off the beach, the Second Marine Division (Reinforced) became a highly vulnerable target for devastating Japanese fire. Dauntlessly advancing in spite of rapidly mounting losses, the Marines fought a gallant battle against crushing odds, clearing the limited beachheads of snipers and machine-guns, reducing powerfully fortified enemy positions and completely annihilating the fanatically determined and strongly entrenched Japanese forces. By the successful occupation of Tarawa, the Second Marine Division (Reinforced) has provided our forces with highly strategic and important air and land bases from which to continue future operations against the enemy; by the valiant fighting spirit of these men, their heroic fortitude under punishing fire and their relentless perseverance in waging this epic battle in the Central Pacific, they have upheld the finest traditions of the United States Naval Service."*

> *For the President,*
> */S/ JAMES FORRESTAL*
> *Secretary of the Navy*

• • •

Name: General Alexander A. Vandegrift, USMC, (Retired)

Biography: Written October, 1962.
General Alexander Archer Vandegrift, who earned the Medal of Honor in World War II, served as the eighteenth Commandant of the Marine Corps,

from January 1, 1944 to January 1, 1948. The general commanded the First Marine Division, Reinforced, in the battle for Guadalcanal, and the First Marine Amphibious Corps in the landing at Empress Augusta Bay, Bougainville, during World War II.

For outstanding services as Commanding General of the First Marine Division, Reinforced, during the attack on Guadalcanal, Tulagi, and Gavutu in the Solomon Islands on August 7, 1942, he was awarded the Navy Cross, and for the subsequent occupation and defense from August 7, 1942 to December 9, 1942, was awarded the Medal of Honor.

General Vandegrift was born on March 13, 1887, in Charlottesville, Virginia. He attended the University of Virginia and was commissioned in the Marine Corps as a second lieutenant on January 22, 1909.

Following instruction at the Marine Officers' School, Port Royal, South Carolina, and a tour of duty at the Marine Barracks, Portsmouth, New Hampshire, he went to foreign shore duty in the Caribbean area, where he participated in the bombardment, assault and capture of Coyotepe in Nicaragua. He further participated in the engagement and occupation of Vera Cruz, Mexico.

In December, 1914, following his promotion to first lieutenant, he attended the Advance Base Course at the Marine Barracks , Philadelphia. Upon completion of schooling, he sailed for Haiti with the First Brigade and participated in action against hostile Cacos bandits at LeTrou and Fort Capois.

In August, 1916, he was promoted to captain and became a member of the Haitian Constabulary at Port au Prince, where he remained until detached to the United States in December, 1918. He returned to Haiti again in July, 1919, to serve with the Gendarmerie d' Haiti as an Inspector of Constabulary. He was promoted to major in June, 1920.

Major Vandegrift returned to this country in April, 1923, and was assigned to the Marine Barracks at Quantico, Virginia. He completed the Field Officers' Course, Marine Corps Schools in May, 1926, following which he went to the Marine Corps Base, San Diego, California, as Assistant Chief of Staff.

In February, 1927, he sailed for China where he served as Operations and Training Officer of the Third Marine Brigade with Headquarters at Tientsin. He was ordered to Washington, D.C., in September, 1928, where he became Assistant Chief Coordinator, Bureau of the Budget. Following duty in Washington, he joined the Marine Barracks, Quantico, Virginia, where he became Assistant Chief of Staff, G-1 Section, Fleet Marine Force. During this assignment, he was promoted to lieutenant colonel in June, 1934.

Ordered to China in June, 1935, Lieutenant Colonel Vandegrift served successively as Executive Officer and Commanding Officer of the Marine Detachment at the American Embassy in Peiping. He was promoted to colonel in September, 1936.

Colonel Vandegrift reported to Headquarters Marine Corps, Washington, D.C., in June, 1937, where he became Military Secretary to the Major General Commandant, and the following month was promoted to brigadier general.

General Vandegrift was detached to the First Marine Division in November, 1941 shortly before the outbreak of World War II. He was promoted to major general in March, 1942, and in May sailed for the South Pacific area as Commanding General of the first Marine division to ever leave the shores of the United States. On August 7, 1942, in the Solomon Islands, he led ashore the First Marine Division, Reinforced, in the first large scale offensive action against the Japanese.

In July, 1943, he assumed command of the First Marine Amphibious Corps, and commanded this organization in the landing at Empress Augusta Bay, Bougainville, Northern Solomon Islands, on November 1, 1943. Upon establishing the initial beachhead, he relinquished command and returned to Washington, D.C., as Commandant-designate.

On January 1, 1944, as a lieutenant general, he was sworn in as the eighteenth Commandant of the Marine Corps. On April 4, 1944, he was appointed general, with date of rank from March 21, 1945, the first Marine officer on active duty to attain four-star rank.

For outstanding services as Commandant of the Marine Corps from January 1, 1944 to June 30, 1946, the general was awarded the Distinguished Service Medal. He left active service on December 31, 1947, and was placed on the retired list, April 1, 1949.

-USMC-

The following are General Vandegrift's Medal of Honor, Navy Cross, and Distinguished Service Medal citations:

The president of the United States takes pleasure in presenting the MEDAL OF HONOR to:

MAJOR GENERAL ALEXANDER A. VANDEGRIFT
UNITED STATES MARINE CORPS

for service as set forth in the following citation:

"For outstanding and heroic accomplishment above and beyond the call of duty as Commanding Officer of the First Marine Division in operations against enemy Japanese forces in the Solomon Islands during the period of August 7, 1942 to December 9, 1942. With the adverse factors of weather, terrain, and disease making his task a difficult and hazardous undertaking, and with his command eventually including sea, land, and air forces of the Army, Navy, and Marine Corps, Major General Vandegrift achieved marked success in commanding the initial landings of the United States Forces in the Solomon Islands and their subsequent occupation. His tenacity, courage, and resourcefulness prevailed against a strong, determined, and experienced enemy, and the gallant fighting spirit of the men under his inspiring leadership enabled them to withstand aerial, land, and sea bombardment, to surmount all obstacles and leave a disorganized and ravaged enemy. This dangerous but vital mission, accomplished at the constant risk of his life, resulted in securing a valuable base for further operations of our forces against the enemy, and its successful completion reflects great credit upon Major General Vandegrift, his command and the United States Naval Service."

/S/ FRANKLIN D. ROOSEVELT

Chapter 1: World War II

The President of the United States takes pleasure in presenting the NAVY CROSS to:

GENERAL ALEXANDER A. VANDEGRIFT
UNITED STATES MARINE CORPS

for service as set forth in the following citation:

"For extraordinary heroism and distinguished devotion to duty as Commander of all ground troops in action with enemy Japanese forces during the attack on the Solomon Islands, August 7, 1942. Though subjected to intense enemy opposition, Major General Vandegrift led his command in superbly coordinated operations with the result that all objectives were captured and opposing enemy Japanese forces were destroyed. His fine spirit of leadership and his courageous determination throughout the engagement were in keeping with the highest traditions of the United States Naval Service."

/S/ SECRETARY OF THE NAVY

The President of the United States takes pleasure in presenting the DISTINGUISHED SERVICE MEDAL to:

GENERAL ALEXANDER A. VANDEGRIFT
UNITED STATES MARINE CORPS

for service as set forth in the following citation:

"For exceptionally meritorious service to the Government of the United States in a duty of great responsibility as Commandant of the United States Marine Corps, from January 1, 1944 to June 30, 1946. General Vandegrift exercised extraordinary foresight, initiative, and judgment in directing the policies and organization of the Corps,

and in continuing without interruption the broad program of expansion and preparation for battle of the specialized branch of our military service. Analyzing the particularized problems incident to Marine Corps participation in large scale joint operations, he successfully carried out a pre-established program for the procurement and training of personnel, determined the design, types, and amounts of combat equipment required by his assault and occupation troops to break the resistance of a determined and deeply entrenched enemy wherever encountered, and effected expedient methods of distribution which made possible the steady flow of men and materials in support of the continued offensive operations of his fighting forces in wide-spread areas. A leader of uncompromising integrity and indefatigable energies, General Vandegrift upheld and quickened the incomparable esprit de corps of his command and developed a level of combat efficiency to the end that the enemy was overwhelmed by the Marines wherever met. By his achievements as Commandant of the United States Marine Corps, General Vandegrift rendered service of an inestimable value to the United States Navy and to his Country. His unfaltering devotion to the honor of the Corps and to the fulfillment of tremendous responsibilities throughout this critical period in the history of the Nation reflects the highest credit upon himself and the United States Naval Service."

• • •

Name: Major Robert W. Vaupell, USMCR.

Biography: Story from Public Relations Office, 1944.
Nearly four years ago Bob Vaupell was a bank teller in Seattle, Washington. Today he is the holder of the Navy Cross, the Air Medal (which was later increased to the Navy Cross), and the Purple Heart for wounds received in action. The story of the years between his leaving the bank, and

becoming a hero, are typical of the average young man who has left his job to fight. Captain Vaupell graduated from the Pensacola, Florida, Naval Air Station in 1941. On Christmas day just after Pearl Harbor, he left the States and was one of the first to prove that young American men, raised in peacetime, can also raise all kinds of hell with the enemy in war-time.

Captain Vaupell left Guadalcanal last October 8th on a scouting mission, in search of Japanese ships. Approximately two hundred and fifty miles from the island, he sighted three destroyers, a cruiser, and a transport. As he was set to dive on them, twenty-two Jap Zeros, in groups of eleven, sighted him.

With Vaupell at the time was his wingman, Lieutenant Jack Blumstein of Pittsburgh, Pennsylvania, who was on his first combat hop.

As the first group of Zeros attacked them, Blumstein got two planes, before his own plane went into a spin. "I thought" commented Vaupell, "that he was a done pigeon, but as a matter of fact, he did pull out, and got back an hour and a half before I did."

How does it feel to play tag with murder? "Well it's like this, when you're a cadet you get lots of training and know that some day you'll have to face the real thing, but when you really get there you have to move so fast you forget any planned procedures. You just do things automatically, the repetition of the things help the most...by that I mean constant practice so you do things right from the first and only chance you get to do them."

Vaupell got four bullets in his leg and six pieces of shrapnel from his encounter with the 22 Jap planes. He didn't start to feel the bullet wounds for about 45 minutes, and didn't know about the shrapnel in him until thirty days later.

Captain Vaupell owes his life to good maneuvering, and the facts that the Japs wasted much ammunition. They would start low and spray lead as they nosed up towards Vaupell's plane, but Vaupell soon caught on to their system and by climbing as fast as he could move, avoided their fire.

"Some funny things happen out there," Vaupell relates. But one big surprise came during the first months of the grim fighting on Guadalcanal. "One night a Jap soldier ran to the American front line with his hands high, and shouting at the top of his lungs....don't shoot!...don't shoot!...hell I'm a damn Yankee from New York City."

Captain Vaupell now, is the Marine Liaison Officer in the Aviation

Cadet Regiment, at the Naval Air Training Center, Corpus Christi, Texas.

-USMC-

The following are Captain Vaupell's two Navy Cross citations:

The President of the United States takes pleasure in presenting the NAVY CROSS to:

CAPTAIN ROBERT W. VAUPELL
UNITED STATES MARINE CORPS RESERVE

for action as set forth in the following citation:

> *"For extraordinary heroism as a pilot in a Marine Scout-Bombing Squadron during action against enemy Japanese forces in the Battle of Midway on June 4 and 5 1942. Participating in a search and attack mission against an enemy aircraft carrier, Captain Vaupell (then Second Lieutenant) brought his plane back to its base under extremely adverse weather conditions. The following day, at great personal risk in the face of tremendous anti-aircraft fire, he took part in an assault which resulted in the severe damaging of a Japanese battleship. His cool courage and conscientious devotion to duty were in keeping with the highest traditions of the United States Naval Service."*

> */S/ W. F. HALSEY*
> *Admiral, U.S. Navy*

The President of the United States takes pleasure in presenting the GOLD STAR in lieu of a second NAVY CROSS to:

LIEUTENANT ROBERT W. VAUPELL
UNITED STATES MARINE CORPS RESERVE

for service as set forth in the following citation:

"For meritorious achievement while participating in an aerial combat against the enemy in the British Solomon Islands area. Lieutenant Robert W. Vaupell, as leader of a two plane formation making a search of the New Georgia channel, sighted one enemy cruiser and three or four destroyers in the afternoon of October 8, 1942. Immediately on sighting the ships, Lieutenant Vaupell and his wingman were attacked by two flights, of eleven each, land-based army type Zeros. As one Zero pulled up in front of him, Lieutenant Vaupell pulled up the nose of his plane and caught the Zero with his front guns, bringing it down in flames. Lieutenant Vaupell was shot through the arm during this engagement. The enemy, meanwhile, brought Lieutenant Vaupell's plane under anti-aircraft fire. In getting out of range of the anti-aircraft fire he was again attacked by Zeros which pressed their attack for 90 miles down the coast of Santa Isabel. With great presence of mind Lieutenant Vaupell continued sending contact reports until his radio was disabled and with great skill and fortitude brought his plane to a safe landing on his home field."

/S/ W.F. HALSEY
Admiral, U.S. Navy

• • •

Name: Lieutenant Colonel Kenneth A. Walsh, USMC (Retired).

Biography: Revised September 1974.
Lieutenant Colonel Kenneth Ambrose Walsh, who wears the Medal of Honor for World War II heroism, retired from active service in the Marine Corps in January 1962, after over 28 years of continuous active duty as a Marine.

A veteran of both World War II and the Korean Conflict, Colonel Walsh rose from a flying private to fourth-ranking Marine Corps Ace in World

War II with a record of 21 enemy planes destroyed.

Colonel Walsh was born in Brooklyn, New York, on November 24, 1916. He was graduated from Dickinson High School, Jersey City, New Jersey, in 1933 where he had been an outstanding track athlete. He enlisted in the Marine Corps on December 15, 1933, and underwent recruit training at Parris Island, South Carolina. Upon graduation, he spent two years as an aviation mechanic and radioman at Marine Corps Base, Quantico, Virginia.

In March 1936, Colonel Walsh was selected for flight training and was transferred to Pensacola, Florida. He won his wings there as a private in April 1937, and spent four years in scout and observation flying. During this time he served aboard aircraft carriers *YORKTOWN, WASP* and *RANGER*. Meanwhile the aviator was promoted through the enlisted ranks to master technical sergeant then to Marine gunner, equivalent to the present rank of warrant officer. The latter promotion took place on May 11, 1942, while he was serving with Marine Aircraft Group 12, 1st Marine Aircraft Wing, Fleet Marine Force, San Francisco, California.

In October 1942, he was commissioned second lieutenant and, in June 1943, was promoted to first lieutenant. He was promoted to captain (temporary) in February 1944 (this appointment became permanent November 13, 1948); to major in April 1955; and to lieutenant colonel in October 1958.

When the Japanese attacked Pearl Harbor, Colonel Walsh was serving on the East Coast with Marine Fighting Squadron 121. He transferred to Marine Fighting Squadron 124 in September 1942, to be shipped overseas in January 1943, for duty in the Solomon Islands area. He was particularly active in aerial combat in the Vella LaVella vicinity in August 1943, while a division leader in his squadron. He scored all his 21 victories in the Vought 'Corsair" F4U fighter.

Colonel Walsh returned to the United States October 15, 1943, and was assigned special temporary aviation duty with the Division of Aviation, Headquarters Marine Corps. He received the Medal of Honor February 8, 1944.

In January 1944, he was assigned to the Naval Air Operational Training Command, Naval Air Station, Jacksonville, Florida, to serve as flight instructor. In April 1945, he was transferred to the Philippine Islands and served in that area and in the Okinawa campaign as Operations Officer for

Marine Fighting Squadron 222 and, later, as Assistant Operations Officer of Marine Aircraft Group 14. He returned to Headquarters Marine Corps in March 1946, to be reassigned with the Bureau of Aeronautics, Navy Department.

After nearly three years with the Bureau, Colonel Walsh joined the 1st Marine Aircraft Wing, Fleet Marine Force, in January 1949, at El Toro, Santa Ana, California, as Assistant Group Engineering Officer, Marine Aircraft Group 12. He transferred from there in July 1949, to Marine Corps Air Station, Quantico, Virginia, as an aircraft engineering and maintenance student. Upon completion, he returned to El Toro and Marine Aircraft Group 25 as Assistant Engineering Officer in Marine Transport Squadron 152.

With this squadron Colonel Walsh went overseas on July 15, 1950, shortly after the outbreak of the Korean Conflict. He served in Korea until July 1951, and was awarded a gold star in lieu of his fifteenth Air Medal, "for outstanding performance of duty in aerial flight against the enemy in Korea."

Colonel Walsh returned to El Toro in late July 1951, remaining there until April 1, 1952, when he was transferred to Staff, Commander Air Force, United States Atlantic Fleet, Norfolk, Virginia, as Marine Liaison Officer for Aircraft Material and Maintenance. He remained there until September 28, 1955, when he was assigned to the 3d Marine Aircraft Wing, Aircraft, Fleet Marine Force, Pacific, El Toro, as Aircraft Maintenance and Repair Officer in Marine Transport Squadron 152.

In January 1959, Colonel Walsh was assigned to the 1st Marine Aircraft Wing, Aircraft, Fleet Marine Force, Pacific, as Wing Aircraft Maintenance Officer. He held this assignment until April 1960, and the following month returned to the 3d Marine Aircraft Wing at El Toro, serving consecutively as Executive Officer and Operations Officer of Marine Transport Squadron 352 until October 1961. That month he was assigned to Headquarters and Headquarters Squadron, Marine Wing Service Group 37, 3d Marine Aircraft Wing.

Besides the Medal of Honor, some of Colonel Walsh's other awards include: the Distinguished Flying Cross with six Gold Stars, the Air Medal with 14 Gold Stars, the Presidential Unit Citation with one bronze star, the Army Distinguished Unit Citation with emblem, the Good Conduct Medal with one bronze star, the American Defense Service Medal with base clasp, and the World War II Victory Medal.

-USMC-

The following are a newspaper article about Colonel Walsh, his Medal of Honor, and one of his Distinguished Flying Cross citations:

DISTRICT MARINE ACE DIFFIDENTLY RECALLS
DOWNING 20 JAP PLANES SINCE APRIL FOOL'S DAY

America's second ranking Marine air ace, Lieutenant Kenneth A. Walsh, 27, of 1222 Newton St. NE, with 20 Jap planes to his credit, not counting 4 "unconfirmed" diffidently told his story of air combat in South Pacific skies at a Navy press meeting, yesterday.

It was a story climaxing the life of a little shy lad on a bicycle who many years ago pedaled nightly to "Newark Airport in New Jersey" to watch the evening mail plane take off, and only eclipsed by Marine air fighter, Major Joe Foss, who has 26 Japs to chalk up on the fuselage of the ships he flies.

"On April Fool's Day, this year," the ace began shyly, "a large force of Jap fighters and bombers came down from the northern Solomons to raid Guadalcanal. I went up on my first combat mission. We jumped a flock of 25 Zeros and I shot down two in my first five minutes of fighting."

"Greatest Sport in World"

Lieutenant Walsh went on to tell of a Jap 20-millimeter blasting the hood of the cockpit; of his mounting excitement in what proved "to be the greatest sport in the world, air fighting," and downing a dive bomber before shoving off for home.

Thirteen Jap planes were knocked down by Corsair fighters in his maiden essay at air slaughter, Walsh revealed.

"After that taste of fighting, wild horses couldn't keep me on the ground," the flier said.

Chapter 1: World War II

Lieutenant Walsh's records reveal that he never missed a scheduled flight mission and that he has flown more than 250 hours in actual combat.

Three times death reached across the skies for him, but each time he lived to fight again, to, as he grinned, "come back for more."

Once, August 12, Walsh was in formation with 13 Corsairs covering a 24 Liberator bomber flight traveling slow because one of their numbers was crippled.

A superior force of Zeros came gunning down from high. Walsh got on the tail of one, sent a stream of bullets into him, and was turning to attack another when..."I heard sounds like hail hitting a tin roof. A Zero was on my tail pouring lead into me."

With his plane nearly out of control, Walsh thought it was curtains for him. However, his wingman, Lieutenant Bill Johnson of Birmingham, dove into and shot the Jap away.

The ace crash landed on the beach of New Georgia Island, got another plane and went back into the fight.

Two days later above Vella LaVella Island 20-millimeter shells severed his hydraulic line, blew up the right wing gas tank and bullets shot away his aileron controls.

Fell Out of Control

Walsh again fell out of control, but righted his ship to come in at flight speed to land on Munda. Mechanics took one look at the plane and consigned it to base junk heap! Again he took another plane and resumed the battle.

The Marines got 20 Japs that day.

The third brush with death was over Bougainville. Five Japs ganged Walsh. He got two, but "they chewed my ship up so badly I crashed into the sea where shore troops rescued me with a Higgins boat."

Starting with the April Fool's Day initial flight, Lieutenant Walsh's box score of Jap death reads: April 1, 2 Jap Zeros, 1 dive-bomber; April 13, 3 Zeros; June 5, 1 Zero, and float plane; August 12, 2 Zeros; August 15, 1 Zero and 2 dive-bombers; August 21, 1 Zero; August 23, 2 Zeros, and August 30, "a hot day for me," he said, "4 Zeros over Ballale and Vella LaVella."

He wears the Distinguished Flying Cross for the April 1 victories.

Also on his record is the sinking of a Jap supply ship, something he admitted in characteristic afterthought: "that was just sort of extra."

• • •

The President of the United States takes pleasure in presenting the MEDAL OF HONOR to:

FIRST LIEUTENANT KENNETH A. WALSH
UNITED STATES MARINE CORPS

for service as set forth in the following citation:

"For extraordinary heroism and intrepidity above and beyond the call of duty as a pilot in Marine Fighting Squadron 124 in aerial combat against enemy Japanese forces in the Solomon Islands area. Determined to thwart the enemy's attempt to bomb Allied ground forces and shipping at Vella Lavella on August 15, 1943, 1st Lt. Walsh repeatedly dived his plane into an enemy formation outnumbering his own division 6 to 1 and, although his plane was hit numerous times, shot down 2 Japanese dive bombers and 1 fighter. After developing engine trouble on August 30, during a vital escort mission, 1st Lt. Walsh landed his mechanically disabled plane at Munda, quickly replaced it with another, and proceeded to rejoin his flight over Kahili. Separated from his escort group when he encountered approximately 50 Japanese Zeros, he unhesitatingly attacked, striking with relentless fury in his lone battle against a powerful force. He destroyed 4 hostile fighters before cannon shellfire forced him to make a dead-stick landing off Vella Lavella where he was later picked up. His valiant leadership and his daring skill as a flier served as a source of confidence and inspiration to his fellow pilots and reflect the highest credit upon the U.S. Naval Service."

Chapter 1: World War II

/S/ FRANKLIN D. ROOSEVELT

In the name of the President of the United States, the Commander South Pacific Area and South Pacific Force takes pleasure in awarding the DISTINGUISHED FLYING CROSS to:

SECOND LIEUTENANT KENNETH A. WALSH
UNITED STATES MARINE CORPS

for service as set forth in the following citation:

"For heroism and extraordinary achievement in aerial attacks against Japanese shore installations, shipping, and aircraft while serving with a Marine aircraft wing in the Solomon Islands area during the period from March 3 to April 1, 1943. Lieutenant Walsh led two planes in a highly successful strike on the first of the above mentioned dates against a schooner at Vella LaVella, which was strafed and destroyed. On March 19, 21, and 23, respectively, he participated in successful escort missions over the Shortland and Munda areas. Lieutenant Walsh led a flight of fighter planes against a superior number of Japanese aircraft on April 1st, and attacked with such skill and aggressiveness that he destroyed three Zero type fighters. His courageous conduct was in keeping with the highest traditions of the United States Naval Service."

/S/ J. F. SHAFROTH
Rear Admiral, U. S. Navy

• • •

Men of Honor

Name: General Lewis W. Walt, USMC (Deceased).

Biography: Revised February, 1971.

General Lewis W. Walt, who led Marines during three wars, retired from active service in the Marine Corps on February 1, 1971. General Walt earned numerous personal awards during his more than 34 years as a Marine Officer. These include two Navy Crosses and the Silver Star Medal during World War II; a Legion of Merit and Bronze Star Medal in the Korean War; a Distinguished Service Medal in Vietnam, and a Gold Star in lieu of a second Distinguished Service Medal as assistant Commandant of the Marine Corps from January 1, 1968 to February 1, 1971.

Lewis William Walt was born February 16, 1913, in Wabaunsee County, Kansas. He graduated from high school in Fort Collins, Colorado, then entered Colorado State University and was awarded a Bachelor of Science Degree in chemistry upon graduation in 1936. He enlisted in the Colorado National Guard at the age of 17. Upon graduation he was commissioned a second lieutenant in the Army Field Artillery Reserve, but resigned that commission to accept an appointment as a Marine second lieutenant, July 6, 1936.

Lieutenant Walt completed Basic School at Philadelphia, and in April, 1937, was assigned to the Sixth Marine Regiment in San Diego, California, as a machine-gun platoon leader. Embarking for China in August, 1937, he took part in the defense of the International Settlement of Shanghai until February, 1938, at which time he returned to San Diego. In June, 1939, he began his second tour of overseas duty when he was assigned to the Marine Barracks, Guam, Marianas Islands. He was promoted to first lieutenant in October, 1939.

Returning to the United States in June, 1941, shortly before this country's entry into World War II, Lieutenant Walt was assigned as a Company Commander in the Officer Candidates' Class, Marine Corps Schools, Quantico, Virginia. He was promoted to captain in December, 1941.

Early in 1942, Captain Walt volunteered to join the First Marine Raider Battalion, and in April, 1942, arrived with the battalion on Samoa.

On August 7, 1942, as Commander of Company A, 1st Raider Battalion, in landed with his company in the assault on Tulagi Island in the British Solomon Islands. He was awarded the Silver Star Medal for conspicuous gallantry during this landing. Following this, he joined the Fifth Marine Regiment on Guadalcanal where he took part in combat as Commanding Officer of the 2d Battalion, Fifth Marines. He was promoted to major in September, 1942.

In October, 1942, as Battalion Commander, 2d Battalion, Fifth Marines, 1st Marine Division, Major Walt was wounded in action but continued in combat. On December 22, 1942, he was spot promoted to lieutenant colonel for distinguished leadership and gallantry in action during the Guadalcanal campaign.

In December, 1943, following hospitalization and training in Australia, Lieutenant Colonel Walt led the 2d Battalion, Fifth Marines, in the assault at Cape Gloucester, New Britain and shortly thereafter was assigned as Regimental Executive Officer. In the middle of this campaign he was ordered to take over command of the 3d Battalion, Fifth Marines, during its intense battle for Aogiri Ridge. During this action, he earned his first Navy Cross and the Aogiri Ridge was named "Walt Ridge" in his honor by General Lemuel C. Shepherd, Jr., Division Commander.

Departing Cape Gloucester in late February, 1944, Lieutenant Colonel Walt was ordered to the Naval Hospital, Oakland, California, for treatment of wounds and malaria. In June, 1944, he returned to the Pacific area. That September, he landed at Peleliu as Regimental Executive Officer, Fifth Marines. On D-day he was ordered, again, to take over command of the 3d Battalion, Fifth Marines, in the midst of the battle for the beachhead when the Commanding Officer and the Executive Officer were both killed. His second Navy Cross was awarded him during this action.

In November, 1944, Lieutenant Colonel Walt returned to the United States, and the following month assumed duty at Marine Corps Schools, Quantico, as Chief of the Officer Candidates' School Tactics Section.

Assigned to Camp Pendleton in January, 1947, Lieutenant Colonel Walt served as Assistant Chief of Staff, G-3, 3d Marine Brigade, and then as G-3, 1st Marine Division. In November, 1947, he assumed duties as Operations and Training Officer, 1st Provisional Marine Brigade on Guam, and served as Chief of Staff of that organization from February to April, 1949. Returning to Marine Corps Schools, Quantico, in May, 1949, he saw duty as battalion commander with the Special Training Regiment; and in September, he entered the Amphibious Warfare School, Senior Course. On completing the course in June, 1950, he remained at Marine Corps Schools serving as Chief of Tactics Section, S-3, and finally, Executive Officer of the Basic School. He was promoted to colonel in November, 1951.

Colonel Walt was ordered to Korea in November, 1952. He was in combat with the 1st Marine Division until August, 1953, serving consecutively as Commanding Officer, Fifth Marines; Assistant Chief of Staff, G-3, and Chief of Staff of the Division. The Legion of Merit and the Bronze Star Medal, both with a combat "V", were awarded him for exceptionally meritorious service during this assignment. Also, the Korean government awarded Colonel Walt the Ulchi Medal and Ulchi Medal with Silver Star for this period of combat.

On arrival at Marine Corps School, Quantico, in August, 1953, Colonel Walt saw duty as Director, Advanced Base Problem Section, Marine Corps Educational Center, through May, 1954, followed by duty as Commanding Officer, Officers' Basic School, until August, 1956; and Member of the Advanced Research Group, Marine Corps Educational Center, until June, 1957.

Transferred to Washington, D.C., Colonel Walt served as Assistant Director of Personnel until August, 1959, then entered the National War College, Washington, D.C., completing the course in June, 1960.

In July, 1960, Colonel Walt began a one-year assignment as Marine Corps Representative on the Joint Advanced Study Group of the Joint Chiefs of Staff. Upon completing this assignment, he was promoted to Brigadier General and reported for duty at Camp Lejeune as Assistant Division Commander, 2d Marine Division.

In September, 1962, General Walt returned to Marine Corps Schools, Quantico, serving as the Director of the Marine Corps Landing Force Development Center there until May, 1965. That same month, he was promoted to Major General, and in June, 1965, assumed command of the III Marine Amphibious Force and 3d Marine Division in Vietnam. He was also Chief of Naval Forces, Vietnam and Senior Advisor, I Corps and I Corps Coordinator, Republic of Vietnam.

Ten months later, General Walt was nominated for Lieutenant General by President Lyndon B. Johnson, and his promotion was approved by the Senate, March 7, 1966. He continued in Vietnam as Commanding General, III Marine Amphibious Force until June, 1967. For exceptionally meritorious service in a duty of great responsibility as Commanding General, III Marine Amphibious Force; Senior Advisor, I Corps and as I Corps Coordinator, Republic of Vietnam, General Walt was awarded his first Distinguished Service Medal. In addition, the Vietnamese government awarded General Walt the Vietnamese National Order, 3rd Class; the Vietnamese National Order, 4th Class; the Gallantry Cross with Palm; the Chuong My Medal, and the Vietnamese Armed Forces Meritorious Unit Citation of Gallantry Cross with Palm. He was also awarded the senior Ulchi Medal by the Government of South Korea.

Upon his return to the United States, General Walt saw duty from June, 1967 until the following December as Deputy Chief of Staff (Manpower) / Director of Personnel, at Headquarters Marine Corps. On January 1, 1968, he was designated Assistant Commandant of the Marine Corps.

In April, 1969, the Senate passed and sent to the White House a bill to make the Assistant Commandant of the Marine Corps a general when active duty strength of the Corps exceeds 200,000. On May 5, President Richard M. Nixon signed the bill, and General Walt was promoted to four-star rank on June 2, 1969, thus becoming the first Assistant Commandant of the Marine Corps to attain that rank. He retired from active duty February 1, 1971.

General Walt, the first commander of the III Marine Amphibious Force in Vietnam (1965-1967), has written a comprehensive book on the Vietnam War, entitled, "Strange War, Strange Strategy", New York: Funk and Wagnalls, 1970.

General Walt's medals include two Navy Crosses, two Distinguished Service Medals, the Silver Star Medal, the Legion of Merit with Combat "V", the Bronze Star Medal with Combat "V", and the Purple Heart.

(General Walt died March 26, 1989).

-USMC-

The following are General Walt's two Navy Cross and Silver Star Medal citations:

The President of the United States takes pleasure in presenting the NAVY CROSS to:

LIEUTENANT COLONEL LEWIS W. WALT
UNITED STATES MARINE CORPS

for action as set forth in the following citation:

"For extraordinary heroism while attached to the Third Battalion, Fifth Marines (Reinforced), First Marine Division, in action against enemy Japanese forces in the Borgen Bay Area, Cape Gloucester, New Britain, on January 10, 1944. When all six members of a 37-mm. gun crew were killed or wounded while moving the weapon up the steep slope of a ridge to provide support for advanced assault units pinned down by heavy enemy fire, Lieutenant Colonel Walt unhesitatingly rushed forward alone and, completely disregarding his own personal safety, began to push the gun up the hill. Inspired by his initiative and valor, several other men came to his assistance and laboriously worked their way up the slope in the face of terrific hostile fire until the gun was in position to enfilade the enemy lines. Courageously leading his men against five counterattacks made by the Japanese during the night in an effort to regain control of one end of the ridge, Lieutenant Colonel Walt enabled his forces to repulse the attacks with great losses to the enemy and, resuming the battle the next morning, skillfully directed the battalion in the capture of the entire ridge. By his brilliant leadership and expert tactical knowledge, Lieutenant Colonel Walt contributed materially to the success of our forces in this area and upheld the highest traditions of the United States Naval Service."

For the President,
/S/ JAMES FORRESTAL
Secretary of the Navy

The President of the United States takes pleasure in presenting the GOLD STAR in lieu of a second NAVY CROSS to:

Chapter 1: World War II

LIEUTENANT COLONEL LEWIS W. WALT
UNITED STATES MARINE CORPS

for service as set forth in the following citation:

"For extraordinary heroism as Executive Officer of the Fifth Marines, First Marine Division, during operations against enemy Japanese forces on Peleliu, Palau Islands, from 15 to 30 September, 1944. When the Commanding Officer of the Third Battalion was wounded and the Executive Officer killed during an engagement with the enemy in thick jungle on the evening of 15 September, Lieutenant Colonel Walt assumed command of the Battalion and, by his aggressive and tireless leadership in the face of hostile small-arms, mortar, and artillery fire, reorganized the Battalion and enabled it to repulse a heavy Japanese counterattack during the night and push forward to its objective the following morning. On the morning of 20 September, as Regimental Executive Officer, he made his way to the northern tip of the Island to direct the installation of a gun and, although under heavy sniper and machine-gun fire, remained at the gun and supervised the firing on a cave until this strong point was neutralized. His courage and inspiring leadership throughout were in keeping with the highest traditions of the United States Naval Service."

For the President,
/S/ JOHN L. SULLIVAN
Secretary of the Navy

The President of the United States takes pleasure in presenting the SILVER STAR MEDAL to:

CAPTAIN LEWIS W. WALT
UNITED STATES MARINE CORPS

133

for service as set forth in the following citation:

> *"For conspicuous gallantry and intrepidity while com-*
> *manding an assault company of the First Marine Raider*
> *Battalion during action against enemy Japanese forces on*
> *Tulagi, Solomon Islands, August 7, 1942. Exercising keen*
> *judgment and distinctive leadership, Captain Walt, with*
> *complete disregard for his own safety, directed the attack*
> *by his company on a strongly entrenched and cleverly con-*
> *cealed Japanese force, ultimately compelling the enemy to*
> *retire. In the same action, observing that several men of*
> *his assault force were seriously wounded by hostile fire,*
> *Captain Walt, although he himself was exposed to intense*
> *machine-gun and sniper fire, rushed forward and person-*
> *ally dragged two of his men to cover, thereby saving their*
> *lives. His inspiring heroism was in keeping with the high-*
> *est traditions of the United States Naval Service."*

For the President
/S/ FRANK KNOX
Secretary of the Navy

2

KOREA

STATEMENT BY PRESIDENT TRUMAN

Washington, June 26, 1950 – Following is the text of President Truman's statement on Korea:

I conferred Sunday evening with the Secretaries of State and Defense, their senior advisors and the Joint Chiefs of Staff about the situation in the Far East created by unprovoked aggression against the Republic of Korea.

The Government of the United States with the speed and determination with which the United Nations Security Council acted to order a withdrawal of the invading forces to positions north of the Thirty-eighth Parallel. In accordance with the resolution of the Security Council, the United States will vigorously support the effort of the Council to terminate this serious breach of the peace.

Our concern over the lawless action taken by the forces of North Korea, and our sympathy and support for the people of Korea in this situation, are being demonstrated by the cooperative of American personnel in Korea, as well as steps taken to expedite and augment assistance of the type being furnished under the Mutual Defense Assistance Program.

Those responsible for this act of aggression must realize how seriously the Government of the United States views such threats to the peace of the world. Willful disregard of the obligation to keep the peace cannot be tolerated by nations that support the United Nations Charter.

• • •

When the Korean War started, in June, 1950, the only units of the 1st Marine Division on active duty were the Fifth Marine Regiment and units of the Eleventh Marine Artillery Regiment. The First and Seventh Marine Regiments were deactivated after World War II and had to be reassembled.

The Fifth Marines participated, as part of the 1st Provisional Marine Brigade, in the defense of the Pusan (Naktong) perimeter.

The Fifth Marines then joined up with the newly formed First Marines and took part in the landings at Inchon on September 15, 1950 and, later joined by the Seventh Marines on September 21st, the First Marine Division moved on to participate in the recapture of the South Korean Capitol of Seoul on September 27, 1950.

The First Marine Division, after reembarking on October 12, 1950, landed at Wonsan and moved up Korea's eastern coast toward the Chosin Reservoir with the Seventh Marines on the point followed by the Fifth Marines then the First Marines.

"Chesty" Puller's First Marines were stationed at Koto-ri as a rear guard and to keep the main supply route open. Eleven miles north the Division Headquarters was set up at Hagaru-ri. The Seventh and the Fifth Marines continued their push toward Yudam-ni, on the west side of the Chosin Reservoir, with the goal of eventually reaching the Yalu River.

On November 27, 1950, the Chinese Army, some 120,000 strong, attacked and surrounded the Marines.

On November 30th, the Seventh and Fifth Marines began their breakout, through the Toktong Pass, towards Hagaru-ri and the last of them arrived there on December 4th. After reorganizing, they started their long trek, in the bitter cold, to Koto-ri on December 6th.

Eleven miles and 38 hours of vicious fighting later they moved into Koto-ri then continued the journey south toward the port of Hungnam.

On December 11th, the First Division, intact, arrived at Hungnam thus ending the battle of the Chosin Reservoir, one of the greatest battles in the history of the United States Marine Corps.

Chapter 2: Korea

The First Division was shipped to Pusan then moved into the defensive line in the "Punch Bowl" area.

In March, 1952, the Division was moved to defensive positions blocking the enemy's route to Seoul and remained there until after the war ended on July 27, 1953.

During the Korean War the First Marine Division suffered over 25,000 wounded, more than 4,000 killed in action, and received 42 Medals of Honor.

• • •

Name: General Raymond G. Davis, USMC, (Retired)

Biography: Revised April, 1972.

General Raymond G. Davis, who earned the Medal of Honor in Korea in 1950, retired from active duty March 31, 1972, after more than 33 years on active duty. His last assignment was as Assistant Commandant of the Marine Corps from March 12, 1971 until March 31,1972.

As a lieutenant colonel in Korea, General Davis earned the Nation's highest decoration for heroism during the First Marine Division's historic fight to break out of the Chosin Reservoir area. There, against overwhelming odds, he led his battalion in a terrific four-day battle which saved a rifle company from annihilation and opened a mountain pass for the escape of two trapped Marine regiments. The award was presented by President Truman in a White House ceremony on November 24, 1952.

Raymond Gilbert Davis was born on January 13, 1915, in Fitzgerald, Georgia, and graduated in 1933 from Atlanta Technical High School, Atlanta, Georgia. He then entered the Georgia School of Technology, graduating in 1938 with a Bachelor of Science Degree in Chemical Engineering. While in college he was a member of the Reserve Officers Training Corps unit. After graduation, he resigned his commission in the U.S. Army Infantry Reserve to accept appointment as a Marine second lieutenant on June 27, 1938.

In May, 1939, Lieutenant Davis completed the Marine Officers' Basic School at the Philadelphia Navy Yard, and began a year of service with the Marine Detachment on board the *USS PORTLAND* in the Pacific. He returned to shore duty in July, 1940 for weapons and artillery instruction at

Quantico, Virginia and Aberdeen, Maryland. Completing the training in February, 1941, he was assigned to the 1st Antiaircraft Machine-gun Battery of the 1st Marine Division at Guantanamo Bay, Cuba. He returned to the United States with the unit in April, and the following month was appointed battery executive officer, serving in the capacity at Parris Island, South Carolina and Quantico. He was promoted to first lieutenant in August, 1941. That September, he moved with the battery to the Marine Barracks, New River (later Camp Lejeune), North Carolina. Upon his promotion to captain in February, 1942, he was named battery commander.

During World War II, he participated in the Guadalcanal-Tulagi landings, the capture and defense of Guadalcanal, the Eastern New Guinea and Cape Gloucester campaigns, and the Peleliu operation. Beginning in June, 1942, he embarked with his unit for the Pacific area, landing at Guadalcanal two months later. After that campaign, he was appointed Executive Officer of the 1st Special Weapons Battalion, 1st Marine Division. In October, 1943, Major Davis took over command of the battalion and served in that capacity at New Guinea and Cape Gloucester. In April, 1944 while on Cape Gloucester, he was named Commanding Officer, 1st Battalion, 1st Marines, 1st Marine Division.

Major Davis' action while commanding the 1st Battalion at Peleliu in September, 1944 earned him the Navy Cross and the Purple Heart. Although wounded during the first hour of the Peleliu landing, he refused evacuation to remain with his men; and, on one occasion, when heavy Marine casualties and the enemy's point-blank cannon fire had enabled the Japanese to break through, he personally rallied and led his men in fighting to re-establish defense positions. In October, 1944, he returned to Pavuvu and was promoted to lieutenant colonel.

Returning to the United States in November, 1944, Lieutenant Colonel Davis was assigned to Quantico, as Tactical Inspector, Marine Corps Schools. He was named Chief of the Infantry Section, Marine Air-Infantry School, Quantico, in May, 1945, and served in that post for two years before returning to the Pacific area in July, 1947 to serve with the 1st Provisional Marine Brigade on Guam. He was the 1st Brigade's Assistant Chief of Staff, G-3 (Operations and Training), until August, 1948, and from then until May, 1949, was Assistant Chief of Staff, G-4 (Logistics). Upon his return from Guam in May, 1949, he was named Inspector-Instructor of the

Chapter 2: Korea

9th Marine Corps Reserve Infantry Battalion in Chicago, Illinois. He served there until August, 1950 when he embarked for Korea.

In Korea, Lieutenant Colonel Davis commanded the 1st Battalion, 7th Marines, from August to December, 1950. Besides receiving the Medal of Honor for action during that period, he twice earned the Silver Star Medal by exposing himself to heavy enemy fire while leading and encouraging his men in the face of strong enemy opposition. He also received the Legion of Merit with a Combat "V" for exceptionally meritorious conduct and professional skill in welding the 1st Battalion into a highly effective combat team.

Later, as Executive Officer of the 7th Marines, from December, 1950 to June, 1951, Lieutenant Colonel Davis earned the Bronze Star Medal with a Combat "V" for his part in rebuilding the regiment after the Chosin Reservoir campaign. He returned from Korea in June, 1951.

Ordered to Headquarters Marine Corps, Washington, D.C., Lieutenant Colonel Davis served in the Operations Subsection, G-3, Division of Plans and Policies, until February, 1952, when he took charge of the subsection. In April, 1953, he became Head of the Operations and Training Branch, G-3 Division. While serving in this capacity, he was promoted to colonel in October, 1953.

The following July Colonel Davis attended the Special Weapons Employment Course, Fleet Training Center, Norfolk, Virginia, under instruction. In September, 1954, he entered the Senior Course, Marine Corps Schools, Quantico. Upon completing the course in June, 1955, he served consecutively as Assistant Director and, later, Director of the Senior School. In October, 1957, he was again transferred to Washington, D.C., and served there as Assistant G-2, Headquarters Marine Corps, until August, 1959. The following June, he completed the course at the National War College in Washington. Assigned next to Headquarters, United States European Command, in Paris, France, he served from July, 1960 through June, 1963, as chief, Analysis Branch, J-2, Staff of the Commander in Chief, Europe. On July 1, 1963, he was promoted to brigadier general while en route to the United States.

General Davis' next assignment was in the Far East where he served as Assistant Division Commander, 3rd Marine Division, FMF, on Okinawa, from October, 1963 to November, 1964. During this period, he also performed additional duty as Commanding General, SEATO Expeditionary Brigade, EXLIGTAS, in the Philippines, during June, 1964; and as Commanding General, 9th Marine Expeditionary Brigade, in China Sea Contingency Operations, from August 2 to October 16, 1964.

In December, 1964, he was assigned to Headquarters Marine Corps. He served as assistant Director of Personnel until March, 1965, then served as Assistant Chief of Staff, G-1, until March, 1968. For his service in the latter capacity, he was awarded a second Legion of Merit. He was promoted to major general in November, 1966.

Ordered to the Republic of Vietnam, General Davis served briefly as Deputy Commanding General, Provisional Corps, then became Commanding General, 3rd Marine Division. For his service in the latter capacity from May 22, 1968 until April 14, 1969, he was awarded the Distinguished Service Medal, and three personal decorations by the Vietnamese Government.

Upon his return to the United States in May, 1969, he was assigned duty as Deputy for Education with additional duty as Director, Education Center, Marine Corps Development and Education Command, Quantico, Virginia. After his promotion to lieutenant general, July 1, 1970, he was reassigned duty as Commanding General, Marine Corps development and Education Command.

On February 23, 1971, President Nixon nominated Lieutenant General Davis for appointment to the grade of general and assignment to the position of Assistant Commandant of the Marine Corps. His nomination was confirmed by the Senate and he received his fourth star on assuming those duties, March 12, 1971.

For his service as Deputy for Education and subsequently as Commanding General, Marine Corps Development and Education Command, Quantico, Virginia, during the period May, 1969 to March, 1971, and as Assistant Commandant of the Marine Corps, from March, 1971, to March, 1972, he was awarded a Gold Star in lieu of a second Distinguished Service Medal.

-USMC-

Chapter 2: Korea

The following are General Davis' Medal of Honor, two Silver Star, and Legion of Merit citations:

The president of the United States takes pleasure in presenting the MEDAL OF HONOR to:

LIEUTENANT COLONEL RAYMOND G. DAVIS
UNITED STATES MARINE CORPS

for service as set forth in the following citation:

> *"For conspicuous gallantry and intrepidity at the risk of his life above and beyond the call of duty as Commanding Officer of the First Battalion, Seventh Marines, First Marine Division (Reinforced), in action against enemy aggressor forces in Korea from 1 through 4 December, 1950. Although keenly aware that the operation involved breaking through a surrounding enemy and advancing eight miles along primitive icy trails in the bitter cold with every passage disputed by a savage and determined foe, Lieutenant Colonel Davis boldly led his battalion into the attack in a daring attempt to relieve a beleaguered rifle company and to seize, hold, and defend a vital mountain pass controlling the only route available for two Marine regiments in danger of being cut off by numerically superior hostile forces during their re-deployment to the port of Hungnam. When the battalion immediately encountered strong opposition from entrenched enemy forces commanding high ground in the path of the advance, he promptly spearheaded his unit in a fierce attack up the steep, ice-covered slopes in the face of withering fire, and, personally leading the assault groups in a hand-to-hand encounter, drove the hostile troops from their positions, rested his men and reconnoitered the area under enemy fire to determine the best route for continuing the mission. Always in the thick of the fighting, Lieutenant Colonel Davis led his*

battalion over three successive ridges in the deep snow in continuous attacks against the enemy and, constantly inspiring and encouraging his men throughout the night, brought his unit to a point within 1500 yards of the surrounded rifle company by daybreak. Although knocked to the ground when a shell fragment struck his helmet and two bullets pierced his clothing, he arose and fought his way forward at the head of his men until he reached the isolated Marines. On the following morning, he bravely led his battalion in securing the vital mountain pass from a strongly entrenched and numerically superior hostile force, carrying all of his wounded with him, including 22 litter cases and numerous ambulatory patients. Despite repeated savage and heavy assaults by the enemy, he stubbornly held the vital terrain until the two regiments of the division had deployed through the pass and, on the morning of 4 December, led his battalion into Hagaru-ri intact. By his superb leadership, outstanding courage, and brilliant tactical ability, Lieutenant Colonel Davis was directly instrumental in saving the beleaguered rifle company from complete annihilation and enabled the two Marine regiments to escape possible destruction. His valiant devotion to duty and unyielding fighting spirit in the face of almost insurmountable odds enhance and sustain the highest traditions of the United States Naval Service."

/S/ HARRY S. TRUMAN

The President of the United States takes pleasure in presenting the SILVER STAR MEDAL to:

LIEUTENANT COLONEL RAYMOND G. DAVIS
UNITED STATES MARINE CORPS

for service as set forth in the following citation:

Chapter 2: Korea

"During the period 2 November 1950 to 8 November 1950, Lieutenant Colonel Davis was serving as Commanding Officer of the 1st Battalion, 7th Marines, 1st Marine Division in Korea. At 0130 hours 3 November 1950, the enemy conducted a fierce coordinated night attack against his battalion. Lieutenant Colonel Davis moved from point to point on the line wherever there was danger of the enemy breaking through, continually exposing himself to heavy enemy small-arms and mortar fire. His display of leadership, initiative, and courage was a constant inspiration to his officers and men and through his actions the lines held and the enemy was repulsed. During the daylight hours of 3 November 1950, Lieutenant Colonel Davis maneuvered elements of his command in such a manner as to route the enemy and again his display of leadership and courage acted as an inspiration to the officers and men of his command. A direct result of Lieutenant Colonel Davis' was that the 1st Battalion was able to break through and continue the attack in its zone of action. Lieutenant Colonel Davis upheld the highest traditions of the United States Naval Service."

BY COMMAND OF MAJOR GENERAL ALMOND

The President of the United States takes pleasure in presenting the GOLD STAR in lieu of a second SILVER STAR MEDAL to:

LIEUTENANT COLONEL RAYMOND G. DAVIS
UNITED STATES MARINE CORPS

for service as set forth in the following citation:

"For conspicuous gallantry and intrepidity as Commanding Officer of the First Battalion, Seventh Marines, First Marine Division (Reinforced), in action against enemy aggressor forces in Korea on 30 September 1950. Assigned

the task of seizing two hills at the southern of the Seoul-Uijongbu corridor, Lieutenant Colonel Davis boldly led his battalion against a well-entrenched enemy force in the face of hostile small-arms, automatic-weapons, and mortar fire. Keenly aware that the unit had been assembled and organized only six weeks previously and that this was its first attack, he advanced with the assault elements and, moving from platoon to platoon to encourage the men, inspired his battalion to rout the enemy and capture its objective quickly. By his marked courage, brilliant leadership, and steadfast devotion to duty, Lieutenant Colonel Davis upheld the highest traditions of the United States Naval Service."

For the President,
/S/ C. S. THOMAS
Secretary of the Navy

The President of the United States takes pleasure in presenting the LEGION OF MERIT to:

LIEUTENANT COLONEL RAYMOND G. DAVIS
UNITED STATES MARINE CORPS

for service as set forth in the following citation:

"For exceptionally meritorious conduct in the performance of outstanding services to the Government of the United States as Commanding Officer, First Battalion, Seventh Marines, First Marine Division (Reinforced), during operations against enemy aggressor forces in Korea from 21 September to 10 October 1950. Assuming control of a newly organized battalion, Lieutenant Colonel Davis discharged his many responsibilities with meticulous attention to detail and effectively coordinated the units under his command into a smoothly functioning combat team. A capable

144

*and resourceful officer, he successfully led his battalion in
the advance from Seoul to Uijongbu, seizing all assigned
objectives in a minimum of time and with a minimum of
casualties. By his inspiring leadership, sound tactical judgment, and unswerving devotion to duty, Lieutenant Colonel Davis contributed substantially to the success achieved
by his battalion and upheld the highest traditions of the
United States Naval Service." Lieutenant Colonel Davis
is authorized to wear the Combat "V."*

*For the President,
/S/ C. S. THOMAS
Secretary of the Navy*

•••

Name: Lieutenant Colonel John L. Hopkins, USMC.

Biography: Written 1952.
Lieutenant Colonel John L. Hopkins, USMC, 34, holder of the Navy Cross
for heroism in the Korean fighting, was decorated five times for valor during that war.

Lieutenant Colonel Hopkins was born November 28, 1918, at
Marshfield, Oregon. Following graduation from Stanford University in June,
1940, he entered the Officers Candidates Class at Quantico, Virginia. Upon
successful completion of the training, he was commissioned a Second Lieutenant in the United States Marine Corps Reserve.

After further training at the Marine Corps Schools, Quantico, and at
the Marine Corps Base, San Diego, California, he was ordered overseas
with the Second Marine Brigade for duty in American Samoa.

As a First Lieutenant, he accepted a regular commission in the United
States Marine Corps. He moved with the Second Marine Brigade to New
Zealand, where he served as Aide-de-Camp to Major General Charles F.
Price.

After his first tour of duty overseas, he served at Marine Corps installations on the West Coast and at Staff and Command School, Quantico,
Virginia.

Promoted to Captain, he again went overseas to join the Sixth Marine Division in time to participate in the Okinawa Campaign. He remained overseas in occupation duty in Japan and received the Letter of Commendation for his outstanding work.

Prior to returning to the United States, he was appointed to the rank of Major on August 7, 1947.

Until the Korean War started, he served as Inspector-Instructor in Los Angeles, California, and Minneapolis, Minnesota.

After being promoted to Lieutenant Colonel on October 13, 1950, he was ordered overseas to the First Marine Division on January 1, 1951. As executive Officer and later Commander of the First Battalion, Fifth Marines, he engaged in five campaigns with the enemy, and earned the Navy Cross, the Silver Star Medal, a Gold Star in lieu of a second Silver Star Medal, the Legion of Merit, and the Air Medal.

-USMC-

The following are Lieutenant Colonel Hopkins' Navy Cross, two Silver Star, and Legion of Merit citations:

The President of the United States takes pleasure in presenting the NAVY CROSS to:

LIEUTENANT COLONEL JOHN L. HOPKINS
UNITED STATES MARINE CORPS

for action as set forth in the following citation:

> *"For extraordinary heroism as Commanding Officer of the First Battalion, Fifth Marines, First Marine Division (Reinforced), in action against enemy aggressor forces in Korea on 2 June, 1951. Assigned the extremely difficult mission of seizing Hill 611, a heavily fortified and bitterly defended hostile position commanding a vital enemy lateral supply route, Lieutenant Colonel Hopkins skillfully directed and coordinated the attack, fearlessly moving in*

close proximity to the assaulting elements and, although his forward units were subjected to intense hostile mortar, artillery, automatic-weapons, and small-arms fire, courageously advanced to a fire-swept observation post where he remained throughout the day-long engagement. Despite the strength of the enemy's defense which consisted of cleverly placed land mines and mutually supporting log and earth bunkers, he expertly controlled the battalion's action, utilizing supporting arms to maximum advantage, skillfully directing the movements of his assault companies and exercising his vast tactical knowledge in decisions regarding the commitment of his reserves. By his coolness and outstanding professional ability, he was responsible for the success of his battalion in wresting the objective from an enemy force estimated at regimental strength, thereby successfully dominating the enemy's supply route in his zone of action. His exceptional courage, inspiring leadership, and valiant devotion to duty reflect the highest credit upon Lieutenant Colonel Hopkins and the United States Naval Service."

/S/ DAN A. KIMBALL
Secretary of the Navy

The President of the United States takes pleasure in presenting the SILVER STAR MEDAL to:

LIEUTENANT COLONEL JOHN L. HOPKINS
UNITED STATES MARINE CORPS

for service as set forth in the following citation:

"For conspicuous gallantry and intrepidity as Commanding Officer of the First Battalion, Fifth Marines, First Marine Division (Reinforced), in action against enemy aggressor forces in Korea on 22 April 1951. Assigned the

mission of protecting the right sector of the regimental zone, Lieutenant Colonel Hopkins skillfully organized the defensive position. During the hours of darkness, a large enemy force succeeded in penetrating the friendly unit on the right, posing a serious threat to the regiment. Although exposed to continuous hostile mortar and automatic-weapons fire, he ably deployed his reserves and launch a devastating counterattack against the enemy force, successfully restoring the friendly positions. By his outstanding courage, quick actions and resolute determination, Lieutenant Colonel Hopkins materially aided in preventing the enemy from exploiting the penetration and overrunning the supporting-arms positions, thereby upholding the highest traditions of the United States Naval Service."

For the President,
/S/ R. B. ANDERSON
Secretary of the Navy

The President of the United States takes pleasure in presenting the GOLD STAR in lieu of a second SILVER STAR MEDAL to:

LIEUTENANT COLONEL JOHN L. HOPKINS
UNITED STATES MARINE CORPS

for service as set forth in the following citation:

"For conspicuous gallantry and intrepidity as Commanding Officer of the First Battalion, Fifth Marines, First Marine Division (Reinforced), in action against enemy aggressor forces in Korea from 25 to 29 April 1951. When a savage attack by numerically superior enemy forces exposed the flanks of his battalion, Lieutenant Colonel Hopkins led his men in a highly complicated and difficult retrograde movement. Constantly exposing himself to intense and accurate hostile mortar, artillery, automatic-

weapons, and small-arms fire, he directed the defense of successive blocking positions and, at all times, inspired his units to greater efforts in inflicting heavy casualties on the enemy. Laboring untiringly, he devised intricate maneuvers to delay and confuse the hostile forces, and devoted himself to insuring adequate medical care for the battalion casualties. By his aggressive leadership, decisive actions, and thorough understanding of the multitudinous problems confronting his battalion, he aided immeasurable in the success achieved by the regiment. His outstanding courage, daring initiative, and devotion to duty reflect the highest credit upon Lieutenant Colonel Hopkins and the United States Naval Service."

For the President,
/S/ R. B. ANDERSON
Secretary of the Navy

The President of the United States takes pleasure in presenting the LEGION OF MERIT to:

MAJOR JOHN L. HOPKINS
UNITED STATES MARINE CORPS

for service as set forth in the following citation:

"For exceptionally meritorious conduct in the performance of outstanding services to the Government of the United States as Executive Officer of the Second Battalion, Fifth Marines, First Marine Division (Reinforced), during operations against enemy aggressor forces in Korea from 18 November to 15 December 1950. Exercising outstanding skill and exceptional foresight throughout this period, Major Hopkins discharged his responsibilities with diligence, providing his commanding officer with a constant flow of accurate information despite frequent exposure to

intense enemy fire. A capable and inspiring officer, he expertly handled tactical and logistical problems and was directly instrumental in maintaining maximum combat efficiency in his battalion, thereby contributing essentially to its success. His professional ability, resourceful initiative and unwavering devotion to duty reflect great credit upon Major Hopkins and the United States Naval Service."
Major Hopkins is authorized to wear the Combat "V."

For the President,
/S/ R. B. ANDERSON
Secretary of the Navy

• • •

Name: Lieutenant General Homer L. Litzenberg, USMC.

Biography: Written July 1, 1963:
WASHINGTON, D. C., June 28—Retired Marine Lieutenant General Homer L. Litzenberg died of cancer last night at Bethesda Naval Hospital, Bethesda, Maryland.

A veteran of 37 years Marine enlisted and officer service, General Litzenberg retired from active duty on May 31, 1959.

Born January 8, 1903, at Steelton, Pennsylvania, the general enlisted in the Marine Corps on October 5, 1922. Following a tour of duty in Haiti, he was commissioned in February, 1925, and later saw expeditionary duty in Nicaragua in 1928-29.

During the early days of World War II, and later from 1944-46, General Litzenberg served in Washington in the War Plans Sections of the offices of Chief of Naval Operations, the Commander in Chief, United States Fleet, and the Joint Chiefs of Staff.

While assigned to the office of the Commander in Chief, U.S. Fleet, he served in England during combined planning with the British on the conduct of the war, and participated in the amphibious assault on Casablanca, French Morocco, in November 1942.

Chapter 2: Korea

He later landed with the Fourth Marine Division on Roi-Namur, Kwajalein Atoll in the Marshall Islands, and as Assistant Operations Officer of the Fifth Amphibious Corps, participated in the Saipan and Tinian campaigns.

After the cessation of hostilities, General Litzenberg served as the Seventh Fleet Liaison Officer with General of the Army George C. Marshall and the Chinese Ministry of Defense in Nanking, China.

Following the outbreak of the Korean Conflict, he formed and assumed command of the Seventh Marine Regimental Combat Team, which sailed for duty in Korea on September 1, 1950.

He later commanded the Seventh Regiment in the Inchon-Seoul campaign, at the Chosin Reservoir, and during operations in Central Korea.

He was senior officer present when the Fifth and Seventh Marines repulsed repeated attacks by elements of five Chinese divisions at Yudam-ni, west of the Chosin Reservoir, in November-December 1950. His regiment later formed the advance guard of the First marine Division in its advance from Hagaru-ri to the sea at Hungnam.

General Litzenberg returned to Korea in March, 1957, as Senior Member of the United Nations Command component of the Military Armistice Commission, negotiating with the Communists at Panmunjom. On his return from Korea, he was assigned his last tour of duty in December, 1957, as Inspector General of the Marine Corps at Headquarters Marine Corps. He remained in that post until his retirement in May, 1959.

Among the many decorations and medals presented the General are the Navy Cross, Distinguished Service Cross (Army), Silver Star Medal with Oak Leaf Cluster and Gold Star, Legion of Merit with Combat "V", Navy Letter of Commendation and Army Letter of Commendation with Oak Leaf Cluster.

The General is survived by a son, Captain Homer L. Litzenberg III and a daughter, Betty Lee (Mrs. Filbert R. Boston).

USMC

The following are a short newspaper article concerning General Litzenberg, his Navy Cross, two Silver Star, and Legion of Merit citations:

Men of Honor

NOW, THAT'S ONE TOUGH MARINE!

News reports that a U.S. Marine Captain turned back three Israeli tanks at pistol point have reminded me of a memorable anecdote.

The late Marine Major General Homer Litzenberg, when a lieutenant colonel, was assigned to help the U.S. Army plan the intricate World War II amphibious invasion of North Africa. He later told me that he wrangled orders to accompany the landing force as an observer.

After the Army was ashore, he dressed in his regular Marine uniform and began a tour of the battle areas. Caught in the open by enemy fire, he dived into a nearby foxhole already occupied by an Army private.

During a lull in the shelling, the young Army man examined the unfamiliar Marine greens, the globe and anchor buttons, and the gleaming leaves of rank and asked, "what are you?"

Litzenberg explained that he was a U.S. Marine. The kid's eyes lit up and he asked, how many Marines are here?" Colonel Litzenberg replied "just me."

The astounded private said, "how come we launch a major expedition with thousands of soldiers and the Marines send only one man?"

Litzenberg answered, "well, you only have one invasion don't you?"

H. P. Newson
Chevy Chase, MD

The President of the United States takes pleasure in presenting the NAVY CROSS to:

COLONEL HOMER L. LITZENBERG, JR.
UNITED STATES MARINE CORPS

for service as set forth in the following citation:

"For extraordinary heroism as Commanding Officer of the Seventh Marines, First Marine Division (Reinforced), in action against enemy aggressor forces in Korea on 6 and 7 December 1950. Confronted with tremendous difficul-

*ties imposed by several days of continuous fighting in sub-
zero temperatures against a numerically superior enemy
force which had severely depleted his regiment, Colonel
Litzenberg unhesitatingly proceeded to carry out his orders to attack from Hagaru-ri to Koto-ri and to join other
units there. With the only route of attack blocked and strong
elements of two hostile divisions holding positions to his
front and flanks, he skillfully directed the assault from a
position exposed to vicious enemy artillery, mortar and
machine-gun fire. Expertly supervising the care and evacuation of casualties and moving tirelessly among his men to
inspire and exhort them to heroic efforts, he finally succeeded in pressing through to his objective with an offensive so devastating that the enemy was unable to recover
rapidly enough to deliver concerted attacks against the
flanks of the rear guard regiment which followed his unit.
His great personal courage, daring initiative and indomitable fighting spirit in the face of overwhelming odds reflect the highest credit upon Colonel Litzenberg and the
United States Naval Service."*

/S/ DAN A. KIMBALL
Secretary of the Navy

The President of the United States takes pleasure in presenting an OAK
LEAF CLUSTER in lieu of a second SILVER STAR MEDAL to:

COLONEL HOMER L. LITZENBERG, JR.
UNITED STATES MARINE CORPS

for service as set forth in the following citation:

*"For conspicuous gallantry and intrepidity as Command-
ing Officer of the Seventh Marines, First Marine Division
(Reinforced), in action against enemy aggressor forces in
Korea from 12 November to 19 November 1950. During*

this period Colonel Litzenberg, though frequently exposed to enemy mortar, automatic weapons and small-arms fire, continually visited and supervised the movements of his front line units in their advance along the Hamhung-Hagaru-ri road to the Chosin Reservoir area in North Korea. The route of advance was over a narrow, mountainous road with the enemy being well-entrenched and possessing excellent observation thereby making movement difficult. The constant display of personal courage and aggressive leadership by Colonel Litzenberg were instrumental in the rapid advance of his unit to assigned objectives. The actions by Colonel Litzenberg reflect great credit upon himself and are in keeping with the highest traditions of the United States Naval Service."

/S/ R. B. ANDERSON
Secretary of the Navy

The President of the United States takes pleasure in presenting the GOLD STAR in lieu of a third SILVER STAR MEDAL to:

COLONEL HOMER L. LITZENBERG, JR.
UNITED STATES MARINE CORPS

for service as set forth in the following citation:

"For conspicuous gallantry and intrepidity as Commanding Officer of the Seventh Marines, First Marine Division (Reinforced), in action against enemy aggressor forces in Korea on 1 October 1950. While his regiment was advancing from Seoul to Uijongbu in an advance guard formation, the leading battalion was opposed by an estimated infantry battalion reinforced by anti-tank guns, tanks and heavy mortars. With the enemy unit entrenched in well-camouflaged positions and delivering heavy fire on the friendly elements, Colonel Litzenberg unhesitatingly moved

forward to determine first hand the nature and strength of the hostile forces. When the enemy launched a concerted counterattack supported by heavy mortar and anti-tank gun fire, he skillfully directed the employment of his units in the face of the heavy fire and effectively called for and controlled supporting fires to repulse the counterattack, thereby allowing his forces to continue their attack. By his aggressiveness, courageous leadership and unwavering devotion to duty, Colonel Litzenberg served to inspire all who observed him and upheld the highest traditions of the United States Naval Service."

/S/ R. B. ANDERSON
Secretary of the Navy

The President of the United States takes pleasure in presenting the LE-GION OF MERIT to:

COLONEL HOMER L. LITZENBERG, JR.
UNITED STATES MARINE CORPS

for service as set forth in the following citation:

"For exceptionally meritorious conduct in the performance of outstanding services to the Government of the United States as Commanding Officer of the Seventh Marines, First Marine Division (Reinforced), while engaged in combat operations against enemy aggressor forces in Korea from 21 September to 2 November 1950. Exercising sound judgement, exceptional organizational ability and a keen perception of operational requirements, Colonel Litzenberg expertly organized, trained and directed his newly formed regiment into a smoothly functioning and highly efficient organization. Often subjected to enemy fire during the advance upon and capture of Seoul, and the subsequent advance to the north, he was in large measure responsible

for the success of his regiment in executing all assigned missions and for the decisive defeat of the enemy on each occasion. His outstanding professional ability, aggressive determination and courageous devotion to duty served as a constant inspiration to his command and reflect the highest credit upon Colonel Litzenberg and the United States Naval Service." Colonel Litzenberg is authorized to where the Combat "V."

/S/ R. B. ANDERSON
Secretary of the Navy

• • •

Name: First Lieutenant Frank N. Mitchell, USMC (Deceased).

Biography: Written 1953.
Frank Nicias Mitchell was born August 18, 1921 at Indian Gap, Texas, and was a 1938 graduate of Roaring Springs High School.

Lieutenant Mitchell enlisted in the Marine Corps in 1939, and was commissioned a second lieutenant in 1945, following World War II service aboard the aircraft carrier *USS ENTERPRISE* at Wake Island, and additional service at the Marshall Islands, and occupation duty in China. He was also attached to Fleet Marine Force Pacific as a member of its rifle and pistol team.

Lieutenant Mitchell attended Colorado College under the Navy V-12 program, and also attended Southwestern University and North Texas Agriculture and Mechanical College. He played varsity football in college for two years.

Lieutenant Mitchell was a member of Company A, 1st Battalion, 7th Marines, when he was posthumously awarded the Medal of Honor in Korea for sacrificing his life in action against the enemy. He was cited for extraordinary heroism for waging a singlehanded battle against the enemy on November 26, 1950 near Hansan-ni, to cover the withdrawal of wounded Marines, despite multiple wounds to himself.

Chapter 2: Korea

The Medal of Honor was presented August 6, 1952 to Lieutenant Mitchell's widow and daughter by Lieutenant Colonel Henry D. Strunk, the acting director of the Sixth Marine Corps Reserve District, at their home in Atlanta, Georgia.

In addition to the Medal of Honor, some of Lieutenant Mitchell's other awards include the Silver Star Medal, the Bronze Star Medal with Combat "V", and the Purple Heart with Gold Star in lieu of a second Purple Heart.

-USMC-

The following are Lieutenant Mitchell's Medal of Honor and Silver Star Medal citations:

The President of the United States takes pleasure in presenting the MEDAL OF HONOR to:

FIRST LIEUTENANT FRANK N. MITCHELL
UNITED STATES MARINE CORPS

for action as set forth in the following citation:

"For conspicuous gallantry and intrepidity at the risk of his above and beyond the call of duty as Leader of a rifle platoon of Company A, 1st Battalion, 7th Marines, 1st Marine Division (Reinforced), in action against enemy aggressor forces in Korea on 26 November, 1950. Leading his platoon in point position during a patrol by his company through a thickly wooded and snow-covered area in the vicinity of Hansan-ni, First Lieutenant Mitchell acted immediately when the enemy suddenly opened fire at point-blank range, pinning down his forward elements and inflicting numerous casualties in his ranks. Boldly dashing to the front under blistering fire from automatic weapons and small-arms, he seized an automatic rifle from one of the wounded men and effectively trained it against the attackers and, when his ammunition was expended, picked

up and hurled grenades with deadly accuracy, at the same time directing and encouraging his men in driving the outnumbering enemy from his position. Maneuvering to the front and left flank, First Lieutenant Mitchell, despite wounds sustained early in the action, reorganized his platoon under the devastating fire and spearheaded a fierce hand-to-hand struggle to repulse the onslaught. Asking for volunteers to assist in searching for and evacuating the wounded, he personally led a party of litter bearers through the hostile lines in growing darkness and, although suffering intense pain from multiple wounds, stormed ahead and waged a singlehanded battle against the enemy, successfully covering the withdrawal of his men before he was fatally struck down by a burst of small-arms fire. Stouthearted and indomitable in the face of tremendous odds, First Lieutenant Mitchell, by his fortitude, great personal valor, and extraordinary heroism, saved the lives of several Marines and inflicted heavy casualties among the aggressors. His unyielding courage throughout reflects the highest credit upon himself and the United States Naval Service. He gallantly gave his life for his country."

/S/ HARRY S. TRUMAN

The President of the United States takes pleasure in presenting the SILVER STAR MEDAL to :

FIRST LIEUTENANT FRANK N. MITCHELL
UNITED STATES MARINE CORPS

for service as set forth in the following citation:

"First Lieutenant Frank N. Mitchell, a member of the 7th Marine Regiment, distinguished himself by conspicuous gallantry and intrepidity in action against the enemy near Hamhung, North Korea on 3 November, 1950 as a rifle

*platoon leader occupying a position in his company's de-
fensive sector. While making a short reconnaissance to
improve his position, his platoon was suddenly and vi-
ciously attacked by the enemy. Immediately returning to
his platoon, which was on the verge of being overrun, he
rallied his men to repel the attack and he, although painfully wounded in the ensuing action, refused to be evacuated until the danger of a serious break-through was
averted. First Lieutenant Mitchell's heroic actions were in
keeping with the highest traditions of the United States
Naval Service."*

BY COMMAND OF MAJOR GENERAL ALMOND

• • •

Name: Captain Raymond G. Murphy, USMCR.

Biography: Revised February, 1967.
Captain Raymond G. Murphy, former member of the United States Marine
Corps Reserve, was the thirty-ninth Marine to be awarded the Medal of
Honor for heroism in Korea. He was decorated by President Eisenhower in
a White House ceremony on October 27, 1953.

Captain Murphy, son of Mr. and Mrs. Thomas M. Murphy, of Pueblo,
Colorado, won the Nation's highest decoration for heroic action and leadership in the "Reno-Las Vegas" fighting of February, 1953.

Raymond Gera Murphy was born in Pueblo, Colorado, January 14,
1930, and was graduated from Pueblo Catholic High School in 1947. He
attended Fort Lewis Junior College, Durango, Colorado; Colorado A&M,
and is a 1951 graduate of Adams State College, Alamosa, Colorado, where
he majored in physical education.

While in college, he played varsity football, basketball, and baseball,
and worked as a swimming instructor at Durango in the summer of 1950.
He enrolled in the Marine Corps Reserve in May, 1951 and entered Officers Candidate School at Parris Island, South Carolina, the following month.

Commissioned a second lieutenant in September, 1951, he then was ordered to Officers Basic School at Quantico, Virginia. Completing the course the following February, he was transferred to Camp Pendleton, California, for further training before embarking for Korea in July, 1952.

In Korea, Lieutenant Murphy served with the 5th Marine Regiment of the 1st Marine Division until he was wounded. After treatment aboard the Danish hospital ship *JUTLANDIA*, the American hospital ship *REPOSE*, and later in Japan, he was returned to the United States Naval Hospital, Mare Island, California, in March, 1953. He was promoted to First Lieutenant that same month.

He returned to Pueblo after his discharge from the hospital, and was released from active duty April 7, 1953. He was promoted to Captain on December 31, 1954. He was discharged from the Marine Corps Reserve on December 28, 1959.

In addition to the Medal of Honor, Captain Murphy's awards include the Silver Star Medal and the Purple Heart.

-USMC-

The following are a newspaper article about Captain Murphy, his Medal of Honor and Silver Star citations:

TWO WOUNDS MADE HIM STRONGER

On February 3, 1953, Raymond G. Murphy, then a second lieutenant, USMC, had the task of seeing that all the Marines who got hit in an attack on a strong enemy trench line got out.

His platoon was detailed to get out the wounded. Right at the start of the action Murphy was painfully wounded by fragments from a mortar shell, but he refused medical aid and worked his forward through the barrage.

As the fight got hotter he took some of his men in as supports, killing two Chinese with his pistol.

When the wounded had been evacuated, he took part in the rear guard action, first with a carbine, then, as the enemy swept forward, an automatic rifle.

Major Kenneth Bailey. (U.S. Marine Corps)   *Sergeant John Basilone. (U.S. Marine Corps)*

Sgt. Basilone (left) poses with another Medal of Honor recipient Pfc. Richard Sorenson. (U.S. Marine Corps)

Colonel Gregory "Pappy" Boyington being presented the Navy Cross by Gen. A.A. Vandegrift. (U.S. Marine Corps)

Colonel Evans F. Carlson on May 13, 1944. (U.S. Marine Corps)

Colonel Justice M. Chambers. (U.S. Marine Corps)

Major General Merritt A. Edson on November 28, 1952. (U.S. Marine Corps)

Lt. Robert M. Hanson on Bougainville on November 14, 1943. (U.S. Marine Corps)

Brigadier General Louis R. Jones. (U.S. Marine Corps)

Captain Joseph J. McCarthy. (U.S. Marine Corps)

Brig.Gen. Harry B. Liversedge. (U.S. Marine Corps)

Below: Col. H.B. Liversedge (left) and Lt.Col. R.H. Williams looking over maps of Iwo Jima. (U.S. Marine Corps)

Lt.Col. Lewis B. Puller, 1945. (U.S. Marine Corps)

Below: Lt.Col. "Chesty" Puller with regimental staff of the 7th Marines (not shown is regimental commander Col. Frisbie). Left to right: Maj. Victor Streit, Puller, Lt. Frank Farrell, Maj. Claude Cross, Capt. R.T. Musselwhite, Lt. John Aubuchon. Photo taken at Cape Gloucester on January 10, 1944. (U.S. Marine Corps)

Major Alan Shapley on September 12, 1957. (U.S. Marine Corps)

James V. Shanley. (U.S. Marine Corps)

Capt. Carlton R. Rouh (right) greeting General A.A. Vandegrift. (U.S. Marine Corps)

General David M. Shoup on January 1, 1960. (U.S. Marine Corps)

General Alexander A. Vandegrift. (U.S. Marine Corps)

Robert W. Vaupell. (U.S. Marine Corps)

Kenneth A. Walsh. (U.S. Marine Corps)

Col. John L. Hopkins. (U.S. Marine Corps)

Below: Lt.Col. John L. Hopkins, commanding the 1st Battalion, 5th Marines leads in singing of the "Star Spangled Banner" at memorial services during the Korean War. Photo taken on June 21, 1951. (U.S. Marine Corps)

General Lewis W. Walt on May 20, 1969. (U.S. Marine Corps)

Brigadier General Raymond G. Davis. (U.S. Marine Corps)

General Homer L. Litzenberg, Jr. (U.S. Marine Corps)

Colonel Litzenberg commanding the 7th Marine Regiment in Korea. (U.S. Marine Corps)

Frank N. Mitchell. (U.S. Marine Corps)

1st Lt. Raymond G. Murphy on October 27, 1953.
(U.S. Marine Corps)

Major General Raymond L. Murray in February
1963. (U.S. Marine Corps)

Colonel Harold S. Roise in November 1958. (U.S.
Marine Corps)

Colonel W.D. Sawyer. (U.S. Marine Corps)

Master Sergeant Stanley Wawrzyniak shortly after receiving his second Navy Cross on January 16, 1953. (U.S. Marine Corps)

Colonel Harvey C. Barnum, Jr. on June 14, 1983. (U.S. Marine Corps)

Lt.Gen. Martin L. Brandtner. (U.S. Marine Corps)

Above: Left to right – Gunnery Sgt. Leroy Paulson, Lance Cpl. John Phelps, Capt. R.E. Fairfield, and Capt. Steven Pless. (U.S. Marine Corps) Below: Army Staff Sgt. Lawrence H. Allen (right) was glad to see Capt. Pless as his crew literally swooped Allen away from the Viet Cong on August 21, 1967. (U.S. Marine Corps)

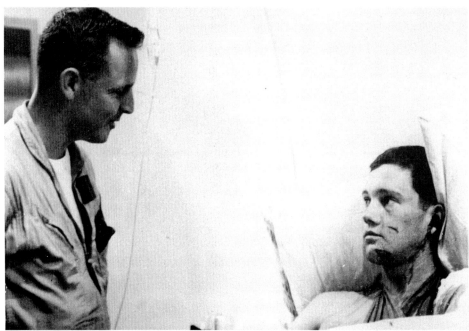

General Ray L. Smith. (U.S. Marine Corps)

Below: Flag ceremony, Quantico, Virginia, 1991. Former Marines of Alpha Company, 1st Battalion, 1st Marines turn over an NVA flag to the 1st Marine Division Museum. The flag was captured at Hue City in February 1968 and is the only documented captured NVA flag of the Vietnam War. From left to right: James Sullivan, Ray Smith (shown here as Maj.Gen., then 2nd Lt.), Herb Watkins, Bill Stubbs, Pat Fraleigh, Ed Neas, Paul Brown, John Ligato, and Gordon Batchelor. (Courtesy of John Ligato)

Lt.Colonel William G. Leftwich, Jr., 1968. (U.S. Marine Corps)

Major Gen. James E. Livingston. (U.S. Marine Corps)

Major Howard V. Lee wearing the Medal of Honor just presented to him by President Johnson on October 25, 1967. (U.S. Marine Corps)

Jay R. Vargas. (U.S. Marine Corps)

Capt. Wesley Fox. (U.S. Marine Corps)

Below: Joseph Donovan (right) being congratulated by Gen. Walt. (U.S. Marine Corps)

Marines storm Tarawa, November, 1943. (U.S. Marine Corps)

Flak-vested 1st Regiment Marines move a 106mm recoilless rifle into position during house-to-house fighting in Hue, February, 1968. (U.S. Marine Corps)

Ranging over the battlefield, he brought back the bodies of a Marine machine-gun crew, then, although a second time wounded, led the whole force back to its point of departure.

Retired as a captain, he now lives in Santa Fe, New Mexico, where he runs a bowling alley.

• • •

The President of the United States takes pleasure in presenting the MEDAL OF HONOR to:

SECOND LIEUTENANT RAYMOND G. MURPHY
UNITED STATES MARINE CORPS RESERVE

for service as set forth in the following citation:

"For conspicuous gallantry and intrepidity at the risk of his life above and beyond the call of duty as a Platoon Commander of Company A, First Battalion, Fifth Marines, First Marine Division (Reinforced), in action against enemy aggressor forces in Korea on February 3, 1953. Although painfully wounded by fragments from an enemy mortar shell while leading his evacuation platoon in support of assault units attacking a cleverly concealed and well-entrenched hostile force occupying commanding ground, (the then) Second Lieutenant Murphy steadfastly refused medical aid and continued to lead his men up a hill through a withering barrage of hostile mortar and small-arms fire, skillfully maneuvering his force from one position to the next and shouting words of encouragement. Undeterred by the increasingly intense enemy fire, he immediately located casualties as they fell and made several trips up and down the fire-swept hill to direct evacuation teams to the wounded, personally carrying many of the stricken Marines to safety. When reinforcements were needed by the assaulting elements, Second Lieutenant

Murphy employed part of his unit as support and, during the ensuing battle, personally killed two of the enemy with his pistol. With all wounded evacuated and the assaulting units beginning to disengage, he remained behind with a carbine to cover the movement of friendly forces off the hill and, though suffering intense pain from his serious wounds, seized an automatic rifle to provide more fire-power when the enemy reappeared in the trenches. After reaching the base of the hill, he organized a search party and again ascended the slope for a final check on missing Marines, locating and carrying the bodies of a machine-gun crew back down the hill. Wounded a second time while conducting the entire force to the line of departure through a continuing barrage of enemy small-arms, artillery, and mortar fire, he again refused medical assistance until assured that every one of his men, including all casualties, had preceded him to the main lines. His resolute and inspiring leadership, exceptional fortitude, and great personal valor reflect the highest credit upon Second Lieutenant Murphy and enhance the finest traditions of the United States Naval Service."

/S/ DWIGHT D. EISENHOWER

The President of the United States takes pleasure in presenting the SILVER STAR MEDAL to:

SECOND LIEUTENANT RAYMOND G. MURPHY
UNITED STATES MARINE CORPS RESERVE

for service as set forth in the following citation:

"For conspicuous gallantry and intrepidity as a Platoon Commander of Company A, First Battalion, Fifth Marines, First Marine Division (Reinforced), in action against en-

emy aggressor forces in Korea on 22 November 1952. As-
signed the extremely hazardous mission of assaulting a
strong point on the enemy main line of resistance, Second
Lieutenant Murphy courageously exposed himself to dev-
astating enemy mortar and artillery fire to press the as-
sault on the objective. On three separate occasions, when
the enemy attempted to prevent him from accomplishing
his mission, he skillfully coordinated and utilized support-
ing arms to repulse the foe. Although the platoon suffered
severe casualties by the time the objective was reached,
the unit succeeded in evacuating the wounded in the face
of continuous enemy fire. Upon successful completion of
the mission, he ordered the withdrawal and personally re-
mained behind until assured that all of his men had with-
drawn. By his outstanding courage, superb leadership, and
indomitable spirit, Second Lieutenant Murphy served to
inspire all who observed him and upheld the highest tradi-
tions of the United States Naval Service."

For The President,
/S/ C. S. THOMAS
Secretary of the Navy

• • •

Name: Major General Raymond L. Murray, USMC (Retired).

Biography: Written 1968.
Major General Raymond L. Murray, who earned two Navy Crosses, one
during World War II, and the second during the Korean Conflict, retired
from active duty August 1, 1968.

As a lieutenant colonel on Saipan during World War II, General Murray
was awarded his first Navy Cross for extraordinary heroism under fire,
June 15, 1944, while commanding the 2d Battalion, 6th Marines, 2d Marine Division. During the Korean Conflict, he was twice again cited for
extraordinary heroism, earning the Army Distinguished Service Cross dur-

ing the period November 29 to December 4, 1950, as commander of the Fifth Marines, First Marine Division (Reinforced).

Raymond Leroy Murray was born June 30, 1913, at Los Angeles, California. He attended schools in Alhambra, California, and Harlingen, Texas, graduating from the latter in 1930. On July 9, 1935, following graduation from Texas A&M College, he accepted his commission as a Marine second lieutenant.

After completing Basic School at the Philadelphia Navy Yard in March, 1936, Lieutenant Murray joined the 2d Marine Brigade in San Diego, California. Embarking with the brigade for China in September, 1937, he served for a short time with the 2d Battalion in Shanghai. In January, 1938, he joined the Marine Detachment at the American Embassy in Peiping. He was promoted to first lieutenant in August, 1938. Upon his return to San Diego in September, 1940, he again saw duty with the 2d Brigade. While there, he was promoted to captain in March, 1941.

That May Captain Murray sailed for duty in Iceland with the Sixth Marines (Reinforced), 1st Provisional Marine Brigade, and later graduated from the British Force Tactical School. After the brigade was disbanded, he returned to San Diego in April, 1942, and the following month was promoted to major.

In October, 1942, Major Murray embarked with the Sixth Marines for the Pacific area. For conspicuous gallantry on Guadalcanal in January, 1943, as commander of the 2d Battalion, 6th Marines, he was awarded his first Silver Star Medal. He was promoted to Lieutenant Colonel in June, 1943.

Lieutenant Colonel Murray was awarded a second Silver Star Medal for conspicuous gallantry while commanding the same unit on Tarawa in November, 1943. Serving in this same capacity on Saipan, his heroism in remaining at his post although seriously wounded and continuing to direct his battalion during the initial assault, earned him his first Navy Cross on June 15, 1944.

Returning to the United States in August, 1944, Lieutenant Colonel Murray entered the Command and Staff School at Quantico the following month. After brief duty as an instructor, he was named Assistant Chief of Staff, G-3, 1st Special Marine Brigade, moving with brigade to Camp Lejeune, North Carolina, in February, 1946. In October, 1946, in departed for duty in the Pacific area as Deputy Chief of Staff, Headquarters Marine

Garrison Forces, Pacific, and the following April was named Inspector of Marine Garrison Forces. He returned to Quantico in July, 1948 for temporary duty on the Marine Corps Board at Marine Corps Schools.

Transferred to Camp Pendleton, California in January, 1949, Lieutenant Colonel Murray served consecutively as Assistant Chief of Staff, G-4; as Commanding Officer, Third Marines; and as Executive Officer, Fifth Marines, First Marine Division. In July, 1950, when the 1st Provisional Marine Brigade was formed for duty in Korea, he was ordered overseas with the Fifth Marine Regiment which was to be the nucleus for the brigade. As Commanding Officer, Fifth Marines, he was awarded his third and fourth Silver Star Medal (Army) and the Legion of Merit during action in August and September, 1950.

With his unit, he participated in the battles of the Naktong River perimeter, Wolmi-Inchon, Seoul, and Wonsan; and in the Marine advance north toward the Yalu River. He was subsequently awarded the Army Distinguished Service Cross for extraordinary heroism in the 1st Division's historic breakout from the Chosin Reservoir area to the sea at Hamhung, and two days later took part in the action which earned him his second Navy Cross. Shortly afterward, with his regiment committed to fighting on the Central Korean front, he was advanced to the rank of colonel, in January, 1951.

Following his return from Korea, Colonel Murray served from May until August, 1951 at Headquarters Marine Corps, Washington, D.C., then entered the National War College. On completing the course in June, 1952, he saw two years duty as Commanding Officer, Basic School, Marine Corps Schools, Quantico. In July, 1954, he was ordered to the Marine Corps Base, Camp Pendleton.

Colonel Murray remained at Camp Pendleton four years, serving first as Commanding Officer, 1st Infantry Training Regiment, until February, 1955; then as Chief of Staff of the Marine Corps Base, until July, 1957. During his final year there, he was assigned to the 1st Marine Division, serving as Division Inspector, Assistant Chief of Staff, and Chief of staff, respectively. In July, 1958, he assumed duties as Chief of Staff, Marine Corps Base, Camp Lejeune. He was promoted to brigadier general in June, 1959.

General Murray departed for Okinawa the following month and assumed duties as Assistant Division Commander, 3d Marine Division, in August, 1959. In July, 1960, he reported to Camp Pendleton, as Deputy Base Commander, and subsequently, in March, 1961, became Commanding General of the Marine Corps Base, Camp Pendleton. He served in the latter capacity until June, 1962. On July 1, 1962, he began a two year assignment as Commanding General, Marine Corps Recruit Depot, Parris Island. While serving in this capacity, he was promoted to major general February 1, 1963.

Transferred to Headquarters Marine Corps in June, 1964, General Murray was assigned as Inspector General of the Marine Corps. In August, 1966, he assumed duties as Assistant Chief of Staff, G-3. Detached from Headquarters in December, 1967, he reported to the Far East the following month and began his last tour of active duty as Deputy Commander, III Marine Amphibious Force. He returned to the United States in February, 1968 and entered the United States Naval Hospital at Bethesda, Maryland, where he remained until he retired from active duty August 1, 1968.

-USMC-

The following are General Murray's Navy Cross, two Silver Star, and Legion of Merit citations:

The President of the United States takes pleasure in presenting the GOLD STAR in lieu of a second NAVY CROSS to:

LIEUTENANT COLONEL RAYMOND L. MURRAY
UNITED STATES MARINE CORPS

for service as set forth in the following citation:

> *"Or extraordinary heroism as Commanding Officer of the Fifth Marines, First Marine Division (Reinforced), against enemy aggressor forces in Korea on 6 and 7 December 1950. Charged with the tremendous responsibility of taking over the perimeter defense of Hagaru-ri, and subse-*

quently pressing the attack to Koto-ri in conjunction with another Marine regiment, Lieutenant Colonel Murray, with his ranks depleted by casualties and all his officers and men exhausted from several days of fierce fighting in sub-zero temperatures, launched vigorous attacks to the east-ward to seize a vital enemy-held ridge and consolidate his positions as the leading regiment moved out in the initial advance the early morning of 6 December. Affording pro-tection for the airstrip where approximately one thousand vehicles containing division supplies, ammunition, and equipment were assembled, he remained until all the wounded had been evacuated and the leading regiment had gained sufficient distance in the direction of the ob-jective to permit the vehicle train to proceed, before di-recting his regiment in forming a rear guard for the entire column. Throughout the night, he beat off vicious on-slaughts continuously launched by the enemy and, on the following morning, carried out a brilliantly executed coun-terattack, taking two hundred prisoners and leaving an ineffective and decimated enemy in his wake as he contin-ued on to his destination, arriving that evening with units intact and ready to continue the attack to the south. By his great personal valor, daring combat tactics, and superb leadership throughout this bitter offensive and defensive action, Lieutenant Colonel Murray served as a constant inspiration to his regiment in completing this extremely hazardous mission against tremendous odds, and his cou-rageous devotion to duty reflects the highest credit upon himself, his gallant officers and men, and the United States Naval Service."

For the President,
/S/ DAN A. KIMBALL
Secretary of the Navy

The President of the United States takes pleasure in presenting an OAK-LEAF CLUSTER in lieu of a third SILVER STAR MEDAL to:

LIEUTENANT COLONEL RAYMOND L. MURRAY
UNITED STATES MARINE CORPS

for service as set forth in the following citation:

> *"Lieutenant Colonel Raymond L. Murray, Commanding Officer, 5th Regiment, 1st Marine Division, United Nations Command, distinguished himself by conspicuous gallantry in action in the amphibious landing resulting in the capture of Inchon, Korea, on 15 September 1950 in the Inchon-Seoul operation. His actions contributed materially to the success of this operation and were in keeping with the highest traditions of the military service."*

> *BY COMMAND OF GENERAL MacARTHUR*

The president of the United States takes pleasure in presenting an OAK-LEAF CLUSTER in lieu of fourth SILVER STAR MEDAL to:

LIEUTENANT COLONEL RAYMOND L. MURRAY
UNITED STATES MARINE CORPS

for service as set forth in the following citation:

> *"Lieutenant Colonel Murray distinguished himself by gallantry in action against an armed enemy of the United Nations in Korea during the period 3 August to 6 September 1950. While serving as Commanding Officer of the Fifth Marine Regiment, Colonel Murray displayed exceptional ability in directing the operations of his regiment against organized enemy resistance of superior strength. With complete disregard for his own safety, Colonel Murray made numerous visits to forward elements of his assault*

*battalions to obtain first hand information necessary for
sound tactical judgment in the employment of his regiment.
On 11 August, as the regiment was advancing along the
road to Sachon, it was halted by heavy enemy fire directed
from well-concealed emplacements on high ground overlooking the route of movement. Moving up to the front,
constantly exposed to enemy small-arms fire, Colonel
Murray personally directed the tactical employment of his
troops until the situation became stabilized. His cool and
positive control of the command, fearless determination,
and indomitable courage were an inspirational propellant
for his valiantly fighting men and furthered the United
Nations campaign for peace. Colonel Murray, through his
valor and notable proficiency as a combat commander,
reflects great credit on himself and the Military Service."*

BY COMMAND OF GENERAL MacARTHUR

The President of the United States takes pleasure in presenting the LE-
GION OF MERIT to:

LIEUTENANT COLONEL RAYMOND L. MURRAY
UNITED STATES MARINE CORPS

for service as set forth in the following citation:

*"For exceptionally meritorious conduct in the perfor-
mances of outstanding services to the Government of the
United States as Commanding Officer of the Fifth Marines,
First Marine Division (Reinforced), while engaged in combat operations against enemy aggressor forces in Korea
from 15 September to 2 November 1950. Displaying sound
judgment, exceptional ability as a troop leader and a keen
perception of operational requirements, Lieutenant Colonel Murray landed with the assault waves of his regiment
in the engagement at Inchon and participated in the ad-*

vance to and crossing of the Han River, the capture of Seoul and subsequent operations against the enemy to the northwest. Frequently receiving sudden orders for the movement and commitment of his regiment to action, he was directly instrumental in the success of his regiment in executing all assigned missions and in the decisive defeat of the enemy in each engagement. His outstanding professional skill, foresight, and courageous devotion to duty, often in the face of heavy enemy fire, served as a constant inspiration to his command and reflect the highest credit upon Lieutenant Colonel and the United States Naval Service." Lieutenant Colonel Murray is authorized to wear the Combat "V."

For the President,
/S/ R. B. ANDERSON
Secretary of the Navy

• • •

Name: Colonel Harold S. Roise, USMC (Retired)

Biography: Revised 1965.
Colonel Harold S. Roise, twice decorated with the Nation's second highest decoration, the Navy Cross, retired from active service in the Marine Corps June 1, 1965.

Colonel Roise was born February 27, 1916, in Moscow, Idaho. Upon graduation from high school, he attended the University of Idaho, where he earned a Bachelor of Science Degree in Education.

He was commissioned a second lieutenant in the United States Marine Corps on July 1, 1939, and was assigned to Officers' Basic School, Quantico, Virginia.

Lieutenant Roise reported to his first Marine Corps duty station in 1940, the 8th Marine Regiment. Assigned until 1941, he served first as a platoon leader, then as a company commander.

From 1941 until 1942, he served with Marine detachments aboard ship at Pearl Harbor and in the Marianas Islands. He first served aboard the *USS MARYLAND* as a detachment officer. He was then ordered aboard the *USS ALABAMA*, serving as a Marine detachment commander.

He reported to the 22nd Regiment, 6th Marine Division in the Far East in 1945, serving with Regimental S-4 (Logistics) and later as Division Assistant G-4 (Logistics) Officer.

He returned to the United States in 1946, reporting for duty with the Naval Academy, at Annapolis, Maryland.

Before reporting to Headquarters, Fleet Marine Force, Pacific, in 1951, he served as commanding officer, 2d Battalion, 5th Marine Regiment, in Korea, as a lieutenant colonel.

Returning to the United States again in 1953, Colonel Roise reported as a student to the Senior School, Quantico, Virginia. He remained upon graduation to become Director, Marine Corps Extension Schools, in 1954.

In 1956, he reported to Marine Corps Headquarters in Washington, D.C., where he served two years with the Promotion Branch and a year with the Personnel Procurement Branch.

He was promoted to his present rank on July 1, 1956.

He reported to the 1st Marine Division in August, 1959, serving with Exercising Control and Inspection Group. Subsequently, he has been Commanding Officer, 7th Marine Regiment, November, 1959, until October, 1960, Assistant Chief of Staff, G-2, November, 1960 until June, 1961, and Commanding Officer, 1st Service Battalion, July, 1961.

A list of Colonel Roise's medals include two Navy Crosses, Silver Star, Legion of Merit, and Purple Heart.

-USMC-

The following are Colonel Roise's two Navy Cross and Silver Star citations:

The President of the United States takes pleasure in presenting the NAVY CROSS to ;

LIEUTENANT COLONEL HAROLD S. ROISE
UNITED STATES MARINE CORPS

for service as set forth in the following citation:

> *"For extraordinary heroism as Commanding Officer of the Second Battalion, Fifth Marines, First Marine Division (Reinforced), in action against enemy aggressor forces in Korea from 15 to 25 September 1950. With hid battalion assigned the lead position during the amphibious assault at Inchon the night of 15 September, Lieutenant Colonel Roise hit the beach in darkness under heavy enemy fire. Maintaining superb control of his companies in the bitter action that followed, he took position on the beachhead line in a heavy rainstorm and personally directed his units into a defensive perimeter to drive off repeated counterattacks launched by the fanatical aggressors. Continually subjecting himself to devastating artillery, mortar, automatic-weapons, and small-arms fire, he pressed forward in his rapid advance to the city, expeditiously capturing assigned objectives and, on one occasion, leading a brilliantly executed maneuver to repulse a heavy counterattack with six hostile tanks and approximately 100 of the enemy destroyed without a single loss among his own units. Seriously wounded in a mortar barrage against his forward observation post as he directed his assault companies against the enemy's main line of resistance outside the city of Seoul on 24 September, Lieutenant Colonel Roise refused medical attention for his own wounds and diligently supervised the care and evacuation of all the wounded. Calling for and briefing his executive officer in the tactical situation, he submitted to emergency first aid but refused evacuation and, although suffering severe pain, encouraged and deployed his men in routing and destroying the enemy in each fierce encounter on their drive to capture the city. His gallant leadership, great personal valor, and cool courage, maintained against tremendous odds, served to inspire all of the men of his battalion and reflect*

the highest credit upon Lieutenant Colonel Roise, his heroic command and the United States Naval Service."

For the President,
/S/ DAN A. KIMBALL
Secretary of the Navy

The President of the United States takes pleasure in presenting the GOLD STAR in lieu of a second NAVY CROSS to:

LIEUTENANT COLONEL HAROLD S. ROISE
UNITED STATES MARINE CORPS

for service as set forth in the following citation:

"For extraordinary heroism as Commanding Officer of the Second Battalion, Fifth Marines, First Marine Division (Reinforced), in action against enemy aggressor forces in Korea from 27 November to 11 December 1950. With his battalion in point position in defense of Yudam-ni as Marine elements moved out in the attack to Koto-ri on 27 November, Lieutenant Colonel Roise consistently remained with the leading assault forces under heavy enemy fire emanating from hostile positions deeply entrenched on commanding ground, personally deploying and directing his companies and utilizing all available supporting fires in defeating the outnumbering enemy in each furious encounter. Realizing the impossibility of gaining the assigned objective before nightfall in the face of the fierce resistance and treacherous terrain conditions, he ordered his units to set up a hasty defense on the ice and snow-covered hillside and, throughout the night as wave after wave of outnumbering forces persisted in their attempts to penetrate the area, expertly shifted elements of his command from one portion of the perimeter to another and supervised each maneuver to prevent the enemy from breaching his

lines. Assigned as rear guard commander for his regiment's withdrawal from Yudam-ni on 1 December, Lieutenant Colonel Roise welded his remaining men and reinforcing units into an impregnable defense of several key terrain features imperative to the continued drive to the sea. With the column held up by a roadblock following an all-night march in bitter sub-zero weather over a narrow, frozen path along the mountain north of Hagaru-ri, he formulated and directed a brilliantly executed maneuver to wipe out the obstruction and enable the entire column to proceed. Inculcating in his officers and men his own courageous spirit of heroism and determination, he again employed his "moving perimeter" to cover the retrograde movements of all elements of the First Marine Division from the Chosin Reservoir area and, on 11 December, arrived at Hungnam with his battalion an intact, fighting organization. His brilliant combat tactics, inspiring leadership, and great personal valor against tremendous odds reflect the highest credit upon Lieutenant Colonel Roise, his intrepid command, and the United States Naval Service."

For the President,
/S/ DAN A. KIMBALL
Secretary of the Navy

The President of the United States takes pleasure in presenting the SILVER STAR MEDAL to:

LIEUTENANT COLONEL HAROLD S. ROISE
UNITED STATES MARINE CORPS

for service as set forth in the following citation:

"For conspicuous gallantry and intrepidity in action against the enemy while serving with a Marine infantry

battalion in Korea on 17 September 1950. Lieutenant Colonel Roise, Commanding Officer of the 2d Battalion, 5th Marines, leaving the western outskirts of Pupyong after successfully repelling an enemy counterattack at dawn, aggressively led his battalion in an attack over a distance of about eight miles to seize the vital objective of Kimpo Airfield. During this attack Lieutenant Colonel Roise remained well forward, constantly exposing himself to enemy fire, without regard for his own personal safety, so as to expedite and control the advance of his assault elements. When darkness approached he aggressively directed his companies to continue forward, and as darkness fell his assaulting companies, using attached tanks, advanced and seized Kimpo Airfield. Due to the excellent disposition and control of all elements in his command, Lieutenant Colonel Roise seized the objective and established a night defense that was successful in repelling a night counterattack of several hundred enemy just before dawn. By his audacious and superb leadership and his heroic bravery, Lieutenant Colonel Roise successfully attained this important objective thereby materially contributing to the success of this campaign. His actions throughout were in keeping with the highest traditions of the United States Naval Service."

BY COMMAND OF MAJOR GENERAL ALMOND

• • •

Name: Brigadier General Webb D. Sawyer, USMC.

Biography: Revised June, 1969.
Brigadier General assumed his current assignment as Assistant Chief of Staff, G-3, at Headquarters Marine Corps, in May, 1969. He had served as Deputy Chief of Staff, G-3, since April, 1968. During the Korean conflict, he earned the Navy Cross, three awards of the Silver Star Medal, and the

Purple Heart for wounds received in action.

Webb Duane Sawyer was born August 31, 1918, in Toledo, Ohio and was graduated from Waite High School in 1936. In June, 1940, he was graduated from the University of Toledo where he was president of his class during his junior year and of the Chi Beta Chi fraternity. Enlisting in the Marine Corps Reserve in January, 1941, he entered the 2d Officer Candidate Class at Quantico, Virginia, the following month, and was commissioned a Marine second lieutenant on May 29, 1941.

After completing the Reserve Officers' Class, he was detached to New River (later Camp Lejeune), North Carolina, and served with the 1st Scout Company, 1st Marine Division, until December, 1941. In January, 1942 he embarked for the Panama Canal Zone where he was assigned to the Marine Detachment guarding ships passing through the Canal, before becoming Executive Officer of the 2d Guard Company, Balboa, Canal Zone.

In January, 1943, he returned to Camp Lejeune as a captain and became a company commander with the 3d Separate Battalion. The unit moved to Camp Pendleton in April and became the 3d Battalion, 24th Marines, 4th Marine Division. With this unit he embarked for the Central Pacific the following January and on arrival in the Marshall Islands, participated in the Roi-Namur campaign, and later in the battles for Saipan and Tinian in the Marianas. When the battalion executive officer became a casualty on Saipan, Captain Sawyer assumed this duty in addition to his own assignment, which earned him the Bronze Star Medal with a Combat "V."

Upon being promoted to major, he became Regimental Plans and Training Officer, prior to the Iwo Jima landing. During the bitter campaign that followed, he earned a second Bronze Star Medal. He returned to the United States in October, 1945 to serve as a tactics instructor at the Officers' Basic School, Quantico, until September, 1948. He subsequently served at Camp Pendleton as technical advisor in filming the "Marine Rifle Squad" training film series. In July, 1949, he became Commanding Officer, Marine Barracks, Long Beach, California.

At the outbreak of hostilities in June, 1950, he received orders to take the 1st Replacement Draft to the 1st Provisional Marine Brigade in Korea. The decision to move the entire 1st Marine Division to Korea caused the draft to be diverted to Camp Pendleton. Major Sawyer became Executive Officer, 1st Battalion, 7th Marines, and sailed for Korea in September, 1950.

A month later he became Commanding Officer of the regiment's 2d Battalion.

Serving briefly as Commanding Officer and then Executive Officer, he returned to the 1st Battalion, 7th Marines, to lead the division's advance guard from Koto-ri at the Chosin Reservoir to the eventual link-up with other division elements. During the period November 5 - December 11, 1950, he was awarded two Silver Stars and the Purple Heart Medal.

He continued to command the 1st Battalion, 7th Marines, during the "Pohang Guerrilla Hunt," operations "Ripper," and "Killer," until the Chinese Spring counter-offensive in April, 1951. For actions protecting the division's left flank and rear during that battle, he was awarded the Nation's second highest decoration – the Navy Cross.

Promoted to lieutenant colonel in January, 1951, he left Korea in April to become the planning officer of the Public Information Division at Marine Corps Headquarters in Washington, D.C. In Late 1952, Lieutenant Colonel Sawyer was assigned to the General Supply Section, Assistant Chief of Staff, G-4, and later became head of that section. In 1955, he left for Venezuela to serve as technical advisor to the Venezuelan Marine Corps and as Executive Officer of the U.S. Naval Mission there.

Lieutenant Colonel Sawyer returned to the United States in July, 1957 for duty under instruction in the Senior Course, Marine Corps Schools, Quantico, Virginia. He reported to the 1st Marine Division in July, 1958, becoming Commanding Officer, 1st Battalion, 1st Marines, and later serving as Executive Officer of the Division's G-3 Section. He was promoted to colonel in August, 1959.

Colonel Sawyer was named Commanding Officer of the 5th Marine Regiment in April, 1960. After serving more than a year in this capacity, he was detached in April, 1961 to attend the Army War College at Carlisle Barracks, Pennsylvania. Upon graduation he reported to Headquarters Marine Corps, Washington, D.C., in July, 1962, where he served first as Assistant, then as Head of Operations Branch, Assistant Chief of Staff, G-3. Colonel Sawyer reported to the Military Assistance Command, Vietnam, in February, 1965 to serve as Chief, Plans Division, Assistant Chief of Staff, J-4. His duties encompassed all logistics planning in the current contingency and SEATO. The Legion of Merit was awarded him for his action in Vietnam.

Men of Honor

The colonel reported to the Marine Corps Recruit Depot, San Diego, California, in March, 1966, where he became Assistant Chief of Staff, G-1. Upon assuming duty as Assistant Division Commander, 5th Marine Division, Camp Pendleton, California, on September 22, 1966, he was advanced to the rank of brigadier general. From March 2, 1967 until April 17, 1967, he served as Commanding General, 5th Marine Division, then reverted to his former duty as Assistant Division Commander, serving in the latter capacity until April, 1968.

Some of General Sawyer's awards include: The Navy Cross, the Silver Star Medal with Gold Star and Oak Leaf Cluster in lieu of a second and third award, the Legion of Merit, the Bronze Star Medal with Combat "V" and Gold Star in lieu of a second award, and the Purple Heart.

-USMC-

The following are General Sawyer's Navy Cross and three Silver Star citations:

The President of the United States takes pleasure in presenting the NAVY CROSS to:

LIEUTENANT COLONEL WEBB D. SAWYER
UNITED STATES MARINE CORPS

for action as set forth in the following citation:

> *"For extraordinary heroism as Commanding Officer of the First Battalion, Seventh Marines, First Marine Division (Reinforced), in action against enemy aggressor forces in Korea from 22 to 25 April, 1951. In the face of mounting enemy resistance on 22 April, Lieutenant Colonel Sawyer courageously moved among the foremost elements of his command, boldly exposing himself to intense hostile fire in order to direct his battalion in attacking and seizing strongly defended enemy positions. When a numerically*

superior enemy force launched a concerted night attack and penetrated an adjacent friendly unit, leaving his left flank completely exposed, he skillfully deployed his men to meet the threat before moving to a forward command post from which he could effectively observe and control the action. Remaining in this exposed position throughout the night and the following morning despite the imminent danger of enemy encirclement, he personally directed the repulse of repeated hostile thrusts and the containing of a dangerous penetration of the center of the line after bitter hand-to-hand fighting. When the enemy withdrew to the immediate front of the battalion shortly before daylight, simultaneously delivering a fierce volume of fire and sending a large force to envelop the penetrated unit on the left flank, he coolly supervised the evacuation of casualties and steadfastly refused to relinquish his exposed position until all had reached safety and he was ordered to assume new defensive positions. Selecting locations for defenses for the night after skillfully guiding the battalion over tortuous mountain trails to the assigned area, he conducted his unit in inflicting severe losses on the hostile force, continuing his engagement of the enemy throughout the night and remaining with the last elements of his command until the withdrawal of two friendly regiments had been covered. His inspiring leadership, aggressive determination, and valiant devotion to duty in the face of constant attack and overwhelming odds were contributing factors in containing the hostile attack and in securing the vital left flank of the Division, thereby reflecting the highest credit upon Lieutenant Colonel Sawyer and the United States Naval Service."

For the President,
/S/ DAN A. KIMBALL
Secretary of the Navy

The President of the United States takes pleasure in presenting the SILVER STAR MEDAL to:

MAJOR WEBB D. SAWYER
UNITED STATES MARINE CORPS

for service as set forth in the following citation:

> *"For extraordinary heroism as Commanding Officer of the 2d Battalion, 7th Marines, 1st Marine Division (Reinforced), in action against enemy aggressor forces in Korea during the period 2 November to 8 November 1950. On 3 November 1950 the enemy conducted a fierce, coordinated night attack against the 2d Battalion, 7th Marines. Major Sawyer moved along the line, constantly closing gaps caused by the enemy action, re-forming the defense to meet the changing situation and continually exposing himself to heavy enemy fire without regard for his own personal safety. Major Sawyer's display of courage, leadership, and initiative, coupled with his ability to coordinate the actions of his battalion, contributed to a high degree to the successful repulsion of the enemy thereby upholding the highest traditions of the United States Naval Service."*

BY COMMAND OF MAJOR GENERAL ALMOND

The President of the United States takes pleasure in presenting the GOLD STAR in lieu of a second SILVER STAR MEDAL to:

MAJOR WEBB D. SAWYER
UNITED STATES MARINE CORPS

for service as set forth in the following citation:

> *"For extraordinary heroism in action against the enemy*

while serving as Commanding Officer of a Marine Infantry Battalion in Korea on 8 December 1950. His battalion had been assigned as the advance guard of an infantry regiment and was ordered to attack, seize, and occupy the vital key terrain feature, Hill 1304, which was being strongly defended by the enemy. This hill controlled the critical passage through which the entrapped 1st Marine Division had to move from Koto-ri to Chinhung-ni. In addition, his battalion was to afford flank protection to the advance elements of the Regimental and Division vehicle train. The morning dawned in a driving snowstorm which limited visibility and ceiling to only a few feet throughout the entire day, and was punctuated by sub-zero temperatures ranging to 22 degrees below zero. His battalion had become severely depleted from casualties and was virtually exhausted after more than eleven days of bitter fighting. During the attack of Hill 1304, which was being defended by a tenacious enemy from deeply entrenched and well camouflaged positions, seeing that one of his rifle companies was being out-flanked by a numerically superior enemy, Major Sawyer, in spite of a painful foot wound received the previous day, traversed the torturous terrain, to reach the dangerous flank. Constantly exposing himself to heavy enemy small-arms, automatic-weapons, and sniper fire, he personally directed and led the attack of his depleted battalion with such calculated precision and aggressiveness as to completely outmaneuver the enemy and in so doing, routed him from his defensive positions, inflicting innumerable casualties upon his foe and captured the vital objective. He then led elements of his battalion down a steep mountain pass for four miles to join friendly forces and open the road for the entrapped 1st Marine Division. Major Sawyer's devotion to duty, his aggressiveness, skill, and heroic action served as a constant inspiration and example to all his officers and men and upheld the highest traditions of the United States Naval Service."

Men of Honor

For the President,
/S/ DAN A. KIMBALL
Secretary of the Navy

The President of the United States takes pleasure in presenting the GOLD STAR in lieu of a third SILVER STAR MEDAL to:

MAJOR WEBB D. SAWYER
UNITED STATES MARINE CORPS

for service as set forth in the following citation:

"For conspicuous gallantry and intrepidity as Executive Officer of the Second Battalion, Seventh Marines, First Marine Division (Reinforced), in action against enemy aggressor forces in Korea on 6 December 1950. When his battalion encountered fierce enemy resistance from strong hostile positions which dominated and blocked the road from Hagaru-ri to Koto-ri, Major Sawyer skillfully led elements of his group in an enveloping movement around the enemy's left flank and, with brilliant leadership, successfully aided in countering and repelling the hostile attack. For twenty-two hours he voluntarily and continually remained exposed to a vicious hail of hostile fire and, though painfully wounded by mortar fire, steadfastly refused evacuation in order that he might assist in the direction and control of the fighting. By his valiant courage, daring initiative, and staunch devotion to duty in the face of overwhelming odds, Major Sawyer contributed materially to the successful accomplishment of the battalion objective, thereby upholding the highest traditions of the United States Naval Service."

For the President,
/S/ DAN A. KIMBALL
Secretary of the Navy

Chapter 2: Korea

. . .

Name: Lieutenant Colonel Stanley Wawrzyniak, USMC.

Biography: Compiled March, 1968.

Lieutenant Colonel Stanley Wawrzyniak, twice decorated with the Navy Cross Medal – this country's second highest award for heroism – is presently serving as Inspector-Instructor of the Marine Corps Reserve's 13th Force Reconnaissance Company, Mobile, Alabama. He has held this assignment since returning from Vietnam in May, 1967.

The 40-year-old native of Gary, West Virginia, also holds the Silver Star Medal, third highest U.S. Military heroism award, and two Bronze Star Medals. The lieutenant colonel was awarded both his Navy Crosses and his Silver Star Medal during two separate tours in Korea. Both Bronze Stars were earned for heroism in Vietnam.

The veteran Marine officer also holds four Purple Heart Medals. Three are for wounds received in Korean fighting and the fourth was awarded after he was wounded while engaged in action against insurgent Communist Viet Cong forces in Vietnam.

On October 12, 1944, 17-year-old Stanley Wawrzyniak, son of Mrs. Elizabeth Sodus, Buffalo, New York, commenced his colorful military career by enlisting in the U.S. Navy. He served 23 months advancing to Boilermaker Third Class before being released from active duty in September, 1946.

Three days later, Wawrzyniak joined the Marine Corps and was on his way to Parris Island, South Carolina, for basic training. During the following four years he served at numerous posts and stations throughout the Marine Corps. When the Korean Conflict erupted in June, 1950, the young Marine had advanced to staff sergeant and was serving with the 2d Marine Division at Camp Lejeune, North Carolina.

S/Sgt. Wawrzyniak's two Korean tours earned him eight battle stars. By the end of the Conflict he was a master sergeant.

In 1953, M/Sgt. Wawrzyniak was commissioned a Marine second lieutenant while serving at Camp Lejeune, North Carolina.

The following 13-years of peacetime duty for the veteran Marine involved routine assignments throughout the United States, plus a 13-month stint in the Far East during 1956-57 as a member of the 3rd Marine Division.

Second Lieutenant Wawrzyniak was promoted to first lieutenant in 1954; to captain in 1956, and to major in 1965.

In July, 1965 Major Wawrzyniak embarked for Vietnam where he served 13-months with the 3rd Marine Division. During this assignment he participated in numerous operations and was wounded in action near Quang Tri Province on March 27, 1967.

(Wawrzyniak retired from the Marine Corps, as a Lieutenant Colonel and passed away in 1995 at the age of 68.)

-USMC-

The following are a newspaper article about Lieutenant Colonel Wawrzyniak, his two Navy Cross, and Silver Star citations:

"I WOULDN'T CHANGE A THING"
PROVOST MARSHAL REVIEWS 28-YEAR CAREER

"I believe he was one of the last Chesty Puller-type Marines left in the Marine Corps," commented William W. Carr. "While in Korea he received two Navy Crosses and was recommended for the Medal of Honor. If I recall correctly, he has 35 awards with 10 battle stars. He's all-Marine."

The Lieutenant is describing Lieutenant Colonel Stanley Wawrzyniak, Cherry Points provost marshal.

Wawrzyniak, who served in the Navy during World War II, joined the Marine Corps as a private after the war. In 1951 he was company gunnery sergeant for "Fox" Company, 5th Marines, when he received his first Navy Cross.

"It was during the capture of Hill 812 on the eastern side of the Punchbowl in Korea. I carried a Thompson sub-machine gun, which fired a .45 caliber bullet," related Wawrzyniak. "That weapon sure made you feel more safe. I was pleased to receive the medal, but lots of other Marines deserved one too!"

The following year, Wawrzyniak was recommended for the Medal of Honor.

Chapter 2: Korea

"We were defending Outpost-3 in Korea," he recalled. "I was company gunny for E Company (5th Marines) during that fight. Somehow we managed to keep our post and resist a couple hundred of the enemy troops. I didn't receive the Medal of Honor, but I was awarded my second Navy Cross."

When asked if he agreed with the statement declaring him one of the last Chesty Pullers in the Marine Corps, Wawrzyniak laughed, "I couldn't shine that man's shoes."

Wawrzyniak earned two Bronze Stars and two Vietnamese Cross of Gallantry awards in Vietnam. He added, "I also received shrapnel wounds in the shoulder blades in Quang Tri Province."

Combat experience was helpful to Wawrzyniak as he instructed platoon leader classes at Quantico, Virginia. "Map reading, signaling, compass usage, patrolling, and just about anything concerning the infantry I taught to young Marines," he said. I've even taught skiing and mountain climbing at the Cold Weather Training Center in Bridgeport, California."

When asked what he considered his best duty assignment, Wawrzyniak replied, "reconnaissance work is my favorite. I love it. I've served as a battalion executive officer for the 2d Marine Division recon battalion and in the Force Recon Company. Its a fast moving job where every day is an adventure. One day you might be parachuting, or scuba diving or participating in field operation. It's an interesting job."

The colonel said that he was pleased when he was selected to be Cherry Point's provost marshal. "Provost marshal work is not new to me. I enjoy working with Traffic Control, Criminal Investigation, Traffic Investigation Division and the Military Police. There's always something to keep me busy."

"The number of serious traffic accidents aboard the air station has dropped since last year," Wawrzyniak reported. "An interest in safety has grown here steadily, or so it seems. The biggest problem we have here is parking lot accidents, where the fender-benders expend manhours and add paper-work to our daily routine."

He continued, "pellet and BB guns are another menace we have. Public Works has to repair the broken lights and windows and that becomes expensive when you total up the loss of heat or air conditioning, or manhours and material."

With 28 years' Marine Corps service, Wawrzyniak said he doesn't foresee retirement in the near future.

"When I do retire I'd like to do juvenile work. I've worked with scouts and high school students in Mobile, Alabama, when I was on I&I (Instructor-Inspector) duty. It seems I have a lot of patience with youngsters. It's funny how a guy can have endless patience with everyone's kids but his own," he sighed.

Lieutenant Colonel Wawrzyniak has been both an enlisted and a commissioned Marine during his career. He stated he wouldn't change a thing regarding his career because he enjoyed his experience as an enlisted man and as an officer. He spoke about the "Old Corps": "We all like to fancy ourselves thinking that we are the best and no one is better ... I don't believe this. I think the young troops are as good as ever. Maybe their ideas are not the same as, say, "my generation", but, then again, this isn't the same world it was twenty years ago."

He concluded, "I only regret that I'm not 17 years old and live my career all over again. I enjoyed it that much."

• • •

The President of the United States takes pleasure in presenting the NAVY CROSS to:

STAFF SERGEANT STANLEY J. WAWRZYNIAK
UNITED STATES MARINE CORPS

for service as set forth in the following citation:

"For extraordinary heroism while serving as Gunnery Sergeant of Company F, Second Battalion, Fifth Marines, First Marine Division (Reinforced), in action against enemy aggressor forces in Korea, on 19 September 1951. Voluntarily joining the leading assault squad in his company's final attack against a heavily fortified and strongly defended enemy hill position, Staff Sergeant Wawrzyniak courageously exposed himself to a hail of in-

*tense, hostile small-arms and grenade fire to move along
the line, encouraging the men and pointing out targets for
their fire. As the unit neared the crest of the hill, he observed an enemy position which threatened the squad's
entire left flank and, singlehandedly charging the emplacement, killed its three occupants. Although painfully
wounded by an enemy grenade during the action, he immediately rejoined the attack and, seizing an automatic-
rifle from a fallen comrade when his own ammunition was
exhausted, aggressively aided the squad in overrunning
the position, directed the pursuit of the fleeing enemy and
consolidated the ground. By his daring initiative, gallant
determination, and steadfast devotion to duty in the face
of heavy hostile opposition, Staff Sergeant Wawrzyniak
served to inspire all who observed him and contributed
materially to the success achieved by his company, thereby
upholding the highest traditions of the United States Naval Service."*

*For the President,
/S/ DAN A. KIMBALL
Secretary of the Navy*

The President of the United States takes pleasure in presenting the GOLD
STAR in lieu of a second NAVY CROSS to:

TECHNICAL SERGEANT STANLEY J. WAWRZYNIAK
UNITED STATES MARINE CORPS
for service as set forth in the following citation:

*"For extraordinary heroism while serving as a member of
Company E, Second Battalion, Fifth Marines, First Marine Division (Reinforced), in action against enemy aggressor forces in Korea on 16 April 1952. When an outpost occupied by his unit was subjected to a fierce assault
by vastly outnumbering enemy forces and the outpost com-*

mander and a section of the area were cut off during the intensive action, Technical Sergeant Wawrzyniak unhesitatingly assumed command of the remaining troops and promptly organized an effective defense against the fanatical attackers. With the position completely encircled and subjected to extremely heavy enemy machine-gun, recoilless-rifle, mortar, and small-arms fire, he repeatedly braved the hail of blistering fire to reach the groups cut off by the enemy, boldly led the men back into the defensive perimeter, replenished their supply of ammunition and encouraged them in repelling the close-in enemy attacks. Although painfully wounded, he refused immediate treatment for himself, dressed the wounds of other casualties and assisted the stricken men to the safety of the bunkers before accepting medical aid. By his outstanding courage, inspiring leadership, and valiant devotion to duty in the face of overwhelming odds, Technical Sergeant Wawrzyniak was greatly instrumental in the successful defense of the outpost and upheld the highest traditions of the United States Naval Service."

For the President,
/S/ DAN A. KIMBALL
Secretary of the Navy

The president of the United States takes pleasure in presenting the SILVER STAR MEDAL to:

STAFF SERGEANT STANLEY WAWRZYNIAK
UNITED STATES MARINE CORPS

for service as set forth in the following citation:

"Staff Sergeant Stanley Wawrzyniak a member of the 2d Battalion, 5th Marines, 1st marine Division distinguished himself by gallantry in action against the enemy near

Chapter 2: Korea

Hoegol, Korea, on 28 May 1951. On that date, Sergeant Wawrzyniak voluntarily accompanied a rifle platoon in an assault against a well-defended enemy position. Without regard for his own personal welfare under heavy enemy fire, he moved forward shouting words of encouragement to the men as they advanced against the hail of enemy mortar and small-arms fire to gain the enemy position. Although painfully wounded, Sergeant Wawrzyniak refused first aid in order that he might remain to supervise the evacuation of all wounded personnel to a position of relative safety. The initiative and aggressiveness displayed by Sergeant Wawrzyniak reflect great credit on himself and the military service."

BY COMMAND OF MAJOR GENERAL BYERS

3

VIETNAM

THE PRESIDENT'S ADDRESS

Following is the text of the President's address on Vietnam last night, as recorded by The New York Times:

My fellow Americans:

As President and Commander in Chief, it is my duty to the American people to report that renewed hostile actions against United States ships on the high seas in the Gulf of Tonkin have today required me to order the military forces of the United States to take action in reply.

The initial attack on the destroyer Maddox on August 2 was repeated today by a number of hostile vessels attacking two U.S. destroyers with torpedoes.

The destroyers and supporting aircraft acted at once on the orders I gave after the initial act of aggression.

We believe at least two of the attacking boats were sunk. There were no U.S. losses.

The performance of commanders and crews in this engagement is in the highest traditions of the United States Navy.

But repeated acts of violence against the armed forces of the United States must be met not only with alert defense but with positive reply.

Chapter 3: Vietnam

Action "Now in Execution"

That reply is being given, as I speak to you tonight. Air action is now in execution against gunboats and certain supporting facilities in North Vietnam which have been used in these hostile operations.

In the larger sense, this new act of aggression aimed directly at our own forces again brings home to all of us in the United States the importance of the struggle for peace and security in Southeast Asia.

Aggression by terror against the peaceful villages of South Vietnam has now been joined by open aggression on the high seas against the United States of America.

The determination of all Americans to carry out our full commitment to the people and to the Government of South Vietnam will be redoubled by this outrage. Yet our response for the present will be limited and fitting.

We Americans know – although others appear to forget – the risk of spreading conflict. We still seek no wider war. I have instructed the Secretary of State to make this position totally clear to friends and to adversaries and, indeed, to all.

I have instructed Ambassador Stevenson to raise this matter immediately and urgently before the Security Council of the United Nations.

Congressional Resolution Asked

Finally, today I have met with the leaders of both parties in the Congress of the United States and I have informed them that I shall immediately request the Congress to pass a resolution making it clear that our Government is united in its determination to take all necessary measures in support of freedom and in defense of peace in Southeast Asia.

I have been given encouraging assurance by these leaders of both parties that such a resolution will be promptly introduced, freely and expeditiously debated, and passed with overwhelming support.

And just a few minutes ago I was able to reach Senator Goldwater and I am glad to say that he has expressed his support of the statement that I am making to you tonight.

It is a solemn responsibility to have to order even limited military action by forces whose over-all strength is as vast and as awesome as those of the United States of America.

But it is my considered conviction, shared throughout your government, that firmness in the right is indispensable for peace.

That firmness will always be measured. Its mission is peace.

• • •

Marine Corps advisors and helicopters were assisting the South Vietnamese Government in 1962.

On June 8, 1965, with units of the 3rd Marine Division in country, a spokesman for the State Department said: "American Forces would be available for combat support together with Vietnamese forces when and if necessary."

By June 22nd of that same year, General Westmoreland was given almost unequivocal authority to commit U.S. Troops to combat with or without South Vietnamese forces.

By August of 1965 the Marines had four regiments in Vietnam. The 3rd Marines were west and north of Da Nang, the 9th Marines were south of Da Nang, the 4th Marines were at Chu Lai, and the 7th Marines were at Chu Lai and Qui Nhon.

Around the first week in August the Marines were authorized to begin offensive operations.

In late August-early September, the Marines engaged in their first large-scale operation in Vietnam when four Marine Battalions attacked a Viet Cong Regiment on the Van Tuong Peninsula, south of Chu Lai. The operation's code name was "Starlight."

Other operations and Marine units involved include: "Operation Blue Marlin", November 10, 1965, a sweep of the area south of Chu Lai, included the Battalion Landing Team 2/7 and the 3rd Battalion, 3rd Marines.

"Operation Double Eagle," in early January of 1966, a search and destroy mission in the Quang Ngai- Binh Dinh area, included the 3rd Battalion, 1st Marines; 2nd Battalion, 3rd Marines, and the 2nd Battalion, 9th Marines.

"Operation Utah," March 4, 1966, an attack southeast of Chau Nhai village, involved the 2nd Battalion, 7th Marines; 3rd Battalion, 1st Marines, and 2nd Battalion, 4th Marines.

Chapter 3: Vietnam

"Operation Hastings," July of 1966, an engagement against a large NVA force in northern Quang Tri Province, included the 2nd and 3rd Battalions, 4th Marines; 1st Battalion, 3rd Marines; 1st Battalion, 1st Marines, and 3rd Battalion, 5th Marines.

"Operation Hickory" and "Operation Belt Tight," May of 1967, operations against the DMZ near Con Thien, involved five Marine Battalions.

"Operation Union II," May 26, 1967, an engagement against two enemy regiments near Tam Ky, involved the 5th Marines.

"Operation Crockett," "Operation Buffalo," and "Operation Hickory II," June and July of 1967, actions in Quang Tri Province, involved three Marine Battalions.

"Operation Kingfisher," July 16, 1967, again in Quang Tri Province, involved units of the 9th Marines.

1968 saw the "Tet" offensive and the siege of the Marine base at Khe Sanh, which lasted 71 days.

The only initial success the enemy had during "Tet" was the capture of the city of Hue, but after three weeks of bitter fighting, in which three Marine Battalions were involved, the city was retaken.

In 1969, although the war was beginning to wind down, the Marines were still very active.

"Operation Dewey Canyon I," January and February of 1969, in southwest Quang Tri Province, involved three Battalions of the 9th Marines.

Other operations in 1969 included "Virginia Ridge," Oklahoma Hills," "Utah Mesa," "Daring Rebel," and "Pipestone Canyon."

1970 and 1971, as forces were being drastically reduced, there were fewer and fewer offensive operations by the Marines.

On the morning of April 30, 1975, a helicopter took the last 11 Marines, from the U.S. Embassy in Saigon, out of Vietnam.

Marine casualties in Vietnam were around 13,000 killed and more than 88,000 wounded.

• • •

Name: Major Harvey C. Barnum Jr., USMC.

Biography: Revised May, 1972.

Major Harvey C. Barnum Jr., the fourth Marine to win the Medal of Honor for valor in Vietnam, is currently serving as Operations Officer, 2nd Battalion, 10th Marine Regiment, 2nd Marine Division, Camp Lejeune, N.C.

Harvey Curtiss Barnum Jr., was born July 21, 1940, in Cheshire, Conn. He was president of his Senior Class at Cheshire High School, where he also played football and baseball. In high school, he was a member of the Boy Scouts of America, the "C" Club and the Gym Leaders Club.

After graduation from high school, he entered St. Anselm's College in Manchester, N.H., where he graduated with a B.A. Degree in Economics in June 1962.

He joined the Marine Corps' Platoon Leaders Class program in November 1958, and attended two summer training sessions, one in 1959 and the other in 1961. Upon graduation from St. Anselm's, he was commissioned a Marine Reserve second lieutenant.

2nd Lt. Barnum was ordered to Marine Corps Schools, Quantico, Va., where he attended The Basic School until December 1962, when he began the Artillery Officers Orientation Course, graduating in February 1963. He was then ordered overseas and joined Battery "A", 1st Battalion, 12th Marines, 3rd Marine Division on Okinawa. He served first as a forward observer and then as the Battalion's liaison officer. In July 1964, he accepted appointment in the regular Marine Corps. Prior to completing his Okinawa tour, he also served as the Battalion liaison officer. He was promoted to first lieutenant in December 1964.

Transferred to the 2nd Marine Aircraft Wing in April 1964, 1st Lt. Barnum was assigned as the Wing's Career Advisory and Personal Affairs Officer. During Exercise "Steel Pike", a landing exercise in Spain, he served as the Wing's Security Officer. Upon returning to the United States from Spain, he was assigned as Officer in Charge, 2nd Marine Aircraft Wing Classified Files.

Detached in March 1965, he then served as Guard Officer, Marine Barracks, U.S. Naval Base, Pearl Harbor, Oahu, Hawaii.

From December 1965 until February 1966, Barnum served on temporary duty in Vietnam. As an artillery forward observer with Company "H",

2nd Battalion, 9th Marines, 3rd Marine Division (Rein), FMF, 1st Lt. Barnum's actions on Dec. 18, 1965, earned him the Nation's highest award for valor, the Medal of Honor. He was promoted to captain in June 1966, after he returned to Hawaii.

From March until August 1967, Capt. Barnum attended the Associate Field Artillery Officers Career Course, Fort Sill, Okla. Transferred to HQMC, Barnum served as Aide-de-Camp for Lieutenant General L. W. Walt then the Assistant Chief of Staff for Manpower and subsequently the Assistant Commandant from September 1967 until October 1968.

In October 1968, Barnum returned to Vietnam where he served as Commanding Officer of Battery "E", 2nd Battalion, 12th Marines, 3rd Marine Division (Rein). With the 3rd Marine Division redeployment from Vietnam to Okinawa in September 1969, he remained with that unit until the following October. For his service in this capacity, he was awarded the Bronze Star Medal with Combat "V" and Gold Star in lieu of a second award, the Navy Achievement Medal with Combat "V", the Purple Heart Medal for wounds received, the Combat Action Ribbon, and the Vietnamese Gallantry Cross with Silver Star.

Upon his return from Okinawa, Barnum was assigned as a weapons instructor at The Basic School, Marine Corps Development and Education Command, Quantico, where he served until August 1970 at which time he entered the Amphibious Warfare School, graduating in February 1972.

He assumed his current assignment in March 1972, and was promoted to major, May 1, 1972.

A complete list of his medals and decorations include: the Medal of Honor, the Bronze Star Medal with Combat "V" and Gold Star in lieu of a second award, the Navy Commendation Medal, the Navy Achievement Medal with Combat "V", the Purple Heart, the Combat Action Ribbon, the Presidential Unit Citation, the Navy Unit Commendation, the National Defense Service Medal, the Vietnam Service Medal with one Silver Star, the Vietnamese Gallantry Cross with Silver Star, the Cross of Gallantry with Palm, and the Republic of Vietnam Campaign Medal.

Major Barnum is married to the former Thelma Lanier of York, S.C. His parents are Mr. and Mrs. H. Curtiss Barnum of 5 Glenbrook Drive, Cheshire. He has one brother, Henry C. Barnum of 5 Log Cabin Circle, Fairborn, N.Y.

Men of Honor

-USMC-

The following are the *narrative description of gallant conduct* for which Major Barnum received the Medal of Honor; and his Medal of Honor and one of his Bronze Star Medal citations:

Narrative description of gallant conduct

Lieutenant Barnum was an artillery forward observer serving with Company H, 2nd Battalion, 9th Marines. The Company itself was attached to the 2nd Battalion, 7th Marines, which was a component of Task Force Delta. At 1300, 18 December 1965, as the 2nd Battalion, 7th Marines was on the third day of a long combat patrol participating in Operation Harvest Moon in Ky Phu, Quang Tin Province, Republic of Vietnam, it came solidly against a battalion of Viet Cong who occupied fortified positions and entrenchment's after a portion of the battalion column had passed them by. The enemy action and the intervening terrain served to sever Company H from the remainder of the battalion. The first fire from ambush hit the radio operator, killed him instantly and critically wounded the Company Commander, Captain Gormley.

Although he was not the senior officer present, nor an infantry officer, Lieutenant Barnum unhesitatingly assumed command of the company and the job of radio operator. When he located the wounded Captain Gormley he ripped off his own pack and cartridge belt, fearlessly exposed himself to the heavy fire which was concentrated on him, and ran to the Company Commander's side. When he found that the Captain was still conscious he called for assistance and brought him back to a sheltered area where he helped to treat his mortal wounds. A Marine who had been shot in the foot was trying to make his way back to safety, and Lieutenant Barnum again went out into the fusillade and brought him back to the protection of a mound of earth.

Lieutenant Barnum ordered all guns and 3.5 rockets forward, then had the 60mm mortars brought up, and their fire directed into Viet Cong positions. He reached the battalion commander by radio and learned that in the forward position they were being hit hard by enemy fire, and that Company H was separated from the main body by an open rice paddy more than

200 meters wide. He called four artillery missions, and in adjusting them he exposed himself repeatedly. His judgment in calling these missions was amazingly accurate in spite of heavy incoming rifle and automatic weapons fire. He set the company up in a perimeter defense, ordered all platoons to pull back on the south side of the trail, and called for an air strike. With the radio strapped to his back and the long antenna prominently exposing his position, he made an inspection of the battle site. He ordered the destruction of all inoperative equipment, machine guns, rocket launchers, and radios. The men of the 2nd and 3rd platoons were instructed to drop and burn their packs to lighten the burden so they could carry the dead and wounded. He went to the top of a hill and directed air strikes. A helicopter pad was then prepared and the dead and wounded were evacuated. He directed two platoon attacks, then an offensive by the remainder of the company to drive the Viet Cong between his company and the rest of the battalion. He assisted in the mopping up and final seizure of the battalion's objective.

Throughout this entire action, Lieutenant Barnum displayed exceptional calm, great professional skill, and a rare ability to inspire others to great heights of performance. His company inflicted heavy losses on a superior enemy force, then joined the main body to continue the fight from a more advantageous position.

The facts as contained in the proposed citation and this narrative account have been substantiated by the statements of eyewitnesses.

The President of the United States takes pleasure in presenting the MEDAL OF HONOR to:

FIRST LIEUTENANT HARVEY C. BARNUM JR.
UNITED STATES MARINE CORPS

for service as set forth in the following citation:

"For conspicuous gallantry and intrepidity at the risk of his life above and beyond the call of duty as Forward Observer for Artillery, while attached to Company H, Second Battalion, Ninth marines, Third Marine Division (Rein-

forced), in action against communist forces at Ky Phu in Quang Tin Province, Republic of Vietnam, on 18 December 1965. When the company was suddenly pinned down by a hail of extremely accurate enemy fire and was quickly separated from the remainder of the battalion by over five hundred meters of open and fire-swept ground, and casualties mounted rapidly, Lieutenant Barnum quickly made a hazardous reconnaissance of the area seeking targets for his artillery. Finding the rifle company commander mortally wounded and the radio operator killed, he, with complete disregard for his own safety, gave aid to the dying commander, then removed the radio from the dead operator and strapped it to himself. He immediately assumed command of the rifle company, and moving at once into the midst of the heavy fire, rallying and giving encouragement to all units, reorganized them to replace the loss of key personnel and led their attack on enemy positions from which deadly fire continued to come. His sound and swift decisions and his obvious calm served to stabilize the badly decimated units and his gallant example as he stood exposed repeatedly to point out targets served as an inspiration to all. Provided with two armed helicopters, he moved fearlessly through enemy fire to control the air attack against the firmly entrenched enemy while skillfully directing one platoon in a successful counter-attack on the key enemy positions. Having thus cleared a small area, he requested and directed the landing of two transport helicopters for the evacuation of the dead and wounded. He then assisted in the mopping up and final seizure of the battalion's objective. His gallant initiative and heroic conduct reflected great credit upon himself and were in keeping with the highest traditions of the Marine Corps and the United States Naval Service."

/S/ LYNDON B. JOHNSON

Chapter 3: Vietnam

The president of the United States takes pleasure in presenting the BRONZE STAR MEDAL to:

CAPTAIN HARVEY C. BARNUM, JR.
UNITED STATES MARINE CORPS

for service as set forth in the following citation:

"For heroic achievement in connection with combat operations against the enemy in the Republic of Vietnam while serving as the Commanding Officer of Battery E, Second Battalion, Twelfth Marines, Third Marine Division. Late in the afternoon of 2 July 1969, the Battery E defensive position at Fire Support Base Spark in Quang Tri Province came under intense mortar and recoilless rifle fire from well-fortified North Vietnamese Army emplacements. With complete disregard for his own safety, Captain Barnum moved across the fire-swept terrain to vantage points from which he could observe the enemy and more effectively direct counterbattery fire. Undaunted by the hostile rounds impacting around him, he resolutely remained in his dangerously exposed position and directed the muzzles of two of his 105mm howitzers to be depressed to deliver direct fire. Ignoring the intense North Vietnamese fire, Captain Barnum fearlessly stood in full view of the enemy to more accurately locate and precisely report the exact positions of the hostile emplacements. As a result of the devastating effectiveness of his artillery fire, the North Vietnamese fire was silenced and the lives of many Marines were saved. Captain Barnum's courage, superb leadership and unwavering devotion to duty in the face of great personal danger inspired all who observed him and were in keeping with the highest traditions of the Marine Corps and of the United States Naval Service." The Combat Distinguishing Device is authorized.

Men of Honor

For the President,
/S/ H. W. BUSE, JR.
Lieutenant General, U.S. Marine Corps

• • •

Name: Lieutenant General Martin L. Brandtner, USMC (Retired)

Biography: Revised June 3, 1993.
Lieutenant General Martin L. Brandtner retired from the Marine Corps on June 1, 1993.

General Brandtner is a native of Minneapolis, Minn. He was commissioned a second lieutenant via the NROTC Regular Scholarship Program following graduation from the University of Minnesota in June 1960. He also holds a master's degree from George Washington University (1973).

Following graduation from The Basic School, Quantico, Va., in March 1961, General Brandtner remained at Quantico where he was assigned to the Officer Candidates School, serving as a Platoon Leader until January 1962.

Reassigned to the 1st Marine Brigade, FMF, in February 1962, he served with the 1st Battalion, 4th Marines as a rifle platoon commander, battalion staff officer, rifle company executive officer and rifle company commander, respectively.

In February 1965, General Brandtner was assigned to the 1st Marine Aircraft Wing, Iwakuni, Japan, serving as the S-1/Adjutant of Marine Wing Headquarters Group 1. Deploying to the Republic of Vietnam in April 1965, he assumed additional duties as Area Defense Coordinator for the Wing Headquarters compound at Da Nang Airbase, RVN.

Returning from overseas in April 1966, he reported to the Landing Force Training Command, Pacific, where he served as Branch Head of the Basic Amphibious Training Branch.

In July 1968, General Brandtner returned to the Republic of Vietnam, where he joined the 1st Battalion, 5th Marines serving as a rifle company commander, and upon promotion to major in November 1968, as Battalion Operations Officer and Battalion Executive Officer. While serving as Commanding Officer, Company D, he was wounded in action and was twice awarded the Navy Cross, the nation's second highest award for valor in combat. He is one of only two Marines to earn that distinction in the Vietnam War.

In August 1969, General Brandtner returned to the United States and assumed duties as the Inspector-Instructor, 26th Rifle Company, USMCR, Minneapolis, Minn., where he served until selected to attend the Naval War College of Command and General Staff, Newport, R.I., in 1972.

Following graduation in July 1973, General Brandtner reported to Headquarters Marine Corps, Washington, D.C., where he served as a Plans Officer in the Plans Division until July 1976.

Again assigned overseas, he reported to the 3rd Marine Division on Okinawa, Japan, where he served as the G-3 Operations Officer until he returned to the United States in July 1977. While overseas, he was promoted to Lieutenant colonel in April 1977.

From July 1977 to June 1980, General Brandtner was assigned to the Marine Corps Recruit Depot, San Diego, Calif., where he served initially as the Executive Officer, Headquarters and Service Battalion. He subsequently was assigned as the Commanding Officer, 1st Recruit Training Battalion, where he served until selected to attend the Air War College in July 1980.

Graduating with distinction from the Air War College in July 1981, General Brandtner was selected to be the Senior Military Assistant to the Under Secretary of Defense for Policy, where he served until July 1984. During this tour, he was promoted to colonel in July 1982.

Returning to the FMF, General Brandtner was assigned as the Assistant Chief of Staff, G-4, I Marine Amphibious Force, Camp Pendleton, Calif., where he served until May 1985. The following month, he assumed command of the 5th Marine Regiment. In July 1986, he was assigned duty as Chief of Staff, 1st Marine Division, FMF. While serving in this capacity, he was selected in December 1987 for promotion to brigadier general. He was assigned duty as the Assistant Division Commander, 2nd Marine Division, FMF Atlantic, Camp Lejeune, N.C., on June 1, 1988, and advanced to brigadier general on July 25, 1988, and assigned duty as the Commanding General, 2nd Force Service Support Group (rein), FMF, Atlantic, Camp Lejeune, N.C., on Sept. 27, 1988. From December 1988 through February 1989, General Brandtner served as the Commanding General, 10th Marine

Expeditionary Brigade, at Camp Lejeune. Advanced to major general on May 11, 1990, he was assigned duty as the Vice Director for Operations, J-3, Joint Staff, on July 3, 1990. General Brandtner was promoted to lieutenant general on March 11, 1991, and assumed duty as Director for Operations, J-3, Joint Staff, Washington. He served in this capacity until his retirement on June 1, 1993.

In addition to the Navy Cross with gold star in lieu of a second award, General Brandtner's decorations and medals include: the Defense Superior Service Medal; Legion of Merit with Combat "V"; Purple Heart; Combat Action Ribbon; Presidential Unit Citation with one bronze star; the Navy Unit Commendation Ribbon; Meritorious Unit Commendation with two bronze stars; and over a dozen campaign and service awards.

Lieutenant General Brandtner is married to the former Sandra Robinson of Salisbury, Pennsylvania. They have a daughter, Cynthia. General Brandtner also has a daughter, Christine, and two sons, Martin Jr., and Mark, who reside in California.

-USMC-

The following are two After Action Reports, one from First Battalion the other from Company D, and General Brandtner's two Navy Cross citations:

A. A. REPORT, 1ST BATTALION, 5TH MARINES

During the period of 2 August through 23 September 1968, the Battalion conducted Search and Destroy missions in the central and southern parts of Dai Loc District and central and northern parts of Duc Duc District in the Quang Nam Province.

Throughout this period the enemy was consistent in the use of sniper tactics (1-8 man teams). The terrain being ideal for such tactics, the enemy used sniper teams continually throughout this period. On numerous occasions, the enemy defended with reinforced platoon to company size units. The enemy was dislodged from his defensive positions with extensive air support, artillery and ground fire. The enemy attacked the Battalion in force (approximately 200 men) on one occasion on the night of 11-12 September and was defeated with heavy losses. Battalion victory is attributed to sound defensive tactics and excellent air and artillery support.

Enemy operations during daylight hours were characterized by platoon to company strength defensive positions heavily entrenched and fortified with well constructed bunker complexes. The enemy forces would engage at extremely close range (within 150 meters), seriously limiting the use of supporting arms, and continue to hold the position until maneuver of friendly units would permit employment of air and artillery. Enemy forces would engage in the late afternoon and conduct withdrawals subsequent to darkness.

The Battalion Operations scheme emphasized night maneuver throughout the period 2 August through 23 September 1968. Capitalizing on intelligence gained by operating units, the Battalion kept the enemy off balance by dual-axis night maneuvers and extensive night ambush activities. On numerous occasions, night marches in excess of 6,000 meters were conducted to exploit information relative to enemy movement and disposition, with good success.

The enemy's determination to hold and dislodge friendly forces from the Dai Loc and Duc Duc Districts tends to support the vital importance of this area to the enemy for the following tactical and logistical reasons: The approaches to other friendly forces and the Da Nang area; to deny friendly forces the approaches to the canopy and mountainous area to the west to prevent capture of equipment, supplies, etc.; to control the local area for recruiting labor forces and the procurement of food stores, mainly rice.

A. A. REPORT, COMPANY D, 1ST BATTALION

3 Sept. 1968

0705H - Company D at (AT 837490) (area coordinates) searching for missing Marine received small-arms and M-79 fire from (AT 835490). Fired 400x5.56; 200x7.62; 5xM-79; received 6 fixed wing missions; 12x105mm HE; and 20x81mm HE. Searched area. Results: 7 VC KIA, 7 USMC WIAE.

0915H - Marine from Company D, while in fighting at (AT 837490) was hit in head by metal fragment from a friendly airstrike. Results: 1 USMC WIAE.

1525H - Company D at (AT 837492) received 8 rounds 82mm mortar from suspected position (AT 818498). Fired 16x105mm HE on suspected enemy position. Results: 10 USMC WIAE.

11 Sept. 1968

0330H - Company D perimeter at (AT 856547) received 10 rounds small-arms and 2 grenades from enemy at (AT 856547). Fired 150x5.56. Results: 1 USMC KIA; 1USMC WIAE.

0830H - Company D Fire Team OP at (AT 857546) received 2 rounds small-arms and one M-79 round from enemy at (AT 858547). Fired 150x5.56 and 5x81mm HE. Results: 1 USMC KIA; 1 USMC WIANE.

2030H - Company D Platoon ambush at (AT 857548) received 1,000 rounds small-arms, 20x82mm and 2 RPG rounds from enemy at (AT 858548). Fired 3,000x7.62, 1,000x5,56, 30x60mm HE, 25 M-79, 100x81mm HE, 330x105mm HE and received helicopter gunship. Results: 1 USMC KIA, 14 USMC WIAE, 7 USMC WIANE, 54 NVA KIA; 1 AK-47 captured. Friendly weapons and equipment losses: 1 M-60, 4 M-16 rifles, 1 .45 caliber pistol, 1 PRC 25 radio, 1 starlight scope.

• • •

The President of the United States takes pleasure in presenting the NAVY CROSS to:

CAPTAIN MARTIN L. BRANDTNER
UNITED STATES MARINE CORPS

for service as set forth in the following citation:

"For extraordinary heroism while serving as Command-
ing Officer of Company D, First Battalion, Fifth Marines,
First Marine Division, in connection with operations
against the enemy in the Republic of Vietnam. On 3 Sep-
tember 1968, while conducting a reconnaissance in force
near the village of Lan Phouc in Quang Nam Province,
the lead platoon of Company D became pinned down by
intense automatic weapons fire from a large North Viet-
namese Army force. As he moved forward to assess the

situation, Captain Brandtner was wounded by grenade launcher fire from an enemy soldier standing in a nearby trench. With complete disregard for his own safety, Captain Brandtner boldly exposed himself to the hostile fire and hurling a hand grenade, killed the North Vietnamese soldier. Suddenly, the Marines came under an intense North Vietnamese hand grenade attack, and when one of the lethal objects landed at Captain Brandtner's feet, he unhesitatingly seized the grenade and threw it back at the enemy. On two more occasions he completely disregarded his own safety to seize hand grenades which were thrown near his position and hurl them toward the hostile force. When another grenade landed in the midst of four nearby Marines, Captain Brandtner fearlessly rushed to their position, picked up the lethal object and hurled it away from his companions. Then, concerned only for the welfare for his fellow Marines, he knocked two of the men to the ground and quickly place himself on top of them, thereby absorbing the fragments from the exploding grenade in his protective armor and preventing possible death or serious injury to his companions. Realizing the numerical superiority of the enemy, he consolidated his company's position and skillfully adjusted effective supporting arms fire which caused the hostile force to flee and enabled his Marines to overrun the objective. By his courage, intrepid fighting spirit, and selfless devotion to duty at the risk of his life, Captain Brandtner sustained and enhanced the highest traditions of the Marine Corps and the United States Naval Service."

For the President,
/S/ JOHN M. CHAFEE
Secretary of the Navy

The President of the United States takes pleasure in presenting the NAVY CROSS (GOLD STAR in lieu of the Second Award) to:

Men of Honor

CAPTAIN MARTIN L. BRANDTNER
UNITED STATES MARINE CORPS

for service as set forth in the following citation:

"For extraordinary heroism in action while serving as the Commanding Officer, Company D, First Battalion, Fifth Marines, First Marine Division (Reinforced) in the Republic of Vietnam on 11 September 1968. Assigned a mission to conduct a search and destroy operation near the village of My Binh, Quang Dia Loc District, Quang Nam Province, Captain Brandtner selected his defensive positions and began deploying his platoons for their assigned night activities. As the First Platoon departed, en route to their night ambush site, they began receiving intense small-arms, automatic weapons, and rocket fire from a numerically superior North Vietnamese Army force. Simultaneously, the enemy, approximately the size of two North Vietnamese Army companies, began an attack on the Command Group with 82mm. mortars, intense automatic weapons fire, and P40 rockets. Quickly analyzing the situation and immediately realizing the seriousness and the danger involved, Captain Brandtner disregarded his own personal safety and moved forward to an extremely exposed position in order that he could personally control the battle at hand. When the enemy began the first in a series of "human wave" sapper attacks against the company's position, he calmly and with outstanding presence of mind moved from position to position reorganizing, encouraging, and rallying his outnumbered and dazed company into an inspired fighting unit which completely stopped the momentum of the enemy attack and forced them to withdraw. Realizing the enemy were regrouping for subsequent attacks, he calmly adjusted his supporting artillery fire to within 200 meters of his lines, again raising havoc and confusion within the enemy's ranks. When the North Vietnamese Army

*units began their second attack, the devastating fires of a
well organized Marine Corps rifle company caught them
off balance and inflicted heavy enemy casualties. Twice
more, the determined enemy launched massive "human
wave" assaults on the perimeter of Company D, but the
steadfast efforts of the men of the company proved to be to
much for the now overwhelmed and demoralized enemy.
After more than two hours of persistent attempts to overrun the company, the enemy broke contact. Daylight revealed 67 North Vietnamese dead as mute testimony to the
ferocious encounter that had taken place. The number of
enemy dead and wounded evacuated could not be estimated. Company D suffered only one Marine killed and
fourteen wounds serious enough to require evacuation. By
his outstanding courage, superb leadership, and unswerving devotion to duty, Captain Brandtner served to inspire
all who observed him and upheld the highest traditions of
the Marine Corps and the United States Naval Service."*

For the President,
/S/ JOHN M. CHAFEE
Secretary of the Navy

• • •

Name: Lieutenant Joseph P. Donovan, USMC.

Biography: Written July 24, 1970.
First Lieutenant Joseph P Donovan, a highly-decorated Marine Corps pi-
lot, winner of two Navy Crosses, was presented the 1970 Frederick L.
Feinberg Award.

First Lieutenant Joseph P. Donovan was presented the award by General Lewis W. Walt, Assistant Commandant of the Marine Corps, in his
office today.

The Feinberg award, initiated by Kaman Aircraft Corporation, is
awarded annually by the American Helicopter Society to a helicopter pilot

for outstanding achievement in rescue, flight and test development of new aircraft or general high level of performance in operational flying during the preceding calendar year.

Lieutenant Donovan, who entered the Marine Corps June 5, 1966, was honored for "courage, superior airmanship and unwavering devotion to duty in the face of great personal danger."

On Feb. 22, 1969, while serving as a pilot with Marine Medium Helicopter Squadron 364 in Vietnam, he launched as wingman in a flight of two transport helicopters assigned to emergency medical evacuation of a seriously wounded Marine. When the section leader's aircraft experienced mechanical difficulties and returned to base, Lieutenant Donovan continued the mission.

Approaching the area, he dispatched his gunships to destroy a hostile rocket launching site. Upon landing to embark the casualty, he was wounded by fragments from hostile grenades and mortar rounds which also severely damaged his helicopter and caused it to vibrate violently.

Nonetheless, he maneuvered it to the nearest medical facility and after receiving medical attention, launched a second emergency medical evacuation mission. Again entering an extremely hazardous area, without gunship support, he picked up the wounded men.

He then embarked upon a third mission and brought 10 more wounded men to safety.

Lieutenant Donovan, stationed with the Third Marine Aircraft Wing at El Toro, California, earned during his short time in the Marine Corps, two Navy Cross Medals, a Silver Star Medal, two Distinguished Flying Cross Medals and 35 Strike/Flight Air Medal Awards.

The 28 year old lieutenant, who graduated from the University of Dallas in 1966, is married to the former Eileen R. Donovan of Chicago, Illinois. He is the son of Mrs. Joseph B. Donovan of 405 West Marvin, Waxahachie, Texas.

-USMC-

The following are Lieutenant Donovan's two Navy Cross and Silver Star citations:

Chapter 3: Vietnam

The President of the United States takes pleasure in presenting the NAVY CROSS to:

FIRST LIEUTENANT JOSEPH P. DONOVAN
UNITED STATES MARINE CORPS RESERVE

for service as set forth in the following citation:

"For extraordinary heroism while serving as a Pilot with Marine Medium Helicopter Squadron 364 in the Republic of Vietnam on 22 February 1969. First Lieutenant Donovan launched as Wingman in a flight of two CH-46 transport helicopters assigned the emergency medical evacuation of a seriously wounded Marine from an area north of the Nam O Bridge in Quang Nam Province. When the section leader's aircraft experienced mechanical difficulties and returned to its base, First Lieutenant Donovan resolutely elected to continue the mission. Approaching the designated area, he observed a hostile rocket launching site and dispatched his gunships to destroy the emplacement. When informed that the injured Marine was in a critical condition, First Lieutenant Donovan, undaunted by the extremely heavy volume of enemy fire and lacking gunship support, fearlessly maneuvered to a landing on the fire-swept area and embarked the casualty. Wounded by fragments from hostile grenades and mortar rounds which also severely damaged his helicopter and caused it to vibrate violently as it lifted out of the zone, he ignored his painful injuries as he fought to regain control of the CH-46 and then skillfully maneuvered it to the nearest medical facility. After receiving medical attention and ascertaining that his aircraft was operable, he boldly launched on a second emergency medical evacuation mission and again entered an extremely hazardous area, without gunship support, to take the wounded to a medical facility. Informed that eight seriously injured Marines in another area required immedi-

ate evacuation, First Lieutenant Donovan unhesitatingly proceeded to the site, coordinated his approach with gunship fire, and landed in the perilous zone. He resolutely remained in his dangerously exposed position until all the casualties were embarked, and then lifted out of the area. As he began to depart, he learned that additional casualties had been brought to the landing zone, two of whom were in critical condition. With complete disregard for his own safety, he again braved the heavy volume of enemy fire and landed in the fire-swept area, embarked the wounded Marines, and departed to the nearest medical facility. By his courage, superior airmanship and unwavering devotion to duty in the face of great personal danger, First Lieutenant Donovan was instrumental in the accomplishment of the hazardous mission and upheld the highest traditions of the Marine Corps and the United States Naval Service."

For the President,
/S/ JOHN H. CHAFEE
Secretary of the Navy

The President of the United States takes pleasure in presenting the NAVY CROSS (GOLD STAR in lieu of the Second Award) to:

FIRST LIEUTENANT JOSEPH P. DONOVAN
UNITED STATES MARINE CORPS RESERVE

for service as set forth in the following citation:

"For extraordinary heroism while serving with Marine Medium Helicopter Squadron 364, Marine Aircraft Group Sixteen, First Marine Aircraft Wing during combat operations against the enemy in the Republic of Vietnam. On 21 April 1969, First Lieutenant Donovan launched as pilot of a transport helicopter assigned the mission of medically

evacuating seriously wounded Marines from an open rice paddy northwest of Liberty Bridge in Quang Nam Province. Arriving over the designated area, he commenced a high-speed, low-altitude approach toward a tree line north of the site, and immediately came under machine-gun fire which damaged the forward section of his transport. Undaunted by the hostile fire, he maneuvered the helicopter to the area where the casualties lay, maintaining his helicopter in a hover while the wounded men were embarked. Still taking a heavy volume of enemy fire, First Lieutenant Donovan departed the area and delivered his patients to the hospital at Da Nang. After an inspection of the battle damage revealed that the helicopter was no longer airworthy, he took command of a second aircraft and immediately received a request for another medical evacuation mission from the same area. Proceeding at once to the site, he commenced his second approach into the hazardous zone, again flying through intense enemy fire. As he awaited the embarkation of the casualties, additional enemy fire erupted which prevented the Marines on the ground from embarking the remainder of the casualties. When informed that his starboard gunner had been wounded, First Lieutenant Donovan lifted from the zone to evaluate the man's wound and to appraise the damage to his aircraft. Determining that the aircraft was still capable of accomplishing the evacuation and that his gunner was not seriously wounded, he advised the ground unit that he was again ready to enter the hazardous zone, but was informed that another helicopter had been designated to complete the mission. By his courage, superior aeronautical ability, and unwavering devotion to duty in the face of grave personal danger, First Lieutenant Donovan was directly instrumental in saving the lives of several fellow Marines and upheld the highest traditions of the Marine Corps and of the United States Naval Service."

Men of Honor

For the President,
/S/ JOHN H. Chafee
Secretary of the Navy

The President of the United States takes pleasure in presenting the SILVER STAR MEDAL to:

FIRST LIEUTENANT JOSEPH P. DONOVAN
UNITED STATES MARINE CORPS RESERVE

for service as set forth in the following citation:

> *For conspicuous gallantry and intrepidity in action while serving as a Pilot with Marine Medium Helicopter Squadron 364, Marine Aircraft Group 16, First Marine Aircraft Wing in connection with combat operations against the enemy in the Republic of Vietnam. On 9 May 1969, First Lieutenant Donovan launched as Section Leader of a flight of two CH-46 transport helicopters assigned the emergency medical evacuation of ten casualties from a Marine company which was heavily engaged in combat with a large North Vietnamese Army force near the village of My Heip (3) in Quang Nam Province. Arriving over the designated area, he found that the wounded Marines were located in five separate positions scattered about the open rice paddies and that the proximity of the opposing forces precluded the delivery of suppressive fire by supporting aircraft. Undaunted by the extremely heavy volume of hostile fire directed at his aircraft, First Lieutenant Donovan fearlessly maneuvered into the precarious area, located the first group of casualties, skillfully executed a landing, and resolutely remained in this dangerously exposed position until all the casualties were embarked. With complete disregard for his own safety, he continued to brave the intense North Vietnamese small-arms and automatic weapons fire as he boldly air-taxied his helicopter at low altitude across the*

212

Chapter 3: Vietnam

*rice paddies to each of the four other positions and suc-
ceeded in extracting all of the remaining casualties. By his
courage, superior airmanship, and unwavering devotion
to duty in the face of great personal danger, First Lieutenant Donovan was instrumental in accomplishing the hazardous mission and upheld the highest traditions of the
Marine Corps and of the United States Naval Service."*

*For the President,
/S/ H. W. BUSE, JR.
Lieutenant General, U.S. Marine Corps*

• • •

Name: Captain Wesley L. Fox, USMC.

Biography: Revised March, 1971.
Captain Wesley L. Fox was the 48th Marine to be awarded the Medal of
Honor for outstanding heroism, while serving as Commanding Officer of
Company A, 1st Battalion, 9th Marines, 3rd Marine Division in action
against the enemy in the Republic of Vietnam, on February 22, 1969.

The Medal was presented to Captain Fox by President Nixon during a
joint service ceremony held at the White House on March 2, 1971.

Born September 30, 1931, in Herndon, Virginia, Wesley Lee Fox at-
tended Warren County High School in Front Royal, Virginia, until 1948.
His schooling since entering the Marine Corps includes the Airborne School,
Fort Benning, Georgia, 1961; the Underwater Swimming School at Subic
Bay, Philippine Islands, 1962; the Military Assistance Training Advisors
Course at the JFK Warfare Center, Fort Bragg, North Carolina, 1967; and
the Amphibious Warfare School, Marine Corps Base, Quantico, Virginia,
1970.

Enlisting in the Marine Corps on August 4, 1950, he was ordered to the
Marine Corps recruit Depot at Parris Island, South Carolina, for his recruit
training which he completed in October 1950.

After a brief tour as a rifleman with the 2nd Marine Division at Marine
Corps Base, Camp Lejeune, North Carolina, he next served his initial tour

213

during the Korean conflict as a rifleman with Company "I", 5th Marines, 1st Marine Division. Wounded in action on September 8, 1951, he was evacuated to the U.S. Naval Hospital, National Naval Medical Center, Bethesda, Maryland.

Upon his release from Bethesda in March 1952, he served with the Armed Forces Police, in Washington, D.C., as a Patrolman until September 1953 when he was reassigned to Marine Corps Aircraft Group 11 in Japan.

Returning to Korea for his second tour, Sergeant Fox served as a Platoon Sergeant with Company "G", 5th Marines and, upon returning to the United States, he served briefly at the Marine Corps Base, Camp Pendleton, California, prior to being assigned to Drill Instructors school at the Marine Corps Recruit Depot, San Diego, California.

Completing his course of instruction in August 1955, he remained at San Diego serving as a Drill Instructor until August 1957 when he once again returned to the East Coast to attend Recruiter's School at the Marine Corps Recruit Depot, Parris Island, South Carolina, subsequent to being assigned duty as a Recruiter in the Washington, D.C., and the Baltimore, Maryland areas.

After completing his tour as a recruiter in December 1960, he was ordered back to the West Coast and served as a Platoon Sergeant with the 1st Force Reconnaissance Company at both Camp Pendleton, California, and on Okinawa through November 1962. In December 1962, he was assigned as a Troop Handler at the Marine Air Detachment, in Jacksonville, Florida, and served in this capacity until September 1965.

Gunnery Sergeant Fox next saw duty in the Office of the Provost Marshall, Supreme Headquarters Allied Powers Europe (SHAPE) in Paris, France. In May of 1966, he was promoted to First Sergeant and also commissioned as a Second Lieutenant. Returning to the United States in August of that year, he became a Platoon Commander with the 2nd Force Reconnaissance Company at Camp Lejeune, North Carolina.

Lieutenant Fox was ordered to the Republic of Vietnam where he served as a Battalion Advisor to the Vietnamese Marine Corps for thirteen months. Being reassigned in November 1968, he became the Commanding Officer of Company "A", 1st Battalion, 9th Marines, 3rd Marine Division, serving in this capacity until May 1969. It was during this assignment that he earned the Nation's highest decoration for bravery. He was promoted to his present rank, April 1, 1969.

After his return to the United States, he completed the Amphibious Warfare School, Marine Corps Base, Quantico, Virginia, in January 1970 at which time he assumed his current assignment as a Tactics Instructor, The Basic School at Quantico.

In addition to the Medal of Honor, his medals and decorations include: the Bronze Star Medal with Combat "V", the Navy Commendation Medal with one Gold Star, the Purple Heart with three Gold Stars in lieu of second through fourth awards, the Combat Action Ribbon, the Presidential Unit Citation, the Good Conduct Medal with four Gold Stars in lieu of subsequent awards, the National Defense Service Medal with one Bronze Star, the Korean Service Medal with three Bronze Stars, the United Nations Service Medal, the Vietnam Service Medal with one Silver Star and one Bronze Star in lieu of subsequent awards, two Vietnamese Crosses of Gallantry, the Vietnamese Honor Medal 1st Class, the Vietnamese Unit Cross of Gallantry with Palm, the Korean Presidential Unit Citation, and the Republic of Vietnam Campaign Medal.

-USMC-

The following are six eyewitness accounts of Captain Fox's actions, and his Medal of Honor citation:

Statement of Witnesses

"On February 22, 1969, while on a water run patrol, Alpha Company came under attack by an estimated company, reinforced with mortars, B-40 rockets, and machine guns. Steep terrain, poor visibility, and double canopy jungle made organization and maneuver difficult. Adding to these problems, the North Vietnamese were well entrenched in fortified bunkers.

As Alpha Company proceeded down to the stream, the point element came into contact with enemy snipers. Although taking a few casualties, they quickly over came the NVA.

After completing the water run, and starting up the hill, Alpha Company came into contact with heavy enemy concentrations. As second platoon commander in Alpha Company, I observed the following actions by my company commander, 1st Lt. Fox. As soon as first platoon started up the hill, they came into contact with the enemy. Losses were heavy and only extreme professional leadership could turn the situation into an advantage.

At this time, Lieutenant Fox ran to the front so he could estimate the situation. Accurate grazing enemy fire made this an extremely difficult and dangerous task. He then, from the front, began to organize his platoon.

First platoon was employed to the left flank, third platoon to the right flank, and second platoon through the middle.

Just after the initial organization was ordered, an enemy mortar round landed in the C. P., wounding 1st Lt. Fox and the rest of the C. P. Lt. Fox never hesitated, although wounded and under concussion. He took all the radios and began communication with the Battalion C. P., platoon commanders, and air support.

With the rest of the officers either killed or wounded, Lt. Fox was left in total command of the entire situation. While wounded the second time, he managed, with no regard for his own safety, to route the enemy fortifications, and turn the victory in favor of Alpha Company.

His calm leadership, professional ability, and extreme courage was the deciding factor. Few men could have overcome the strain of wounds and organized a decisive victory under such conditions. I am proud to have been under 1st Lt. Fox on the 22nd of February. He maintained, what in my opinion, was truly the highest tradition of the Marine Corps and its officers."

/S/ James H. Davis

"I was Company Gunnery Sgt. on the 22nd of February 1969, when Alpha Company was assigned the mission of clearing an area east of the Battalion perimeter. We departed the I. P. at approximately 1030. We encountered a bunker complex on the right flank which contained a couple of snipers. Snipers bringing fire on the point were immediately done away with. Continuing on, our mission was to supply water for the Battalion by means of a water detail. While at the creek, Alpha Company came under mortar fire. The water detail was organized and returned to the Battalion perimeter. Upon leaving the creek and heading south, the company came under heavy sniper fire and automatic weapons. Lt. Fox immediately set his plan of action. The company was on line and pushing toward a second bunker complex which contained an estimated NVA Company (Rein). Six machine guns had this company in a cross fire. Lt. Fox had the command post immediately to the rear of the 2nd platoon. The command post received mortar fire, killing or wounding most of the C. P. Lt. Fox was wounded in the shoulder and one leg. Knowing also that his Air Control Operator, Company Operator and the Artillery Operator were also hit, Lt. Fox mounted one radio on his back, carrying another radio, and operating still a third radio, and all this time yelling encouragement to the troops. Though wounded twice at this time, Lt. Fox was still in command and control of his company. Never at one time during this action did the skipper drop below his knees. Working with the skipper, we pulled the able wounded to our rear for security, because at this time, we were also receiving fire from there. The executive officer was killed after assuming command of the Second Platoon, who's platoon leader was wounded earlier. The Third Platoon commander was killed. The First Platoon commander was wounded. Lt. Fox at this point was the only officer remaining in action. The weather most of the day prevented Lt. Fox from using his air support. I believe the success of the 22nd of February was mainly accredited to the leadership shown by the company commander. It's a hard decision to pull out or push on. With the dead and wounded acquired by this time, there was nothing left but to push on. The fire was heavy all through this particular fire fight, but not one time did Lt. Fox hesitate in showing the leadership which this man has so much of. With all disregard for his own life, Lt. Fox knew what had to be done and he did it. Returning to the Battalion perimeter, wounded himself, Lt. Fox personally helped the wounded through the darkness and a somewhat hell of a climb."

/S/ Ronald G. Duerr

"Company "A" was assigned the task of a company size patrol to check out an area we had received contact from the day before. Lieutenant Fox issued the order the night before and we moved out approximately 10:30 on the morning of the 22nd. Our first contact came when first platoon received fire from an enemy position near the stream. The enemy position was destroyed and one automatic weapon captured and one body removed from the bunker. Lieutenant Fox ordered a hasty defense set up to allow the remainder of the company to move down and secure the stream. As C. P. group moved into the area, more sniper fire was received and Lieutenant Fox, with complete command of the situation moved his First Platoon in the direction from which the fire was coming. As the First Platoon moved forward, we began to receive mortar fire on the stream bed and heavier fire from the flank. The water detail was brought back and moved up to join the First. Lieutenant Fox moved in and positioned the Third Platoon with the rest of the company and began the assault of the hill which the enemy held.

As we began the assault, Lieutenant Fox and the C. P. were located on my right and I could see the enemy mortar rounds landing in and all around their area. I could hear the skipper's commands even above the roar of battle and saw him in the lead of his C. P. as we moved forward. When my radio communications with the platoon commander went out, I moved to the right and received orders from Lieutenant Fox to take my platoon on up the hill. At that time, I saw Lieutenant Fox with one radio on his back and one in his hand calling in mortar and artillery in support of our assault. When it seemed the movement was slowing, Lieutenant Fox' cool headed command would be incentive to us all to get going. Lieutenant Fox kept himself positioned at the point of the heaviest fighting and regardless of his own safety, would personally observe the artillery and mortar fire and gave coordinations. He continually reminded us to keep the line moving and to keep our flanks secure while we moved. He also set up, under the direction of the company gunney, a rear security to keep the wounded secure. He never mentioned his own wounds until the battle was over and personally checked our security and lines while we waited for Company D to move down. No company could be more proud of their company commander as they followed him up the hill when the area was secure."

/S/ Robert R. Jensen

"The company was on a company size patrol. We were to check out an area where 3rd Platoon had heavy contact the day before. My platoon had rear security. We were setting up a hasty perimeter when 1st Platoon had contact to the front. We started receiving mortar fire in the rear. I saw Lieutenant Fox on his feet moving all platoons up on line with the 1st Platoon with complete disregard for his own safety.

Once the company was in attack position, the attack started. Now we were receiving mortars, RPGs and very heavy small arms and automatic fire. Lieutenant Fox kept very calm and directed the attack even though all of his C. P. radio men were knocked out. He was on three radios at the same time, directing the company, getting air support, and the battalion net. I feel through his attack we lost fewer men. I saw Lieutenant Fox on his feet even though he was hit with RPGs and mortars that were landing all around him directing the company."

/S/ Michael L. Lane

"On February 22, 1969, while serving as squad leader with Second Platoon, Co. "A", 1st Battalion, 9th Marines, our company was taken under heavy RPG, mortar, and automatic weapon fire from an estimated reinforced company of NVA, who were deeply entrenched in fortified bunkers and spider holes.

In the initial barrage of mortar fire, my platoon commander and platoon sergeant became incapacitated from shrapnel wounds. As I moved forward to assume command of the platoon, I immediately became aware of 1st Lt. Fox, Co. "A"'s commander, as he began to organize the assault which eventually proved to be our ticket to victory.

Let me say here, that due to weather conditions wherein visibility was limited to probably less than 100 feet most of the morning, precluding the possibility of air support, and because of the close quarter at which we were engaging the enemy, making it unfeasible to call on artillery, it became quite evident we would have to fight our way out. However, it was also obvious that because of the large number of casualties sustained in the first few minutes of the attack, it would take nearly a superhuman effort in organizing and leading us in the assault through the hail of machine gun bullets to our objective. But we made it! And it was because of a fantastic effort by 1st Lt. Fox.

Although wounded twice, and with no one left in his command post group as radio operators, he wasted no time setting in motion the product of a quick, yet accurate, assessment of our situation. He became commander, communicator, coordinator, and whatever else was necessary to accomplish that one man show, all rolled into one calm, organized piece of machinery.

When the fight was over, there was one officer left; a limping but victorious Co. "A" commander. Under his inspirational and courageous direction, his company fought their way out of certain annihilation. Certainly his outstanding efforts, much more than outstanding, have earned for 1st Lt. Fox the highest distinction and honor, we as his fellow Marines, especially his Alpha Company Marines, can bestow on him. And in my opinion that distinction should rightfully be the Congressional Medal of Honor."

/S/ David A. Beyerlein

"As senior corpsman of a line company, my primary concern is, and was on that day, the health of the Command Post personnel, to wit, Lt. Wesley L. Fox and his staff.

On the 22nd of February, we met the NVA in strength. The battlefield was not unlike that depicted many times in Hollywood films. There prevailed a low fog around us, and after the first few minutes of combat, the area was littered with Marine casualties. The enemy was hitting us from all sides and with everything they had. Sniper and automatic weapons fire attempted to pin us down while mortar and RPG projectiles exploded in our midst. The battle lasted for several hours, and in the course of this action, my attention was turned to Lt. Fox many times, for he, as the company commander, was my first concern. The following amount of his action was witnessed by me on that day, and I declare it to be true and factual. When an incoming mortar round hit the CP group disabling all of the radiomen, Lt. Fox picked up the company and battalion nets and went into action. There was no cover to be found in that valley, and concealment was to be found only in the form of slender banana palms, but Lt. Fox seemed to desire neither of the protective elements. Though wounded himself in the shoulder, he knelt (under fire which forced everyone else prone) and began to direct the attack. I can never forget the expression written upon his face, for in this initial critical time, he showed no fear, only determination. With his maps spread before him, he would, while coordinating the advance through a radio in each hand, looked first in the direction of the enemy employment, then back to his maps. He never hid his face from the enemy, and his eyes seemed to defy them. As he continued to move the troops forward by command, he received another wound to the legs, which forced him to lie prone but up on his elbows. He did not call me to him, for his wounds were less serious than those of several others, but instead he continued to shout into the radios. Still he never hid his face from the enemy. He was in command, and I could tell he had complete control of the situation by the way the men advanced at his command. Then, as suddenly as it had begun, it was all over. All around lay men killed and wounded. Lt. Fox met the officer in charge of the company that had been sent to help us (though they arrived after the fighting) and I noticed that he limped. I know these wounds were painful, but I cannot recall a grimace during that fight.

We had been victorious, the NVA had failed in their attempt to wipe us out, even though they held command territory and had superior armament. Credit must be given to the men who lost their lives in that action, but it is my considered opinion that the heroic actions of Lt. Wesley L. Fox on that day, in that he kept control of himself and the company, was the most important factor which gave us victory."

/S/ Charles H. Hudson

The President of the United States in the name of The Congress takes pleasure in presenting the MEDAL OF HONOR to:

CAPTAIN WESLEY L. FOX
UNITED STATES MARINE CORPS

for service as set forth in the following citation:

"For conspicuous gallantry and intrepidity at the risk of his life above and beyond the call of duty while serving as Commanding Officer of Company A, First Battalion, Ninth Marines, Third Marine Division, in action against the enemy in the northern A Shau Valley, Quang Tri Province, Republic of Vietnam, on February 22, 1969. Captain (then

First Lieutenant) Fox's company came under intense fire from a large well-concealed enemy force. Captain Fox maneuvered to a position from which he could assess the situation and confer with his platoon leaders. As they departed to execute the plan he had devised, the enemy attacked and Captain Fox was wounded along with all of the other members of the command group, except the executive officer. Captain Fox continued to direct the activity of his company. Advancing through heavy enemy fire, he personally neutralized one enemy position and calmly ordered an assault against the hostile emplacements. He then moved through the hazardous area coordinating aircraft support with the activities of his men. When his executive officer was mortally wounded, Captain Fox reorganized the company and directed the fire of his men as they hurled grenades against the enemy and drove the hostile forces into retreat. Wounded again in the final assault, Captain Fox refused medical attention, established a defensive posture, and supervised the preparation of casualties for medical evacuation. His indomitable courage, inspiring initiative, and unwavering devotion to duty in the face of grave personal danger inspired his Marines to such aggressive actions that they overcame all enemy resistance and destroyed a large bunker complex. Captain Fox's heroic actions reflect great credit upon himself and the Marine Corps, and uphold the highest traditions of the United States Naval Service."

/S/ RICHARD M. NIXON

• • •

Chapter 3: Vietnam

Name: Major Howard V. Lee, USMC.

Biography: Revised November 1971.

Major Howard V. Lee, the seventh Marine to win the Nation's highest award for heroism in Vietnam, the Medal of Honor, is now serving as Operations Officer, G-3 Section, Headquarters, Fleet Marine Force, Atlantic, in Norfolk, Virginia. The Medal was presented to him by President Johnson in ceremonies held at the White House on October 25, 1967.

Born August 1, 1933, in New York City, he graduated from DeWitt Clinton High School in the Bronx, New York in 1951, and from Pace College with a Bachelor's Degree in Business Administration on June 17, 1955. While in his senior year at college, he enlisted as a member of the Platoon Leaders Class in the United States Marine Corps Reserve.

In September 1955, he entered the 14th Officers Candidates' Course, Quantico, Virginia, and upon completing the course the following December, was commissioned a Marine Corps Reserve Second Lieutenant. Lieutenant Lee completed the Basic School, Marine Corps Schools, Quantico, in July 1956 and the Marine Corps Supply School, Marine Corps Base, Camp Lejeune, North Carolina, that September.

Upon completion of these courses, he was transferred to the Marine Corps Supply activity, Philadelphia, Pennsylvania, for duty as Field Inspection Officer, Field Inspection Section and, later, Officer in Charge, Audit Section. He was promoted to first lieutenant in June 1957, and integrated into the Regular Marine Corps in January 1958.

Detached from the Supply Activity in September 1958, he was ordered to the West Coast, and served briefly as Troop Handler, 1st Replacement Battalion, Staging Regiment, Marine Corps Base, Camp Pendleton, California, then was assigned duty as a platoon commander with Company F, 2d Battalion, 9th Marines, 3d Marine Division (Rein), FMF, serving in this capacity until June 1959.

Lieutenant Lee next served as the Battalion S-4 Officer with H&S Company, 3d Battalion, 3d Marines, 3d Marine Division (Rein), FMF, San Francisco, California. In February 1960, he was assigned duty as Guard Officer at the Marine Barracks, U.S. Naval Propellant Plant, Indian Head, Maryland.

After his promotion to captain on July 1, 1961, he was assigned duties as Platoon Commander and, later, Instructor, The Basic School, Marine Corps Schools in Quantico, where he remained until June 1964.

From July 1964 until February 1966, Captain Lee was stationed at Camp Lejeune, North Carolina, serving first as Commanding Officer of Company A, 1st Battalion, then as Battalion S-3 Officer with H&S Company, 1st Battalion (Rein), 2d Marines, 2d Marine Division, FMF. During the latter period, he served aboard the *USS LaSalle (LPD-3)*, and in the Dominican Republic during the crises there (1-29 May 1965).

Ordered to the Republic of Vietnam in April 1966, Captain Lee served as Commanding Officer of Company E, 2 Battalion, 4th Marines, 3d Marine Division. It was on August 8-9 that he distinguished himself above and beyond the call of duty for which he was awarded the Medal of Honor. He received the Bronze Star Medal with Combat "V" for heroic action earlier on 26-27 June 1966. Wounded in action on August the 8th and again on the 9th in the vicinity of Quang Tri, Captain Lee was evacuated to the U.S. Naval Hospital, Bethesda, Maryland. In November 1966, he returned to duty at Headquarters Marine Corps and assigned duty as TO/MOS Coordinator and, later, Assistant FMF Readiness Officer in the Operations Section, G-4 Division. He was promoted to his present rank in July 1966.

Following this assignment, Major Lee completed the Command and Staff College, Quantico, Virginia, in June 1970, then returned to the Republic of Vietnam for his second tour of duty. For his service as Executive Officer, Provisional Headquarters and Service Company and with the 2 Combined Action Group, III Marine Amphibious Force, he earned a Gold Star in lieu of a second Bronze Star Medal with Combat "V."

Upon his return to the United States in May 1971, he assumed his current assignment.

A Complete list of his medals and decorations include: the Medal of Honor, the Bronze Star Medal with Combat "V" and Gold Star in lieu of a second award, the Purple Heart, the Combat Action Ribbon, the Presidential Unit Citation, the National Defense Service Medal, the Armed Forces Expeditionary Medal, the Vietnam Service Medal with two Bronze Stars, the Vietnamese Cross of Gallantry with one Bronze and one Silver Star, and the Republic of Vietnam Campaign Medal.

Chapter 3: Vietnam

-USMC-

The following are four eyewitness accounts of Major Lee's actions, and his Medal of Honor, citation:

Statements of Witnesses

"On the afternoon of 8 August 1966, I was coordinating the extraction of a reconnaissance team and a reaction force from Company E, 2 Battalion, 4th Marines, as Battalion Operations Officer. At about 1730H one half of the personnel were extracted when the helicopters were subjected to a heavy anti-aircraft fire. The Platoon Commander waved the helicopters off because of the severe enemy fire and an enemy attack which had just been launched from three directions. During the attack the Platoon Commander was killed and the remaining two sergeants severely wounded. Upon learning of this Captain Lee recommended that a second platoon be inserted to assist the beleaguered survivors. He discussed the unit's chances with me and we both concluded that if reinforcements were not inserted, the fate of the unit of 21 men would be in grave doubt against the North Vietnamese Company opposing them. Realizing that the situation was critical, being fully aware of the fact that it would be next to impossible to get more men into the area let alone a platoon or larger to reinforce the unit, and of the certain danger to which he was exposing himself with little chance of survival, he prevailed upon the Battalion Commander to allow him to lead the relief unit regardless of the consequences.

Following the reports over the radio I learned that Captain Lee with his radio operator and two other men out of a total of eight fought their way through the encircling enemy to gain the position. Captain Lee received wounds in the head by automatic weapons fire while debarking from the helicopter but refused evacuation. Captain Lee reported that he could receive CH-46A at the position as the fighting was dying down. However, shortly thereafter, a second enemy attack was launched which lasted over two and a half hours preventing the landing of the remainder of the relief force. During this attack he was again wounded, receiving a missile wound in the leg. Later an enemy grenade wounded him with fragments in his body and head, damaging one eye. The enemy came within fifteen meters of the friendly lines firing automatic rifles and throwing grenades. It was later estimated that at least 200 grenades were thrown during the attack.

As night fell a flare ship arrived on station and at 1950H Captain Lee reported that his unit was surrounded by about seventy-five enemy personnel and that enemy heavy weapons were employed on the ridgeline to the north. At 2025H he reported that there were three dead, six critically wounded, and sixteen men able to fight. Forty-five minutes later two U.S. Air Force C-47 gatling gun ships were on station and he adjusted their fire to within 20 meters of his lines, despite his wounds. One half hour later Captain Lee reported that he was still under constant attack. At 2335H the reconnaissance radio operator reported that Captain Lee was almost incapacitated due to his wounds. Twenty-five minutes later a helicopter bringing ammunition resupply was grounded in the position by enemy fire. The enemy attack died short;y thereafter. At about 0200H Captain Lee conferred with me over the radio concerning the plans for the following day and at 0430H he was trying to adjust the fire of the gatling guns closer to his lines. At 0630H Captain Lee was incapacitated due to his wounds and the command relinquished to the pilot of the downed helicopter.

His sustained conspicuous gallantry and intrepidity at the risk of his life above and beyond the call of duty merits consideration for the Nation's highest award."

/S/ Captain J. J. W. Hilgers

"At approximately 1730H, on 8 August 1966, the Second Platoon of Company E, 2d Battalion, 4th Marines was hit by heavy North Vietnamese automatic weapons fire and grenades. Twenty-one men were left from the reaction force to repel the attack. After the initial attack there were only sixteen of us left able to fight. At about 1900H a helicopter brought Captain Lee and three other men to our position. They landed outside our perimeter and had to fight their way to us. When Captain Lee arrived I noticed that he had been wounded in the head. As soon as he reached our positions, he was checking each of us personally to see if we were wounded and if we had enough ammunition. I was on the perimeter and didn't see the Captain all of the time, as a big attack started just after he landed and continued for quite a while. During the attack Captain Lee was wounded at least one more time that I know of. A grenade went off right next to him. With all the lead flying around and with him constantly moving among the men, he could have been wounded again but he stayed on the radio calling in support and tried to get more troops and ammunition. He stayed in command of his troops until the next morning when he grew to weak and the Major, the helicopter took over for him."

/S/ Corporal David A. Smith

"On 8 August 1966 at approximately 1730H, the Second Platoon of Company E, 2d Battalion, 4th Marines was hit by heavy enemy automatic rifle and grenades during an extraction from a mountain top. Due to the heavy fire, all but twenty-one men were extracted.

At approximately 1900H, a helicopter brought Captain Lee, our Commander, and several other men to our position. The helicopter for some reason landed outside the position and the group had to fight their way into our lines. Captain Lee immediately went around the perimeter personally, obtaining information as to our situation and condition. When he came to my position, I saw that he was wounded in the head. When he had finished, he immediately started radioing for resupply, troop assistance, and supporting fire. Right after this the North Vietnamese started a big grenade attack followed by everything they could throw at us, including rockets. Though I was on the perimeter, I could still hear Captain Lee in back of me calling in fire. During the battle, some time around 2000H, Captain Lee was seriously wounded by fragmentation from a grenade and received a missile either earlier or later.

Though wounded and nearly unconscious, he stayed on the radio giving information in support of the hill. He did so until the next morning when he became too weak from his wounds."

/S/ Corporal Douglas H. Van

"On the night of 8 August 1966, we received word that one of our platoons was under a heavy North Vietnamese attack and that the Platoon Commander had been killed. Captain Lee instructed me to accompany him aboard a helicopter to go to their aid with six additional Marines. When we neared the landing zone, we received heavy automatic weapons fire. Captain Lee was wounded in the head. Before we could leave the helicopter, we had to leave another Marine aboard on account of serious wounds. Captain Lee refused to be evacuated. We were landed at the base of a hill outside the perimeter and had to fight our way into the perimeter. When we got to the top of the hill he was calling to and asking team leaders and squad leaders for ammo and personnel reports. At this time, the North Vietnamese were throwing grenades and firing small-arms from about fifteen meters. An air strike was going on at this time. Captain Lee moved about, directing fire and exposing himself to automatic weapons fire and grenades, even though he was wounded again. After this, he tried to find out what direction the main attack was coming from and if it was possible to get a relief force into the area to relieve the pressure from the men on the hill.

The Captain seemed to realize that it was impossible to get troops off the hill before daybreak due to the fact that the helicopters were receiving such heavy fire and four had already been shot down. The Captain called for a resupply of ammo and directed the resupply under continuous attack.

Every time you would talk the North Vietnamese would throw grenades, but the Captain kept both physical and voice contact with the squad leaders for reports and gave them instructions. At this time, a grenade went off near the Captain and he was wounded again with multiple wounds on his complete right side and eyes in addition to another missile wound he had received earlier. Even after receiving these wounds, the Captain kept on the radio in constant contact with Battalion and even helped direct resupply of urgently needed ammo.

Captain Lee remained in command until the battle was over, the helicopter pilot took over the next morning. The next morning we found dead North Vietnamese in, on, and around our positions, plus many automatic weapons and machine-guns. We found out later that we had held off a reinforced North Vietnamese company."

/S/ Lance Corporal Gary N. Butler

• • •

Chapter 3: Vietnam

The President of the United States takes pleasure in presenting the MEDAL OF HONOR to:

MAJOR HOWARD V. LEE
UNITED STATES MARINE CORPS

for service as set forth in the following citation:

"For conspicuous gallantry and intrepidity at the risk of his life above and beyond the call of duty as Commanding Officer, Company E, Second Battalion, Fourth Marines, Third Marine Division. A platoon of Major (then Captain) Lee's company, while on an operation deep in enemy territory, was attacked and surrounded by a large enemy force. Realizing that the unit had suffered numerous casualties, depriving it of effective leadership, and fully aware that the platoon even then was under heavy attack by the enemy, Maj. Lee took seven men and proceeded by helicopter to reinforce the beleaguered platoon. Maj. Lee disembarked from the helicopter with two of his men and, braving withering enemy fire, led them into the perimeter, where he fearlessly moved from position to position, directing and encouraging the overtaxed troops. The enemy then launched a massive attack with the full might of their forces. Although painfully wounded by fragments from an enemy grenade, including his eye, Maj. Lee continued undauntedly throughout the night to direct the valiant defense, coordinating supporting fire, and apprise higher headquarters of the plight of the platoon. The next morning he collapsed from his wounds and was forced to relinquish his command. However the small band of marines had held their position and repeatedly fought off many vicious enemy attacks for a grueling six hours until their evacuation was effected the following morning. Maj. Lee's actions saved his men from capture, minimized the loss of lives, and dealt the enemy a severe defeat. His indomitable fight-

ing spirit, superb leadership, and great personal valor in
the face of tremendous odds, reflect great credit upon him-
self and are in keeping with the highest traditions of the
Marine Corps and the U.S. Naval Service."

/S/ LYNDON B. JOHNSON

• • •

Name: Lieutenant Colonel William Groom Leftwich, Jr., USMC
(Deceased).

Biography: Written July, 1974.
Lieutenant Colonel William G. Leftwich, Jr., was born on April 28, 1931 in
Memphis, Tennessee, and graduated from Central High School in that city.
He was commissioned a Marine second lieutenant on June 5, 1953 upon
graduation from the United States Naval Academy. As brigade captain in
his senior year at the Naval Academy, he was specially commended at graduation for exemplary officer-like qualities which contributed "to the development of naval spirit and loyalty within the brigade."

Upon entering the Marine Corps, he completed the Basic School at
Marine Corps Schools, Quantico, Virginia, in January, 1954, and later served
as a rifle platoon commander with the 2d Marine Division at Camp Lejeune,
North Carolina. During 1955-56, he served with the 3rd Marine Division
on Okinawa. On his return to the United States, he was stationed at Camp
Pendleton, California, where he was promoted to captain in July, 1957. He
then began a three year assignment at the Naval Academy, serving as a
company officer. An excellent athlete himself, he also voluntarily performed
collateral duty as assistant varsity tennis coach and battalion football coach.

In 1960, he rejoined the 2d Marine Division, serving as a company
commander until 1962 when he was named aide-de-camp to the Commanding General. In June, 1963, he was assigned as aide to the Commandant,
Marine Corps Schools, Quantico. He was promoted to major in July, 1964.
He later completed a course of study in the Vietnamese language prior to
reporting for duty in Vietnam in January, 1965 as Assistant Senior Advisor
to the Vietnamese Marine Brigade.

Joining Task Force Alfa, he participated in 27 major operations against the Viet Cong in the central highlands of Vietnam, and spent more than 300 days in the field. He was wounded in the battle of Hoai An, March 9, 1965 and, besides the Purple Heart, was awarded the Navy Cross for extraordinary heroism.

He returned to the United States in January, 1966, served as an instructor at the Basic School, then completed the Command and Staff College in June, 1967 and was named to the School's Honor List. Assigned to Headquarters Marine Corps, he was promoted to lieutenant colonel in November, 1967 while serving as a systems analyst with the Manpower Management Information Branch, G-1 Division. He later became head of the Systems Analysis Section.

In 1968, Lieutenant Colonel Leftwich was selected by the Under Secretary of the Navy to be his Special Assistant and Marine Corps Aide. He served in this capacity under the Honorable Charles F. Baird, and Mr. Baird's successor as Under Secretary of the Navy, the Honorable John W. Warner.

In April, 1970, he began his second tour of duty in Vietnam, serving initially as an infantry battalion commander with the 2d Battalion, 1st Marines. On September 13, he assumed duty as Commanding Officer of the 1st Reconnaissance Battalion, 1st Marine Division (Reinforced).

On November 18, 1970, Lieutenant Colonel Leftwich was killed in a helicopter crash during an emergency extraction of one of his reconnaissance teams. In accordance with the practice of accompanying every emergency extraction called for by his reconnaissance teams, he was serving as senior "extract officer" for such a mission on the day of his death. The team had incurred casualties in an area beginning to be enveloped by dense fog. The team was extracted under Lieutenant Colonel Leftwich's personal supervision, then, as the helicopter began its ascent, it crashed into a mountainside in enemy territory, killing all aboard.

A partial list of his medals and awards includes: the Navy Cross, the Silver Star (posthumous), the Legion of Merit with Combat "V" and two Gold Stars, the Meritorious Service Medal, the Air Medal with one Gold Star, and the Purple Heart with two Gold Stars.

-USMC-

The following are an After Action report for Lieutenant Colonel Leftwich's Silver Star, his Navy Cross, Silver Star, and three Legion of Merit citations:

A. A. REPORT, SECOND BATTALION, FIRST MARINES

4 Aug. 1970

1450H - Heliborne assault of 3rd Platoon, Co. G and attachments landed on VC headquarters bunker complex at 1430H. VC were caught by surprise and attempted to flee. Ensuing chase combined C/C Huey as chase groups. Search and destroy action continued until 1720H when force was extracted by helicopter. 2/1 Recon Squad "Spooky Trip" left behind to ambush. Reaction force of one platoon plus one section of tanks positioned at BT 079641 to support "Spooky Trip" during the night. Engr. squad and demolitions will be flown in at 0630H to destroy bunker complex. Intend to terminate demo operations at 1000H and extract engr. squad and "Spooky Trip." Results of operation are: 12 VC/NVA KIA, 3 POW's, 9detainees, 4 AK-47's, 1 M-16, 1 SKS, 2 K-54 pistols, 12 K-26's, 2 Chi-Com's, 7 AK-47 Mag's, 5 K-16 Mag's, misc. 782 gear, medic supplies, foodstuffs, clothing and 2lbs. of documents.

· · ·

The President of the United States takes pleasure in presenting the NAVY CROSS to:

MAJOR WILLIAM G. LEFTWICH, JR.
UNITED STATES MARINE CORPS

for service as set forth in the following citation:

> *"For extraordinary heroism as the Senior Task Force Advisor to Task Force Alfa, Vietnamese Marine Brigade, in the vicinity of Hoai An Village, Binh Dinh Province, Republic of Vietnam, on 9 March, 1965. Major Leftwich played a major part in all phases of the successful relief of*

*the village of Hoai An, which was under heavy enemy at-
tack by two Viet Cong battalions. Prior to the actual operation, he worked out a plan with the 22d Division Air
Liaison Officer for supporting aircraft to deliver their ordnance in extra-close proximity to the front lines, and then
to continue simulated attacks while the Vietnamese Marines assaulted the enemy positions. He participated in the
planning of the approach march which, by using last minute
intelligence, avoided a massive ambush planned by the Viet
Cong. As lead elements of the Task Force contacted the
Viet Cong from an unexpected direction, he sensed the ideal
opportunity to use the pre-arranged air support plan, and
taking the radio, he moved under heavy fire to the for-
ward-most elements of the Task Force. By his own personal example of shooting point-blank and shouting, he
led the attack which overran the immediate Viet Cong positions and carried the assault to within forty meters of the
crest of a hill overlooking Hoai An. Despite injuries by
enemy machine-gun bullets in the back, cheek, and nose,
he went to the aid of a mortally wounded comrade, and
although bleeding profusely, he refused assistance and
delayed his own evacuation until he could call for additional air strikes and brief the Task Force Commander of
the situation. Through his heroic conduct and fearless devotion to duty in the face of personal risk, Major Leftwich
upheld the highest traditions of the Marine Corps and the
United States Naval Service."*

*For the President,
/S/ PAUL H. NITZE
Secretary of the Navy*

The President of the United States takes pride in presenting the SILVER
STAR MEDAL posthumously to:

Men of Honor

LIEUTENANT COLONEL WILLIAM G. LEFTWICH
UNITED STATES MARINE CORPS

for service as set forth in the following citation:

"For conspicuous gallantry and intrepidity in action while serving as Commanding Officer of the Second Battalion, First Marines, First Marine Division in connection with combat operations against the enemy in the Republic of Vietnam. On 4 August 1970, upon learning from intelligence sources that high level enemy commanders were planning to meet at a designated location in Quang Nam Province, Lieutenant Colonel Leftwich conceived a bold plan for an attack on the meeting place. Through expert analysis of all available intelligence data, he determined the exact location and time schedule of the proposed meeting, formulated a detailed plan, and alerted and briefed his attack force. Fully aware of the danger involved, he elected to forego the normal pre-landing reconnaissance activities and landing zone preparatory fires and, to avoid detection by the enemy, moved his men into the area by helicopters maneuvering at treetop level. Following his plan, Lieutenant Colonel Leftwich surreptitiously deployed his unit around the hostile headquarters and launched an aggressive attack which took the enemy commanders completely by surprise. When the now disorganized enemy attempted to escape, he directed his men in vigorous pursuit and disregarded his own safety as he moved to the most forward position to coordinate supporting arms fire. Under his dynamic and courageous leadership, his unit accounted for twelve enemy commanders killed, twelve others captured, and the seizure of seven weapons, and, according to subsequent intelligence reports, was instrumental in thwarting all planned enemy activity in the area. By his tactical skill, bold fighting spirit, and unflagging devotion to duty, Lieutenant Colonel Leftwich upheld the high-

est traditions of the Marine Corps and the United States
Naval Service."

For the President,
/S/ WILLIAM K. JONES
Commanding General, Fleet Marine Force, Pacific

In the name of the President of the United States, the Commander in Chief
U. S. Pacific Fleet takes pleasure in awarding the LEGION OF MERIT to:

MAJOR WILLIAM GROOM LEFTWICH, JR
UNITED STATES MARINE CORPS

for service as set forth in the following citation:

"For exceptionally meritorious conduct in the performance
of outstanding services as Senior Advisor to the Vietnamese Marine Task Force during operations conducted in
South Vietnam from 8 August to 17 August 1965. An extremely competent and resourceful leader and advisor,
Major Leftwich anticipated the problem of coordination
among three different elements operating simultaneously
and personally provided the missing unity of control by
organizing the advisors of the respective elements. As a
result, when the Viet Cong attacked the column, reaction
was immediate with a minimum of confusion and difficulty.
One of the Marine battalions, composed largely of recruits,
had not been previously battle tested. However, during the
engagement, the entire battalion stood fast and fought effectively as a direct result of the sound advice, and personal example provided by Major Leftwich. During the
course of that day's action, Major Leftwich moved to the
forward elements of his task force and, while under intense fire from the Viet Cong, directed numerous air strikes
on the enemy positions as close as 300 meters to the front

*lines of the Marine elements. By his outstanding leader-
ship, advice and judgment, as well as his inspiring devotion to duty, Major Leftwich upheld the highest traditions
of the United States Naval Service." Major Leftwich is
authorized to wear the Combat "V."*

/S/ ROY L. JOHNSON
Admiral, U.S. Navy

In the name of the President of the United States, the Commander in Chief
U. S. Pacific Fleet takes pleasure in awarding a GOLD STAR in lieu of the
second LEGION OF MERIT to:

MAJOR WILLIAM GROOM LEFTWICH, JR.
UNITED STATES MARINE CORPS

for service as set forth in the following citation:

*"For exceptionally meritorious conduct in the performing
outstanding service while serving with friendly foreign
forces engaged in armed conflict with the enemy from 27
January 1965 to 18 January 1966. As a member of the
Marine Advisory Unit, Naval Advisory Group, Military
Assistance Command, Vietnam, Major Leftwich served as
Senior Advisor to Vietnamese Marine Task Force ALFA.
During the entire period the Task Force was deployed under combat conditions in the hard pressed II Corps of central Vietnam, and participated in 25 major combat operations for a total of 235 days on actual combat operations.
He shared every physical hardship with his counterpart
by living and subsisting with the Vietnamese Marines.
During combat he was habitually exposed to enemy fire
and extremes of climate and rugged terrain. Through personal example, patience, persistence and outstanding professional knowledge, Major Leftwich was able to bring
about many necessary changes in tactics and organiza-*

tion of Vietnamese Marines Task Force ALFA. As Senior Advisor to Task Force ALFA he participated in the planning and execution of all operations, demonstrating rare ability as a leader, staff officer, and advisor. By his outstanding leadership, judgment, inspiring and courageous devotion to duty throughout, Major Leftwich upheld the highest traditions of the United States Naval Service." Major Leftwich is authorized to wear the Combat "V."

/S/ ROY L. JOHNSON
Admiral, U.S. Navy

The President of the United States takes pride in presenting a GOLD STAR in lieu of the third LEGION OF MERIT posthumously to:

LIEUTENANT COLONEL WILLIAM G. LEFTWICH
UNITED STATES MARINE CORPS

for service as set forth in the following citation:

"For exceptionally meritorious conduct in the performance of outstanding service with the First Marine Division in connection with combat operations against the enemy in the Republic of Vietnam from 16 May to 18 November 1970. Throughout this period, Lieutenant Colonel Leftwich performed his demanding in an exemplary and highly professional manner. Initially assigned as Commanding Officer of the Second Battalion, First Marines, he deployed his Battalion over a wide area and planned and supervised the execution of search and destroy operations, ambushes, and patrols which blocked the enemy's persistent attempts to launch offensives against friendly positions. Working tirelessly and with meticulous attention to detail, he implemented sound administrative and logistic procedures, organized a vigorous training program, and initiated several strategic innovations which confused the enemy and

significantly reduced friendly casualties. Under his dynamic and courageous leadership, his Battalion inflicted severe personnel losses on the North Vietnamese Army and Viet Cong forces, destroyed base camps and staging areas, and captured large quantities of supplies. Reassigned as Commanding Officer of the First Reconnaissance Battalion on 14 September, Lieutenant Colonel Leftwich quickly familiarized himself with the mission direction of his large unit and commenced an aggressive program to expand the response capability of his reconnaissance teams. With keen foresight and sound judgment, he established company-sized and platoon-sized patrol bases at key tactical locations to enable him to supply, deploy, and replace his patrols during adverse weather when helicopter support was not available, thus ensuring continuous ground support to his command. In addition, he pioneered the concept of employing reconnaissance teams with quick reaction forces and proved the value of this tactic in a series of combat actions in the Que Son Mountains. On 18 November 1970, Lieutenant Colonel Leftwich was killed when his helicopter crashed in rugged mountainous terrain while en route to extract a reconnaissance team from an enemy infested area. His extraordinary initiative and resourcefulness earned the respect and admiration of all who served with him and contributed immeasurably to the accomplishment of his command's mission. By his leadership, professional acumen, and unflagging devotion to duty, Lieutenant Colonel Leftwich rendered distinguished service to his country and thereby upheld the highest traditions of the Marine Corps and the United States Naval Service." The Combat Distinguished Device is authorized.

For the President,
/S/ WILLIAM K. JONES
Commanding General, Fleet Marine Force, Pacific

Chapter 3: Vietnam

• • •

Name: Major General James E. Livingston, USMC (Retired).

Biography: Revised August 4, 1995.
Major General James E. Livingston retired on September 1, 1995, following over 33 continuous years on active duty in the United States Marine Corps. His last assignment was the Commander of Marine Reserve Force in New Orleans, Louisiana.

He was commissioned a second lieutenant in June, 1962, following graduation from Auburn University. Early assignments included service as a platoon commander, intelligence officer, and as a Recruit Training Regiment series commander.

Promoted to captain in June,1966, General Livingston served as the Commanding Officer of the Marine Detachment aboard the Aircraft Carrier *USS WASP*, before joining the 3d Marine Division (Reinforced) in the Republic of Vietnam in August, 1967.

On May 2, 1968, while serving as Commanding Officer, Company E, 2d Battalion, 4th Marines, he distinguished himself above and beyond the call of duty in action against enemy forces, and earned the Congressional Medal of Honor.

After his second tour in Vietnam, General Livingston served as an instructor in the Army's Infantry School, Director of Division's Schools for the 1st Marine Division and, later, as S-3 of the 3d Battalion, 7th Marines. In March, 1975, he returned to Vietnam and served as Operations Officer for the Vietnam evacuation operations which included Operation "Frequent Wind," the evacuation of Saigon.

He then commanded the Marine Barracks, United Kingdom, London, and served as Commanding Officer, 3d Recruit Training Battalion and then as Assistant Chief of Staff for Operations and Training at the Marine Recruit Depot, Parris Island, South Carolina. During this period, he earned a masters degree in Management from Webster University. General Livingston then served with the 2d Marine Division and commanded the 6th Marines before joining the Joint U.S. Assistance Group in the Republic of the Philippines.

Following advancement to brigadier general on June 10, 1988, he served as Deputy Director for Operations at the National Military Command Center in Washington, D.C. During Operations Desert Shield and Desert Storm, General Livingston commanded the Marine Air Ground Combat Center, 29 Palms, California, and developed the Desert Warfare Training Program. After command of the 1st Marine Expeditionary Brigade, he was advanced to major general on July 8, 1991, and assumed command of the 4th Marine Division (Reinforced). In July, 1992, he assumed command of the newly created Marine Reserve Force, and continued through its reorganization in October, 1994, with its new title, Marine Forces Reserve.

Major General Livingston is a native of Towns, Georgia. He is a graduate of Amphibious Warfare School, the Marine Corps Command and Staff College, and the Air War College. His decorations include: the Medal of Honor; Distinguished Service Medal; Silver Star Medal; Defense Superior Service Medal; Bronze Star Medal with Combat "V"; and the Purple Heart, third Award.

Major General Livingston is married to the former Sara Craft. They have two daughters, Kimberly and Melissa. Kimberly, a graduate of the U.S. Naval Academy and Medical University of South Carolina, is currently assigned with the Portsmouth Naval Hospital. Melissa is attending Clemson University in South Carolina.

-USMC-

The following are the *narrative summary of gallant conduct* for which General Livingston received the Medal of Honor; nine eyewitness accounts; and the Medal of Honor, Silver Star Medal, and Bronze Star Medal citations:

Narrative Summary of Gallant Conduct

At first light on the morning of 2 May 1968, Echo Company, Battalion Landing Team 2/4, commanded by Captain Livingston, launched an assault against the heavily fortified village of Dai Do. The enemy had retaken Dai Do the night before with a strong counterattack which forced Golf Company, Battalion Landing Team 2/4 into a tight perimeter in the northeast corner of the village. Captain Livingston's mission was to drive the enemy from Dai Do, link up with Golf Company and together continue the advance northward into the village of Dinh To.

The assault commenced with Company "E" moving out across 500 meters of open rice paddy and into the enemy's trained and waiting sights. With uncanny employment of screening agents, Captain Livingston maneuvered his entire company through the hail of bullets and incoming rounds and up to the edge of the fortified enemy positions, sustaining only very light casualties in the process. In close quarters with the determined enemy now, Captain Livingston led a systematic, but savage, assault through the well-entrenched North Vietnamese Army positions. Moving fearlessly forward, and constantly exposing himself to enemy fire, he rallied his men to super-human feats in destroying more than a hundred mutually supporting A-frame bunkers, completely annihilating the estimated three companies of NVA who fought bravely and tenaciously for every inch of ground. The enemy was not to be routed without extracting his price from the assaulting Marines, however, and friendly casualties were also high. The loss of key personnel, coupled with the blistering enemy fire, caused the assault to bog down on at least six occasions. Each time, Captain Livingston jumped into the breach and reignited the faltering attack. Shouting words of encouragement, directing friendly fire, calling in supporting arms, he somehow managed to personally account for 14 enemy dead by his own hand. On two occasions he was painfully wounded by grenade fragments but refused treatment or evacuation. His gallantry and complete disregard for his personal safety were more than an inspiration to his men. His actions were the turning point on which the ensuing success hinged.

The village was now secured and the assault force linked up with Golf Company for consolidation. A hasty body count revealed 165 enemy dead with an undetermined number sealed within collapsed bunkers and caved-in trench lines. Captain Livingston still refused evacuation with the other wounded of his company.

Company H, Battalion Landing Team 2/4 continued the attack north to the village of Dinh To, moving through the consolidated positions of Companies E and G. They were immediately met with heavy opposition but pressed on into a steadily worsening situation. Friendly casualties mounted at a staggering rate, enemy obstacles became almost impenetrable, and the attack had lost its momentum. Company H was badly in need of assistance, and the following are the words of an eyewitness, the Executive Officer of the beleaguered company: "The word was passed that Echo was coming up, and I turned and saw Captain Livingston for the first time that day. With the incoming rounds whistling past his ears and kicking up dust at his feet, he walked tall and erect up to our lines at the head of his men. With forces joined Hotel and Echo advanced again into the fire. Captain Livingston and I were in visual contact during most of the fight and I never once saw him take cover on take a backward step. Instead, with complete disregard for his personal safety, he moved among his troops, encouraging, comforting, urging, pushing and pulling them to perform virtually super human feats."

With this new momentum gained, the enemy was driven from its positions, but within moments came back with a fierce battalion-sized counterattack, forcing the friendly forces to withdraw and consolidate. Throughout this action, Captain Livingston repeatedly exposed himself to the withering fire to direct the orderly withdrawal, and personally killed 11 more of the enemy. Again painfully wounded, this time with a machine-gun bullet through his thigh, and though unable to walk and weak from loss of blood, he refused evacuation once more, and continued to direct his unit all casualties were evacuated and his men were safely out of the village, now swarming with enemy troops.

The three day battle, which commenced on 30 April 1968, and in which Captain Livingston's heroism played a vital role, netted 805 NVA killed, as opposed to 72 friendly KIA's.

The facts contained in this narrative summary are based on the statements of eyewitnesses.

Statements of Witnesses

"On May 2, Company E was given the mission to help in the assault of Dai Do. After crossing an open field the company began receiving light small-arms fire from the edge of the village. Captain Livingston continued to maneuver his three platoons and one platoon was able to continue the assault with Company G. The other two platoons were pinned down for a few minutes and lost contact with Company G.

To perform his mission of securing the village, Captain Livingston brought his CP on line with the remainder of the two platoons and continued to sweep through the village. He was constantly in the front line of the assault attempting to get enemy soldiers out of a bunker or just checking a bunker out.

Shortly after securing Dai Do, Company E was sent to assist Company H assault the next village to the north. Upon reaching Company H's position, we found that they were in fairly heavy contact and unable to advance. Again Captain Livingston put his company and CP on line and successfully moved by fire and movement to the next treeline. Again Captain Livingston was at the front of his company exposing himself to enemy fire. After reaching the treeline the company began taking heavy casualties and the decision was made to begin retrograde movements. Captain insured all the casualties were out before anyone else moved. He continued to remain with the last of the company insuring all of his men made it out of the area safely; often he was almost acting as rear security.

He only began moving with the front elements of the company after being wounded and required assistance.

Captain Livingston's actions throughout the day are just another example of his professionalism plus his complete disregard for his own safety while moving his company."

/S/ 1st Lieutenant M. L. Cecil

"On 2 May 1968, Hotel Company was ordered to attack and seize the fortified village of Dinh To which, it turned out, was occupied by a numerically superior force of NVA. Hotel was to advance through Echo Company which was deployed on the northern edge of Dai Do (the village bordering Dinh To on the south) and continue the attack. We were deployed with two platoons up and one back. Although the Executive Officer, I had taken command of our third platoon due to the lack of officers and staff and we were on the left front of Hotel's formation. We were taken under fire immediately upon entering Dinh Do. First sniper fire then rapidly increasing in volume with automatic rifles, machine-guns, RPGs and hand and rifle grenades. Friendly casualties mounted at a staggering rate, it seemed among key personnel: radiomen, squad and fire team leaders, etc. Hotel continued to advance. Movement became increasingly difficult due to the shrubbery and bamboo hedgerows. We would assault across the open then falter at the obstacles. Weapons had begun to jam, ammo was low, men were exhausted, and our numbers were dwindling. In short, against the devastating opposition we were losing our momentum. The word was passed "Echo is coming up" and I turned and saw Captain Livingston for the first time that day. With the incoming rounds whistling past his ears and kicking up dust at his feet, he walked tall and erect up to our lines at the head of his men. With forces joined Hotel and Echo advanced again into the fire. Captain Livingston and I were in visual contact most of the fight and I never once saw him take cover or a backward step, instead with complete disregard for his personal safety he moved among his troops encouraging, threatening, comforting, urging, pushing and pulling them to virtually super human feats. Under his direction Captain Livingston's men repulsed two heavy counterattacks and during the last one he himself was shot through the leg. Even wounded Captain Livingston continued to shout encouragement and guidance until he was evacuated during Hotel and Echo's withdrawal and consolidation. Seldom does one see such unselfish bravery under more difficult circumstances. By his personal example Captain Livingston contributed a great deal to our final success."

/S/ 1st Lieutenant B. V. Taylor

"During Company E's assault on the village of Dai Do on May 2, 1968, the company met heavy resistance from a numerically superior force of regular NVA. Captain Livingston displayed great professionalism in his actions as Company Commander. He was in the front lines directing fire with no apparent concern for his own safety. Captain Livingston once again showed bravery when removing wounded Marines from the field of battle while the enemy still fired a heavy volume of small-arms and automatic weapons fire into the company area."

/S/ PFC. Joseph E. Wood

"On 2 May 1968, Captain Livingston Led his company into the village of Dai Do, Republic of Vietnam. After advancing to the edge of the village the company met heavy resistance with a numerically superior enemy force. The heavy volume of enemy fire and the mounting casualties forced Captain Livingston to pull back and regroup his men to continue the attack.

After regrouping his men, Captain Livingston again entered the village. Through the day-long battle the enemy had provided stiff resistance and it became apparent that the village could not be secured by night. Captain Livingston gave the order to begin a retrograde action making sure all the wounded were evacuated. Captain Livingston and his radio operator were the last to leave the village making sure all Marines were out."

/S/ L/Cpl. Larry R. Mulligan

"On 2 May 1968 at approximately 1015 hours, Company E was in an attack on the village of Dai Do. This was the third day of a continuous battle. Company E was meeting a stiff resistance from a well entrenched enemy. Captain Livingston picked up an M-14 rifle and moved to the head of his assault troops and began shouting orders and words of encouragement. Thus he inspired his company to continue the assault. After we secured the village I was instructed to take care of the casualties and I did not observe Captain Livingston the rest of the day."

/S/ Gunnery Sergeant Roscoe Chandler, Jr.

"On 2 May 1968, Company E assaulted the village of Dai Do. Approximately 150 meters from the village we were taken under fire by enemy small-arms. Captain Livingston successfully maneuvered the company to the village edge where fierce fighting took place. Even though taking many casualties, Captain Livingston continued to encourage his men often at the risk of his own safety. He assured that all the casualties were removed from the battle field and taken to the rear area for evacuation. He continued to maneuver his unit through the village with himself in the lead elements directing fire, shouting encouragement, and throwing grenades. The assault continued until the entire village had been secured.

Later the same day Captain Livingston led the attack on a second objective. The enemy mounted a counterattack and forced the company to begin a retrograde movement. Although painfully wounded in the initial enemy attack, he remained in the village refusing medical evacuation until he assured all casualties were removed."

/S/ Sergeant Kenneth E. Johnson

"On the 2nd of May 1968, at about 0700, Echo Company, BLT, 2d Battalion, 4th Marines departed for their mission, which was to assault and take the village of Dai Do, which at the time was heavily fortified by numerous NVA troops and crew served weapons. Captain Livingston, who was the Company Commander at this time, started moving his men out in an assault formation. As the point elements of the Company started to near the edge of the village they were taken under heavy fire. Taking a large amount of casualties all the time. Captain Livingston continued to encourage his men to continue their assault because we were now overcoming the enemy's main defense and we were pushing them back and the enemy was now suffering numerous casualties. At this the Marines kept pushing the assault until we were inside the village and had taken about half of the village. We also suffered heavy casualties. After this, Captain Livingston himself was carrying wounded Marines to safety. Captain Livingston then regrouped all the remaining troops and got them on line, including the Company CP, in order to make the assault element stretch across the village. After getting all of the troops ready to continue the rest of the assault, Captain Livingston led the assault himself. After finishing the remainder of the assault, Captain Livingston had the remainder of his Company set up security and to rest.

About one hour later we got the order to sweep to a connecting village to reinforce Hotel Company, which was under heavy fire and partly pinned down. At this order Captain Livingston then moved his men out. When we reached Hotel Company we were also taken under heavy enemy fire. At this we tied in with Hotel Company and Captain Livingston started pushing the enemy back, but the enemy force was too large for the remainder of the two companies. Huey Gunships were called in for support and while the gunships were pounding the enemy Captain Livingston started pulling his men back. Not until all casualties were pulled back, and most of the men, did he pull back. While pulling back Captain Livingston, still calling in support for the gunships, was shot and badly wounded to where he had to be medevaced. Throughout the day Captain Livingston showed outstanding leadership, courage, and heroism in leading his Marines."

/S/ L/Cpl. Patrick J. Haines.

"On 2 May 1968, Company E was pinned down in a trench line in the village of Dinh To. All attempts to continue the assault had resulted in the company's sustaining heavy casualties and the company's right flank had been severely threatened. Captain Livingston, who was the Company Commander, passed the word to start pulling out, moving the wounded out first. After personally insuring that all the wounded were removed he remained in the trench line until almost all of his company had pulled back. His enthusiasm at this time and personal leadership were an inspiration to his men and kept the retrograde movement organized even though the enemy continued to fire a heavy volume of small-arms and automatic weapons fire into the company area.

After pulling back a short distance the company was once again hit from the right flank. Captain Livingston personally directed a heavy volume of fire into the flanking element forcing them to retreat. At this time he was wounded in the right leg by enemy small-arms fire. Captain Livingston refused medical evacuation and continued the retrograde movement. His personal enthusiasm and leadership proved essential in the maintaining of unit integrity under counterattack by the enemy."

/S/ Sergeant Albert G. Bothe

The President of the United States in the name of the Congress takes pleasure in presenting the MEDAL OF HONOR to:

CAPTAIN JAMES E. LIVINGSTON
UNITED STATES MARINE CORPS

for service as set forth in the following citation:

"For conspicuous gallantry and intrepidity at the risk of his life above and beyond the call of duty while serving as

Men of Honor

Commanding Officer, Company E, Second Battalion, Fourth Marines, Ninth Marine Amphibious Brigade in action against enemy forces in the Republic of Vietnam. On 2 May 1968, Company E launched a determined assault on the heavily fortified village of Dai Do, which had been seized by the enemy on the preceding evening isolating a Marine company from the remainder of the battalion. Skillfully employing screening agents, Captain Livingston maneuvered his men to assault positions across 500 meters of dangerous open rice paddy while under intense enemy fire. Ignoring hostile rounds impacting near him, he fearlessly led his men in a savage assault against enemy emplacements within the village. While adjusting supporting arms fire, Captain Livingston moved to the points of heaviest resistance, shouting words of encouragement to his Marines, directing their fire, and spurring the dwindling momentum of the attack on repeated occasions. Although twice painfully wounded by grenade fragments, he refused medical treatment and courageously led his men in the destruction of over 100 mutually supporting bunkers, driving the remaining enemy from their positions, and relieving the pressure on the stranded Marine company. As the two companies consolidated positions and evacuated casualties, a third company passed through the friendly lines launching an assault on the adjacent village of Dinh To, only to be halt by a furious counterattack by an enemy battalion. Swiftly assessing the situation and disregarding the heavy volume of enemy fire, Captain Livingston boldly maneuvered the remaining effective men of his company forward, joined forces with the heavily engaged Marines, and halted the enemy's counterattack. Wounded a third time and unable to walk, he steadfastly remained in the dangerously exposed area, deploying his men to more tenable positions and supervising the evacuation of casualties. Only when assured of the safety of his men did he allow himself to be evacuated. Captain

Livingston's gallant action uphold the highest traditions of the Marine Corps and the United States Naval Service."

/S/ RICHARD M. NIXON

The President of the United States takes pleasure in presenting the SILVER STAR MEDAL to:

CAPTAIN JAMES E. LIVINGSTON
UNITED STATES MARINE CORPS

for action as set forth in the following citation:

"For conspicuous gallantry and intrepidity in action while serving as Commanding Officer, Company E, Second Battalion, Fourth Marines, Ninth Marine Amphibious Brigade in connection with operations against the enemy in the Republic of Vietnam. On 18 March 1968, Captain Livingston's company was participating in a battalion assault against North Vietnamese Army positions in the fortified village of Vinh Quan Thoung in Quang Tri Province when a platoon from an adjacent company became pinned down the heavy enemy fire. In an attempt to relieve the beleaguered unit, Captain Livingston maneuvered his company forward until the intensity of the fire from the enemy's well placed, mutually supporting bunkers forced his unit to withdraw to a more advantageous position. Coordinating with the commander of the second company, he then led his unit forward under cover of supporting air strikes and again was halted by the hostile fire. Observing a third company commence an assault against the enemy's flank, Captain Livingston completely disregarded his own safety as he jumped to his feet during a heavy rocket attack, rallied his men and led them in an aggressive charge against the North Vietnamese positions. His bold actions inspired all who observed him as the Marines seized the village,

inflicting 127 North Vietnamese confirmed killed. By his courage, gallant leadership, and selfless devotion to duty at great personal risk, Captain Livingston upheld the highest traditions of the Marine Corps and the United States Naval Service."

For the President,
/S/ V. H. KRULAK
Commanding General, Fleet Marine Force, Pacific

The President of the United States takes pleasure in presenting the BRONZE STAR MEDAL to:

CAPTAIN JAMES E. LIVINGSTON
UNITED STATES MARINE CORPS

for action as set forth in the following citation:

"For heroic achievement in connections with operations against insurgent communist (Viet Cong) forces in the Republic of Vietnam while serving as Commanding Officer of Company E, Second Battalion, Fourth Marines, Ninth Marine Amphibious Brigade. On 13 March 1968, Captain Livingston led his unit in an attack on an enemy occupied position in Quang Tri Province. Immediately after crossing a river, the Marines come under intense small-arms, mortar, and artillery fire, forcing them to seek cover along the river bank. For two hours Captain Livingston repeatedly maneuvered his unit in an attempt to breach the enemy defense. Ordered to withdraw his unit, he fearlessly moved about the fire- swept terrain, supervising the withdrawal and insuring that all of his men, including casualties, had moved from the hazardous area. Observing an amphibian vehicle, he unhesitatingly exposed himself to the hostile fire and, climbing on top of the vehicle, removed two machine-guns, thereby preventing the weapons from

being seized by the enemy. Captain Livingston's courage, superb leadership, and unwavering devotion to duty in the face of great personal danger inspired all who served with him and were in keeping with the highest traditions of the Marine Corps and of the United States Naval Service. "Captain Livingston is authorized to wear the Combat "V."
For the President,
/S/ V. H. KRULAK
Commanding General, Fleet Marine Force, Pacific

• • •

Name: Major Stephen W. Pless, USMC (Deceased).

Biography: Revised November, 1969.

Major Stephen W. Pless, 29, Medal of Honor winner and one of America's most decorated heroes, who survived 780 combat helicopter missions in Vietnam, was killed July 20, 1969, when his motorcycle plunged off an open drawbridge into Santa Rosa Sound which separates Pensacola from Pensacola Beach, Florida.

Pless was the 18th Marine to receive the Medal of Honor for heroism in Vietnam. It was presented to him by President Lyndon B. Johnson in ceremonies held at the White House, January 16, 1969.

Stephen Wesley Pless was born September 6, 1939, in Newnam, Georgia. He attended Decatur High School at Decatur, Georgia, and graduated from Georgia Military Academy, College Park, Georgia, in 1957.

While at Georgia Military Academy, he enlisted in the U.S. Marine Corps Reserve, September 6, 1956, and served with the 1st Motor Transport Battalion, USMCR, Atlanta, Georgia. He received recruit training and advanced combat training at Parris Island, South Carolina, graduating in October, 1957. He then served as an Artillery Surveyor, 10th Marine Regiment, 2d Marine Division, until September, 1958.

While attending flight training at Pensacola, Florida, he was commissioned a Marine Corps second lieutenant, September 16, 1959. He was promoted to first lieutenant March 16, 1960, and designated a Naval aviator upon graduation from flight training April 20, 1960.

Lieutenant Pless next served successively as Squadron Pilot with HMR(L)-262, MAG-26, at New River, North Carolina; with HMR(L)-264 aboard the *USS BOXER*; with HMR(L)-262 aboard the *USS WASP*; again with the HMR(L)-262, MAG-26, at New River; as Assistant Administrative Officer of HMR(L)-262 aboard the *USS SHADWELL*; and as Squadron Adjutant, HMM-162, MAG- 16, at New River.

Ordered to the Far East in June, 1962, he saw duty as Assistant Administrative Officer of HMM-162, MAG-26, in Thailand, and at Da Nang, in the Republic of Vietnam.

Upon his return to the United States in June, 1963, he reported to the Naval Air Station, Pensacola, Florida, and served as Basic Flight Instructor, VT-1, and later as Officer in Charge, Aviation Officer Candidate School. He was promoted to captain July 1, 1964.

After his detachment in April, 1966, Captain Pless was assigned duty as Brigade Platoon Commander, 1st Anglico, Marine Corps Air Station, Kaneohe, Hawaii. In August, 1966, he became Officer in Charge, ROK Detachment, and later Brigade Air Officer, 1st Anglico, Sub Unit 1, with the 2d Brigade Korean Marine Corps, at Chu Lai, in the Republic of Vietnam. For his service in this capacity, he was awarded a Bronze Star Medal and the Korean Order of Military Merit. He was awarded the Medal of Honor, the Silver Star Medal, the Distinguished Flying Cross, the Purple Heart for wounds received, and 32 Air Medals for his service as Assistant Operations Officer, VMD-6, MAG-36, 1st Marine Aircraft Wing, in the Republic of Vietnam, from March 20, 1967 until September 22, 1967.

Upon his return to the United States, he assumed duties as Administrative Assistant, Officer Candidate School, Naval Air Station, Pensacola, Florida. While serving in that capacity he was promoted to major, November 7, 1967. He was killed as a result of a motorcycle accident, July 20, 1969.

Major Pless was awarded the Avco-Aviation/Space Writers Association Helicopter Heroism Award for his heroic rescue of three wounded American soldiers in Vietnam on August 19, 1967.

A list of Major Pless' medals and decorations include: the Medal of Honor, Silver Star Medal, Distinguished Flying Cross, Bronze Star Medal, Air Medal with seven Silver Stars and two Gold Stars in lieu of second through 38 awards, Navy Commendation Medal with Combat "V", and the Purple Heart.

The following are six eyewitness accounts of Major Pless' actions; his Medal of Honor, Silver Star, Distinguished Flying Cross, and Bronze Star citations:

Statement of Witnesses

"I was flying on a Med-Evac mission, with Captain Pless and Captain Fairfield acting as pilot and co-pilot. Lance Corporal Phelps was our crew chief. We received an urgent distress message from "Land Shark" (I believe) to all planes in the area for help. The word was that an Army helicopter had gone down and four men had been captured by the Viet Cong. Captain Pless said "shall we help them" and we all put our "thumbs up" indicating we were with him. When we arrived in the area we could see the Viet Cong down below; I also saw four uniformed men being beaten by the Viet Cong. Captain Pless gave the order for me to fire. I fired close to the perimeter of the Viet Cong and they all took off in a group for a tree line near a village. Captain Pless, with a great show of airmanship, rolled in and shot his rockets into the fleeing Viet Cong. Captain Pless then did a hard left and strafed the 'ville and tree line, while Lance Corporal Phelps and I fired our internal machine-guns. Captain Pless' airmanship was so fantastic in his gun runs and maneuvering of the helicopter, it was hard to believe if you were not there. After several gun runs we landed on the beach. I unplugged my headset, and jumped out of the aircraft to get to the wounded. Lance Corporal Phelps immediately came over to my internal gun and covered me as I went over to check the Med-Evacs. Lance Corporal Phelps did an outstanding job of cover fire and I owe my life to his accurate fire. The first Med-Evac was fairly easy to get to the airplane because he could walk with my aid. After putting him in the aircraft, I went out to get another man. The second man was a large man, and was down in a gully or tide-line type place. I was having a hard time with him. As I bent over to try to pick him up, a round hit right above me. I waved for help, because every time I tried to pick the man up, I would sink into the sand. Captain Fairfield came to my aid and we dragged the man into the aircraft. Captain Fairfield and I went out to get the third man. He was heavier than the second man, so

Lance Corporal Phelps came out to help us. Lance Corporal Phelps and Captain Fairfield were at each arm and I had the man by his legs. At the same time they were carrying the man, they were firing at the enemy with their revolvers. At one time, Lance Corporal Phelps dropped the man we were carrying and shot a Viet Cong that was about ten or fifteen feet from us. This Med-Evac was about thirty to forty feet from the helicopter and was quite difficult to get into the aircraft. We finally got him into the bird. We were receiving heavy automatic fire at all times while we were on the beach. I had determined that the fourth man was dead, for when I checked him, he appeared to have his throat cut and was not breathing and had no heart beat. We did not go back to get him. Captain Fairfield also went over to check this man and also felt he was dead.

As we were putting the third Med-Evac into the aircraft, an Army Huey began to strafe the 'ville and tree lines to keep the enemy away from us. Without their support, we would have been unable to complete our mission.

As we put the Med-Evac in the aircraft, an H-34 landed on the beach. I later found out that it was an ARVN aircraft. We took off, so I cannot say if he picked up the last body. As we took off, we had extreme difficulty getting airborne. We skipped across the water and Captain Pless, with another outstanding show of airmanship, managed to get us airborne. We were taking heavy fire on take-off, but made it. Once we were airborne, we took the wounded men directly to the First Hospital Company at Chu Lai, applying first aid enroute. Following their delivery, we returned to Ky Ha."

/S/ Gunnery Sergeant Leroy N. Poulson

"On 19 August 1967, I was assigned as co-pilot of an armed UH-1E helicopter which was acting as chase aircraft for the Medical Evacuation H-34. Captain Pless was the pilot of the gunship and Gunnery Sergeant Poulson and Lance Corporal Phelps were serving as gunner and crew chief. At approximately 1600, we received an emergency Med-Evac mission and, because the H-34 was experiencing mechanical difficulties, we decided to launch and proceed independently to the Medical Evacuation site. While enroute we heard several transmissions on "Guard" channel to the effect that an aircraft had been badly shot up and was proceeding to Duc Pho following a landing on the beach south of Chu Lai, and that the Viet Cong had taken four Americans prisoner. Captain Pless transmitted on "Guard" that we were a Huey gunship with a full load of fuel and ordnance and asked if we could be of any assistance. Although the transmission was not acknowledged, we had by this time deduced the location of the action and I had also ascertained that our original mission, the evacuation of one wounded Korean Marine, could be accomplished by the H-34 without our escort. I advised the Medical Evacuation helicopter that the zone was secure and that we were proceeding to the area where the four Americans had been captured. As we neared the mouth of the Song Tra Khuc, we observed a number of explosions on the beach approximately one mile north.

The explosions stopped abruptly and thirty to fifty armed Viet Cong ran from the tree-line onto the beach. Captain Pless asked "how we felt about going down", and I turned to give the thumbs-up signal to Gunnery Sergeant Poulson; he and Lance Corporal Phelps quickly returned the signal, and we began preparing our ordnance while Captain Pless dove the aircraft at the Viet Cong on the beach. As we passed directly over the top of the Viet Cong at an altitude of less than fifty feet, we saw the four American prisoners lying on the sand. One Viet Cong had a rifle and was smashing one of the prisoners in the head. However, another prisoner managed to raise his hand and wave.

Captain Pless ordered Gunnery Sergeant Poulson to open fire with his door gun. As he did, the Viet Cong abandoned the four Americans and ran into a tree-line only thirty meters from the beach. Captain Pless immediately pulled the aircraft into a near wingover to the right and fired fourteen rockets into the mass of Viet Cong. Our white phosphorus rockets scored direct hits on the Viet Cong, but the smoke obscured the trees and the enemy. Our rockets expended, Captain Pless repeatedly made machine-gun runs, firing into the smoke and through the trees at an altitude so low that the windscreen quickly became covered with mud. Although we were receiving intense fire from automatic weapons, the smoke and our low altitude must have prevented us from taking any hits. Our ordnance was almost exhausted and Captain Pless transmitted "I'm going to land."

He flared the aircraft to a spot on the beach directly between the four Americans and the Viet Cong and continued firing from a hover. Then he kicked the aircraft around, pointed the nose of the aircraft seaward, and landed, thus utilizing the aircraft itself as a shield for the four Americans.

Gunnery Sergeant Poulson jumped onto the beach and assisted the only American capable of walking back to the helicopter. Lance Corporal Phelps continued firing for a few seconds at several Viet Cong who attempted to close with us from our left rear, and then he, too, jumped from the aircraft to help carry the three remaining men. I also unstrapped and exited the aircraft through the right rear door. As I came out, I suddenly saw three Viet Cong with rifles less than ten feet from the rear of the helicopter. I removed the right door machine-gun and killed them. I then ran out to assist Gunnery Sergeant Poulson and Lance Corporal Phelps. As I reach the beach, I saw more Viet Cong trying to over run us and ordered Phelps back to his machine-gun. The soft, powdery sand made it impossible to carry the largest American, and Gunnery Sergeant Poulson and I literally dragged him to the aircraft. Then Gunnery Sergeant Poulson, Lance Corporal Phelps, and I ran onto the beach and picked up the third American and carried him to the aircraft. All the while, Lance Corporal Phelps and I continued firing with pistols at Viet Cong who kept appearing on the small sand dunes overlooking the beach.

Then, I ran to the fourth man, but failing to detect heartbeat or pulse, I became certain he was dead. He had been badly mutilated and his throat was slashed. I looked for dog-tags but found none. I ran back to the helicopter and noticed that the small-arms fire had intensified. I jumped in and told Captain Pless that the fourth man was dead. Gunnery Sergeant Poulson affirmed that he, too, had checked the man and thought him dead.

Then Captain Pless and I saw a Vietnamese H-34 approaching from the water, and an Army Huey began strafing runs on the Viet Cong positions. I yelled at Captain Pless that the Vietnamese helicopter would pick up the dead man and that we should try to save the three wounded we had with us.

Our aircraft was at least five hundred pounds heavier than maximum take-off weight, and our skids hit the water four times before we finally became airborne. We jettisoned our empty rocket pods, and tossed out all our armor plating. While Captain Pless continued forcing the aircraft to fly, Gunnery Sergeant Poulson and Lance Corporal Phelps rendered first aid to the three wounded men. I contacted our controlling agencies, told them our position, and requested that they cancel all artillery between our position and First Hospital at Chu Lai. We landed at First Hospital a few minutes later, where we discharged our passengers. We then returned to Ky Ha."

/S/ Captain Rupert E. Fairfield

"On 19 August 1967, Captain Pless, Captain Fairfield, Gunnery Sergeant Poulson, and myself were assigned as the crew on an armed UH-1E helo on Med-Evac chase. We had just refueled and headed out on another mission, a Med-Evac pick-up in the ROK area, with the Med-Evac pick-up bird a few minutes behind us. On our way to this next pick-up, we received a call on "Guard" from an unidentified aircraft. The message was that an aircraft had been shot up, and that four of the personnel on board had been taken by the V.C.

We called on "Guard" and answered the call with "we are a fully armed UH-1E gunship and are in the area. Can we give assistance?" Our call was not answered, but we continued to the area. The aircraft in distress had said they were a mile or so north of the mouth of the Song Tra Khuc River.

When we approached the area, Captain Pless asked the crew, "you all with me?" He knew the answer would be yes. As we flew on, we saw four U.S. personnel laying on the beach, and around them, not less than forty or fifty armed Viet Cong. They, the V.C., were beating the helpless personnel. As we flew over the group of people, one of the men laying on the beach waved to us, and for his efforts got a rifle butt in the face. The V.C. were to close to the Americans to safely fire at them, but the V.C. were killing them anyway, so Captain Pless ordered the right door gunner, Gunnery Sergeant Poulson, to fire on them. It took only a short burst to send the V.C. running for cover. When Captain Pless saw this, he immediately rolled in hot with rockets and guns. The smoke from our W.P. rockets obscured the V.C. who were running when we started our attacks, but Captain Pless continued to fire into the smoke, displaying the most remarkable airmanship I have ever seen in my eighteen months in country as an air crewman. As crew chief of the aircraft, and knowing its capabilities, I couldn't believe what he was making the helo do, but when the smoke started to clear, I saw bodies laying everywhere.

We then flew to the edge of the water where the badly hurt Americans were located. Before setting down, Captain Pless pointed the guns of the aircraft into the 'ville and fired off the remaining ammo. In landing, Captain Pless put the aircraft between the wounded men and the Viet Cong. The way he had landed put me facing the V.C.; I started firing my M-60, while the gunner, being on the side next to the wounded, jumped out and ran to the men. Picking up the first man who was the closest, he helped him into the aircraft; this man was still conscious, and didn't seem to be in bad shape. Then the gunner, Gunnery Sergeant Poulson, ran to the next man, tried to pick him up, but found that the man was far to heavy to carry by himself. The co-pilot, Captain Fairfield, and myself seeing this, jumped from the aircraft and started to run over to Gunnery Sergeant Poulson to help him. When several V.C., who were out of my line of fire, came running down the beach, Captain Fairfield pulled the other door gun off its mount and fired at the V.C., killing all with the first short burst. At this time, Captain Fairfield told me to return to the aircraft to provide covering fire.

Then more V.C. came running at the aircraft from the 'ville, shooting as they came. I fired until they all lay on the sand. Some of the V.C. were still shooting at the plane; I couldn't see them, but I could see the sand kicking up all around the plane. I kept my gun going, firing in the tree-line and under bushes at the end of the beach. About this time, the co-pilot and gunner came back to the plane with the second man, then went back for the third. Captain Pless, seeing that the third man was far to much for Captain Fairfield and Gunnery Sergeant Poulson to handle, told me to go out and help them. I gave my gun to the one wounded man who was still conscious, and asked him if he thought he could use it; he said "yes", so I jumped out and ran to the other man. The three of us could move him, and we were about twenty feet from the aircraft, when a lone V.C. with a hand grenade of some kind came running from behind the plane. I let go of the wounded man and drew my pistol, firing all six rounds into the Viet Cong. He was only about ten of fifteen feet away, so I knew I was hitting him. We got the last man into the aircraft, and started to take off, but the plane was so heavy that we could hardly get off the ground. We had to take off over the water because we were taking so much fire. One Army gun bird, a UH-1E like ours, tried to suppress the fire and give us cover. After a few frightening moments, we lifted off. On our way to the 1st Hospital Company, we rendered first aid to the wounded men. We then returned to Ky Ha."

Chapter 3: Vietnam

/S/ Lance Corporal John G. Phelps

On 19 August 1967, our aircraft was struck by ground fire and forced down on the beach south of Chu Lai. The crew chief and myself, along with two other NCOs climbed out to check the extent of the damage. Three of us set up a security guard between the helicopter and the inland position of the beach. At this time, a grenade thrown by a Viet Cong exploded near the front of the aircraft. We attempted to withdraw to the helicopter, but the pilot had already lifted off. We then ran back to our position behind a sand dune. We began to receive a barrage of grenades; we returned fire, but soon ran out of ammo. The Viet Cong then moved in close and threw more grenades. Everyone was wounded by this time, when one Viet Cong appeared on our flank with an automatic weapon. His fire struck everyone but me. I crawled next to the sand dune and tried to pass as dead. I could hear the Viet Cong move among us, removing our weapons. At this time, I heard two explosions. I looked up and saw a Huey gunship making rocket and gun runs on the Viet Cong, who were returning the fire as they attempted to flee into the brush along the beach. At this time, several Hueys were orbiting the area, but Captain Pless' aircraft was the only one to come to our aid. After making several attacks, Captain Pless landed by us on the beach. I was moved to the aircraft, then the crew members of the helicopter moved out to recover my buddies. I could hear small-arms fire all around us. I tried to lay down fire with one of the aircraft's internal guns while the crew members loaded the others aboard. When the other survivors were on the aircraft, we lifted out. If it were not for the actions of Captain Pless and his crew, I am sure all of us would have been killed."

/S/ Staff Sergeant Lawrence H. Allen

"On 19 August 1967, we took off from Ky Ha enroute to the 196th Brigade VIP pad for a 1630 pick-up. On our way, we heard a distress call come over the "Guard" channel. We proceeded directly to the area of the distress call. When we arrived, we saw twenty to thirty people on the beach. We did not know the difference or position of Americans or Viet Cong. We started circling the area. Approximately thirty seconds later, a Marine gunship made a pass and started the attack. We proceeded to cover the gunship with our two door guns. After four or five passes, the gunship landed on the beach, where we saw four bodies laying. As soon as the ship hit the beach, the crew jumped to help the wounded. We gave them as much cover as our couple of door gunners could give. We emptied both guns before the ship left the beach. He was on the beach helping the wounded for at least five to ten minutes. We never had communications with Captain Pless while he was on the beach. We understood that all the Americans were dead.

Without communications and without protection that he knew of, Captain Pless took a gunship down twenty-five meters from hostile fire and performed the most outstanding Med-Evac I have ever witnessed. During his few gun runs, I would estimate five to ten enemy kills."

/S/ Warrant Officer Ronald L. Redeker

"On 19 August 1967, at approximately 1615, we received a "Mayday" call shortly after departing Ky Ha. We went straight to the area that was described as being one mile north of the Quang Ngai River along the beach. When we arrived, we could see four people on the beach under mortar fire. About thirty meters from the four persons on the beach, we could observe approximately thirty-five V.C., with weapons, firing at them. The mortar fire stopped, and about fifteen V.C. ran out towards the people on the beach. It was at this time that a Marine gunship made a very low pass, driving the V.C. back into the tree-line. At this point we began to cover the Marine ship. The Marine ship, after making the first pass, did hovering turns, firing rockets into the retreating V.C., and went up and down the tree-line strafing the V.C. at tree-top level. We could observe the V.C. firing back, but with no apparent effect. The Marine ship then landed next to the four persons on the beach and remained there for five to ten minutes. We circled overhead suppressing the tree-line while the gunner and crew chief scrambled from the Marine ship to help aid the four wounded on the ground. While exposed to enemy fire, the crew helped the wounded aboard and then departed.

In my opinion this was the most heroic action I have witnessed during my eight months in country. The Marine ship's crew did their utmost to save four Americans while under fire from the enemy nearly all the time. I highly recommend that this crew be properly rewarded for their unselfish act of heroism."

Chapter 3: Vietnam

/S/ Warrant Officer James P. Van Duzee

Note: Captain Fairfield, Gunnery Sergeant Poulson, and Lance Corporal Phelps each received the Navy Cross for the preceding action.

The President of the United States takes pleasure in presenting the MEDAL OF HONOR to:

MAJOR STEPHEN W. PLESS
UNITED STATES MARINE CORPS

for action as set forth in the following citation:

> *"For conspicuous gallantry and intrepidity at the risk of his life above and beyond the call of duty while serving as a helicopter gunship pilot attached to Marine Observation Squadron Six in action against enemy forces near Quang Ngai, Republic of Vietnam, on 19 August 1967. During an escort mission, Major (then Captain) Pless monitored an emergency call that four American soldiers stranded on a nearby beach, were being overwhelmed by a large Viet Cong force. Major Pless flew to the scene and found 30 to 50 enemy soldiers in the open. Some of the enemy were bayoneting and beating the downed Americans. Major Pless displayed exceptional airmanship as he launched a devastating attack against the enemy force, killing or wounding many of the enemy and driving the remainder back into the tree-line. His rocket and machine-gun attacks were made at such low levels that the aircraft flew through debris created by explosions from its rockets. Seeing one of the wounded soldiers gesture for assistance, he maneuvered his helicopter into a position between the wounded men and the enemy, providing a shield which permitted his crew to retrieve the wounded. During the rescue the enemy directed intense fire at the helicopter and rushed the aircraft again and again, closing to within a*

*few feet before being beaten back. When the wounded men
were aboard, Major Pless maneuvered the helicopter out
to sea. Before it became safely airborne, the overloaded
aircraft settled four times into the water. Displaying superb airmanship, he finally got the helicopter aloft. Major
Pless' extraordinary heroism coupled with his outstanding flying skill prevented the annihilation of the tiny force.
His courageous actions reflect great credit upon himself
and uphold the highest traditions of the Marine Corps and
the United States Naval Service."*

/S/ LYNDON B. JOHNSON

The President of the United States takes pleasure in presenting the SIL-
VER STAR MEDAL to:

CAPTAIN STEPHEN WESLEY PLESS
UNITED STATES MARINE CORPS

for action as set forth in the following citation:

*"For conspicuous gallantry and intrepidity in action while
serving as a pilot with Marine Observation Squadron Six,
Marine Aircraft Group Thirty-six, First Marine Aircraft
Wing in connection with operations against insurgent communist (Viet Cong) forces in the Republic of Vietnam during the period 2 to 4 June 1967. On 2 June, Captain Pless
launched as Section Leader of two UH-1E armed helicopters escorting five Marine CH-46 aircraft and nine Army
of the Republic of Vietnam UH-34 transport helicopters
assigned the mission of inserting a two platoon size force
deep within enemy controlled territory south of Khe Sanh.
The operation, in support of the U.S. Army Special Forces,
Special Operations Group, was conducted to assess the
damage of a large scale bombing attack. Throughout the
three-day operation, Captain Pless and his crew repeat-*

edly came under small-arms and automatic weapons fire as they determinedly provided supporting fire for the besieged ground troops which had been surrounded by a numerically superior enemy force. Returning to the insertion site on eight separate occasions and even though his aircraft received severe damage from enemy ground fire on three different passes over the hostile positions, he steadfastly continued to provide outstanding support. While making a low altitude ordnance run over the Viet Cong positions, an enemy round struck the aircraft's starboard rocket pod, causing the pod to burst into flames. In an attempt to jettison the pod, Captain Pless activated the electrical and manual release systems, however the pod failed to jettison. Displaying calm presence of mind, he maneuvered his aircraft in preparation for another attack heading and subsequently commenced his firing runs when the crew safely released the burning rockets from the helicopter. Despite severe thunderstorms over the target area and although several aircraft were downed by enemy fire, Captain Pless resolutely ignored the hazardous conditions to deliver effective suppressive fire on the Viet Cong emplacements. In addition, he assisted the tactical Air Controller (Airborne) and thoroughly briefed other helicopter and fixed-wing aircraft pilots on the disposition of enemy and friendly units as they arrived on station. In large measure due to his analysis and comprehensive knowledge of the tactical situation, he was instrumental in planning the extraction of friendly forces from the embattled area. During the retraction operation, Captain Pless led a five aircraft division of UH-1E helicopters into the fire-swept zone, utilizing the fire power of his aerial gunner after he had expended all of his ordnance on the enemy positions. By his determined fighting spirit, exceptional aeronautical ability and courageous actions despite seemingly insurmountable obstacles, Captain Pless contributed significantly to the successful accomplishment of the mission and upheld the highest traditions of the Marine Corps and the United States Naval Service."

For the President
/S/ V. H. KRULAK
Commanding General, Fleet Marine Force, Pacific

The President of the United States takes pleasure in presenting the DISTINGUISHED FLYING CROSS to:

MAJOR STEPHEN W. PLESS
UNITED STATES MARINE CORPS

for service as set forth in the following citation:

"For heroism and extraordinary achievement in aerial flight while serving as a Pilot with Marine Observation Squadron Six in the Republic of Vietnam. On 21 June 1967, Major (then Captain) Pless launched as the Flight Leader of a section of two aircraft assigned as armed escort for a medical evacuation and artillery lift mission in support of Special Landing Force Bravo. Completing his assigned mission, Major Pless diverted his flight to support a Marine outpost which was under intense enemy automatic weapons fire. Displaying exceptional aeronautical ability and professional skill, he quickly located the target and aggressively attacked the enemy positions. Repeatedly maneuvering his aircraft through the hostile ground fire, he delivered accurate rocket and machine-gun fire which resulted in the destruction of three enemy structures. Upon being informed of a critically wounded Marine at the outpost, Major Pless, exhibiting exemplary airmanship and bold initiative, skillfully maneuvered his aircraft to the Marine's position and successfully extracted the injured man despite constant enemy fire. His courageous action and resolute determination were instrumental in saving the

life of the Wounded Marine. Major Pless' courage, outstanding professionalism and selfless devotion to duty were in keeping with the highest traditions of the Marine Corps and the United States Naval Service."

For the President,
/S/ JOHN H. CHAFEE
Secretary of the Navy

The President of the United States takes pleasure in presenting the BRONZE STAR MEDAL to:

MAJOR STEPHEN W. PLESS
UNITED STATES MARINE CORPS

for service as set forth in the following citation:

"For meritorious service while serving as Officer in Charge of Detachment B, Sub-Unit One, First Air and Naval Gunfire Liaison Company and subsequently as Air Liaison Officer to the Second Brigade, Korean Marine Corps from 2 September 1966 to 10 March 1967. Throughout this period, Major (then Captain) Pless performed his demanding duties with outstanding initiative, exceptional professional skill, and resourcefulness. Demonstrating meticulous attention to detail and superior leadership, he skillfully planed and supervised the movement of his detachment from Hawaii to Vietnam. Upon the detachment's arrival in Vietnam, two previously deployed tactical air control parties were integrated into the detachment and the unit was attached to the Second Brigade, Korean Marine Corps. Immediately establishing liaison with the support unit, the detachment began functioning as an efficient team without delay. Realizing that the conventional organization of his unit would not satisfy the requirements of supporting the Korean Brigade, he effectively reorganized his

*unit which resulted in excellent support down to the pla-
toon level, thus enhancing the combat capabilities of the
support unit. As Air Liaison Officer, he organized a vastly
improved centralized brigade resupply system and directed
the training of personnel to ensure efficiency of operations.
The success of several large scale vertical assault operations and troop deployments as well as aerial support for
the brigade were a result of his superior planning ability,
keen perception in changing tactical situations and sound
judgment. Throughout, his professional knowledge and
initiative gained for him the respect of all who served with
him and contributed significantly to the accomplishment
of his unit's mission. Major Pless' inspiring leadership and
unwavering devotion to duty were in keeping with the highest traditions of the Marine Corps and the United States
Naval Service." The Combat "V" is authorized.*

*For the President,
/S/ JOHN H. CHAFEE
Secretary of the Navy*

• • •

Name: Colonel Jay R. (formerly Manuel S.) Vargas, USMC.

Biography: Revised May, 1984.
Colonel Vargas is the son of a Hispanic father and Italian mother, who
came to the United States in late 1917. He is one of four sons that has
served in the United States Armed Forces in time of war (Angelo-Iwo Jima,
WWII; Frank-Okinawa, WWII; Joseph-Korea; and Jay-Vietnam). Like
Colonel Vargas each of his brothers are decorated veterans of war.

He was born July 29, 1938 in Winslow, Arizona and attended high
school there, where he was a standout athlete, achieving All-State recognition in two sports. Attending Arizona State on an academic and athletic
scholarship, he graduated in 1962 with a B.S. Degree in Education. He has
completed his Master of Arts Degree with "Honors" at the U.S. Interna-

tional University, San Diego, California.

After completing the Basic School at Quantico, Virginia in June, 1963, he was assigned to the 1st Battalion, 5th Marines. He is also a graduate of the Amphibious Warfare School, the Command and Staff College, Quantico, Virginia and the National War College, Washington, D.C.

Colonel Vargas has served successfully as a Weapons and Rifle Platoon Commander; Rifle Company Executive Officer; three times as a Rifle Company Commander (two of which were in combat); S-3 Operations Officer; Recruit Depot Series Commander; Instructor, Staff Planning School, LFTCPAC; Headquarters Company Commander, 3rd Marine Division; Commanding Officer and Executive Officer, 3rd Reconnaissance Battalion, 3rd Marine Division; Aide-de-Camp to the Deputy Commanding General, Fleet Marine Force, Pacific; Marine Officer Instructor, NROTC Unit, University of New Mexico; Head, Operations Branch, Headquarters Marine Corps, Washington, D.C.; and as the Assistant Chief of Staff, G-4, 1st Marine Amphibious Force.

His decorations include: the Medal Of Honor, the Silver Star Medal, and Purple Heart with four Gold Stars in lieu of four more Purple Hearts.

Colonel Vargas is one of a few recipients in the United States to be awarded the American Academy of Achievement's "Golden Plate Award" presented to national leaders in all professional fields.

He has also received the National Collegiate Athletic Association's Commemorative Plaque presented by the United States Collegiate Athletic Directors and Coaches, in Houston, Texas, for excelling in collegiate athletics and having made a significant contribution to his country.

Colonel Vargas and his wife Dottie are the parents of three girls, Kris, Julie, and Gina.

-USMC-

The following are the *narrative summary of gallant conduct* for which Colonel Vargas received the Medal of Honor; thirteen eyewitness accounts; and the Medal of Honor and Silver Star Medal citations:

Narrative Summary of Gallant Conduct

At 1600 on 30 April 1968, an intense enemy artillery barrage commenced on the defensive perimeter of Golf Company, 2d Battalion, 4th Marines, located near the village of Lam Uan. At 1730, the company, commanded by Captain Vargas, was ordered to proceed by helicopter to the Battalion CP located at Mai Xa Chanh, in order to prepare to join in a heavy battle the following day involving BLT 2/4 and major elements of the 320th NVA division. The intensity of the artillery barrage increased as the helicopters arrived for lift-out. While constantly exposing himself to the deadly incoming rounds, Captain Vargas ran from unit to unit, organizing helo-teams and supervising the loading of equipment. Only the 81mm. mortars and a portion of the 2d Platoon were able to be placed aboard the helicopters before the barrage became so intense that the scheme had to be abandoned in favor of an overland route to the base camp. At 1925, as darkness was setting in, Captain Vargas organized and executed the withdrawal of his company from the landing zone by foot. During the march overland to the Battalion CP, Company G was subjected to increasingly heavy artillery and mortar fire. Over 1,000 rounds of incoming fell on the men that afternoon and evening. On several occasions, when elements or individuals became disorientated or lost in the darkness, Captain Vargas personally moved through the intense fire, issuing calm and clear orders, encouraging his men, and ensuring an orderly tactical withdrawal. He was wounded by shrapnel during this move, but ignored his wounds, refusing treatment in order to move up and down the column to ensure that his unit was intact. Captain Vargas' cool professionalism enabled Company G to arrive at the BLT CP with light casualties and the remainder of his night was spent organizing and preparing, to the most minute detail, for the planned assault the following day.

At 1040, 1 May 1968, Company G arrived by Mike Boat at a point "1" kilometer southeast of its objective – the village of Dai Do. Disembarking, Captain Vargas skillfully deployed his unit and moved forward across 700 meters of rice paddy, northwest to the objective. From the moment his unit hit the beach they were continuously bombarded with heavy artillery, rocket, and mortar fire. None-the-less, his skill and inspiration enabled the Company to cross the LOD as an effective combat force. Bravo Company 1/3, had made the beach landing in conjunction with Company G and was moving in support of the attack and on their left flank. In the movement toward the objective, this unit also came under intense enemy fire, resulting in the loss of the Company Commander and rendering the Platoon Commanders casualties. The individual that assumed Command of Company B at this point became hysterical on the radio net, expressing the desire to pull back in the face of the intense enemy fire. Captain Vargas broke in on the net, took control of the situation, and began talking the individual down to a level of rationalization. His encouragement brought the man to his senses. Captain Vargas then began issuing orders to the man who in turn responded to them effectively. As they approached the village, the Company came under heavy small-arms and automatic weapons fire from North Vietnamese forces in trench-lines and well fortified positions. Through clever use of artillery, smoke screen, and overhead machine-gun fire, Captain Vargas was able to gain a precious foothold in the first two hedge-rows marking the outer edge of the heavily fortified village. The assault, however, was stalled at this point as friendly casualties began to mount and as his left flank platoon became pinned down by the overwhelming firepower of the well-entrenched enemy. Assessing the situation immediately, Captain Vargas personally led his reserve platoon around to the left and to the aid of his beleaguered men. Swiftly and with calm resolve he led an assault which eliminated one weapons bunker after another, simultaneously guiding the movement of his right flank platoon, thereby keeping a steady pressure on the enemy, thereby enabling the assaulting units to move relentlessly forward. In the close fighting that ensued, Captain Vargas sustained wounds from grenade fragments. Once again completely ignoring them, he moved up and down the assault lines, inspiring his men to superhuman feats and maintaining the momentum of the attack. During this particular action, eight enemy soldiers fell dead at his own hand. Shortly after the objective was secured, the North Vietnamese launched a savage counterattack, and Captain Vargas ordered his men into a tight perimeter defense at the edge of the village. Wave upon wave of the counterattack was beaten off and Company G subsequently held its position after inflicting heavy casualties upon the enemy. Thereafter, throughout the night, the enemy continued heavy probes of the perimeter, but Captain Vargas' well-organized defense prevented any successful penetration. The Company, at this juncture, was isolated from the remaining units which were participating in the encounter. Company B, 1/3, had been ordered to come to their assistance, but was unable to penetrate the heavy enemy opposition, and was ordered to withdraw to a more secure area. Throughout the night, Captain Vargas surrounded himself with artillery fire to protect his small force of sixty-eight men. At times he called in artillery to within 50 meters of his own position. Not a single friendly casualty was taken during the night. The following morning, 2 May 1968, Company E linked up with Company G, and together with Company H in support, the village of Dai Do was again swept of the enemy which had reentered during the night. By 0800, Companies E and G were vigorously engaged with well-fortified North Vietnamese at the northern portion of the village. Heavy casualties were taken by the assault Companies, yet throughout the remainder of the morning they steadily advanced through the entrenched enemy with the assistance of artillery and close air support. By 1300, the village of Dinh To, to the north, had been secured, but a massive enemy counterattack forced the friendly units to pull back to the southern edge of Dai Do to reorganize and consolidate. At 1550, Company G, with an ineffective strength of only fifty-three, and together with Company F in support, spearheaded an attack once again through Dai Do, and on toward the villages of Dinh To and Thoun Do. With the attack in progress, a while Company G was still moving forward, the enemy launched a battalion-sized counterattack. A fierce and brutal hand-to-hand battle ensued. Captain Vargas, remaining in the thick of the battle, rallied his men and directed an orderly withdrawal back through Dai Do. Painfully wounded by shrapnel from an RPG rocket round – his third wound in as many days – he again refused treatment and continued to expose himself and coordinate the activity of those of his men still capable of fighting. Through his inspiration and example, his company fought savagely with grenades, small-arms, and bayonets to contain the enemy attack long enough to make a withdrawal, and to establish a hasty defense. Captain Vargas was everywhere – running 25 meters here, and under direct fire, to clear a jammed M-16 rifle, advancing another 50 meters there, to resupply a grenadier who had completely exhausted his M-79 rounds, and who was totally unarmed. When the Battalion Commander became seriously wounded during this engagement, Captain Vargas carried him to safety and returned to the scene of the fire fight to assist and direct his men. The majority of his Company now within the hastily established perimeter defense, Captain Vargas set about to assist the wounded still within the village. Each time he entered the village, now swarming with enemy troops, he was forced to fight his way in with hand grenades and small-arms fire. With complete disregard for his own personal safety, he made these trips repeatedly, shooting his way in, and carrying the wounded out. He personally accounted for seven enemy dead in this action and more significantly, saved at least as many lives. When all that was humanly possible to assist the wounded had been accomplished, and by now reeling from his own wounds, he still refused evacuation and remained behind to help organize the BLT perimeter defense. At 1130, reinforcements arrived from the Mai Xa Chanh base camp, and by darkness, the BLT maneuver elements had consolidated into a perimeter at the southern edge of Dai Do. The night was quiet and no significant contact with the enemy was experienced the following day. The three day encounter netted 805 enemy KIA. Friendly casualties were 72 KIA and 297 med-evacs. The facts contained in this account have been substantiated by eyewitnesses.

Statement of Witnesses

"On or about 1600 on the 30th of April our defensive perimeter at Lam Xuan West came under heavy and prolonged artillery attack. On or about 1800 of the same day we received the word to move out to the Battalion Base Camp. We were still under intense artillery fire. Captain Vargas displayed outstanding coolness and supervision in withdrawing the company. He acted quickly in getting the company out of the perimeter and down the river. The enemy artillery became more intense at this point. Without regard for personal safety Captain Vargas moved among the troops keeping total command and encouraging the troops.

At this time the artillery was falling among the exposed troops, wounding two or three. The troops were on the verge of panic but Captain Vargas kept good control of the situation and kept moving out for the river. It was his complete control and supervision that kept the troops from panicking or becoming demoralized. He displayed his complete control of the company by his ability to direct the company safely back to the Battalion perimeter while at night and under heavy enemy artillery fire.

On the 1st of May on or about 0900 the company deployed to launch an assault on the heavily defended village of Dai Do. The company came under heavy automatic and artillery fire almost immediately.

Our left flank became pinned down by extremely heavy and accurate small-arms fire. Captain Vargas again displayed his coolness and grasp of the situation by deploying the 1st Platoon to take the place of the pinned down flank and thus kept up pressure on the enemy to our front and flank.

Captain Vargas led the company through our objective and began to clear it of the enemy. The enemy was dug in and fighting to the last man. Captain Vargas deployed the company in such a manner as to retain complete control and keep maximum pressure on the enemy. He also made arrangements to med-evac the many wounded while in the middle of conducting the sweep thus saving the lives of at least two badly wounded troops.

At or about 1600 of the same day the enemy launch a heavy counterattack. The fighting became close and confused. Captain Vargas again regained control of the company displaying extreme coolness and disregard for personal safety. He pulled the company back to the southern edge of the village, under heavy attack, and set up a defensive perimeter. From this point the company successfully fought off the counterattack inflicting heavy casualties on the enemy. He ringed the small perimeter with artillery and set us in for the night, in a very tight company perimeter. All through the night we received heavy probes but successfully repulsed them inflicting heavy casualties.

The next morning we jumped off in the attack again with Echo on our left. Echo became pinned down by heavy fire but Captain Vargas kept the company moving and thus relieved pressure on Echo company.

Due to the extreme coolness of Captain Vargas while under fire, the company inflicted heavy losses on the enemy. His professional knowledge and employment made it possible for the company to secure the objective with maximum loss to the enemy and minimum loss to the company. It was to his complete grasp and control of the situation that the enemy was unable to launch a successful counterattack at any time during the battle.

His coolness and good moral was an example that kept the company in good fighting shape despite heavy casualties."

/S/ James T. Ferland

Chapter 3: Vietnam

"On the night of April 30th, 1968 Golf Company was ordered to draw back from their position at Lam Xaun West to the Battalion perimeter. The order had been given because earlier that day BLT 2/4 had become engaged in heavy combat at the hamlet of Dai Do. Golf Company began their withdrawal movement. The copters went in to evacuate excess ordnance when suddenly enemy artillery began pounding in upon them. Captain Vargas immediately organized and executed a small unit withdrawal to get the company out of the impact zone. Darkness fell rapidly and many were disoriented. Captain Vargas moved about showing the direction of withdrawal and aiding the casualties. After arriving at the Battalion Base Camp, Captain Vargas continued moving about until every man was accounted for. He then reported to Major Warren, the Battalion S-3, after which he received orders to regroup and prepare to move in support of the attack on Dai Do in the morning. All night Captain Vargas moved about giving orders, checking and double checking the most minute details in preparation for the mission to come. I was not personally with the Captain the following morning, but as S-3 Watch Officer, I was afforded the opportunity to monitor a significant event in which Captain Vargas exemplified the presence of mind and professionalism so characteristic of the extraordinary officer he is. Candy Tuff Bravo, Bravo 3/1, had made a beach landing. They immediately received a heavy volume of enemy fire resulting in the loss of their CO and wounding, I believe, all their platoon commanders. Candy Tuff Bravo regrouped and was to move in support of the attack on the left flank of Gulf Company. As Bravo Company began moving they again received heavy enemy fire. The individual in command of Candy Tuff Bravo became hysterical on the radio net. Captain Vargas broke in, took control of the situation, and began steadily talking the individual down to a level of rationalization. His encouragement brought the man to his senses. Captain Vargas then began issuing orders to the man who responded effectively. Throughout this episode Gulf Company had been heavily engaged with a numerically superior enemy and pinned down along with Bravo Company. For me to relate the other events illustrating the magnificent leadership traits of Captain Vargas, would be doing so from here-say of those who fought by his side. However, I'm sure accompanying statements will illustrate the type of Marine Officer Captain Vargas is."

Men of Honor

/S/ 1st Lieutenant Luther L. Lawson III

"On 30 April 1968, Company G was given the order to return to the BLT 2/4 Base Camp Area from Lam Xaun West and Nhi Ha. This was to be accomplished by helo-lift after all of Co. E's gear and 2 sections of 81's had been moved. When the helicopters began to arrive we started receiving incoming artillery rounds. The intensity of the incoming increased and we were only able to helo-lift part of the 81's, part of our 2nd Platoon and the gear we had staged at the LZ. Throughout the incoming, Captain Vargas ran from unit to unit organizing them into helo-teams and supervising the loading of our equipment. When the incoming became to intense to continue bring the helicopters into the LZ, Captain Vargas organized his units and issued the order to move out by foot. He moved fearlessly up and down the column insuring he had everyone. Darkness had fallen and the move was extremely difficult. Captain Vargas' professionalism and devotion to duty enabled him to bring his company back to the BLT 2/4 area with light casualties.

On 1 May 1968, Co. G was given the mission to attack the village of Dai Do. Shortly after crossing the LOD, Company G came under heavy small-arms and automatic weapons fire from NVA forces in trench lines and well-fortified positions. We started taking casualties and Captain Vargas, realizing the seriousness of the situation, rallied his men and continued to attack until the objective had been secured. Shortly after the objective had been secured the NVA commenced a savage counterattack. Captain Vargas with about 45 men pulled into a tight perimeter and repeatedly repulsed the enemy attacks. Company B, 1/3, was called upon to reinforce Co. G but they were unable to reach them because of the heavy fire and they withdrew to a more secure area. Captain Vargas again rallied his men. He supervised the redistribution of ammunition and organized a defensive position which enabled him to hold through the night. He surrounded himself with artillery and at times called it in to within 50 meters of his perimeter. The following morning Co.G was given the mission along with Co. E to continue the attack through Dai Do. Captain Vargas organized the now 68 remaining men in his company into a fighting unit and led then in the attack through Dai Do, then organized the consolidation of that position later that afternoon. Later, Co. G was given the mission to continue the attack to

274

the northwest. Captain Vargas moved his men out and shortly thereafter we encountered a numerically superior force of NVA. Captain Vargas immediately consolidated his position and began laying down a base of fire. When the intensity of the attack became more severe, Captain Vargas was ordered to withdraw to a more secure area. He then had his 3rd Platoon maintain a base of fire, while the remainder of his men commenced the withdrawal. While withdrawing, the CO of BLT 2/4 was seriously wounded. He immediately went to the Colonel's aid and assisted him back to the battalion area. Throughout the withdrawal, Captain Vargas exposed himself on numerous occasions to assist the wounded and to rally his men. After getting the Colonel back to an evacuation point, he again went back out to the men and carried one of them back so he could be med-evaced.

Throughout this 3-day period, Captain Vargas was instrumental in his units success. His outstanding leadership, calm presence of mind, unfaltering devotion to duty, and disregard for his own safety, were inspirational to all who observed him."

/S/ 1st Lieutenant Jack E. Deichman

On 1 May at approximately 1100 hours Company G began an assault on the village of Dai Do in northeast Quang Tri Province. Several casualties were taken but as a whole the casualties were light due to the expert maneuvering of our company upon the objective by Captain Vargas As we entered the ville, Captain Vargas directed the company to form a line to begin an east to west sweep of the entire village of Dai Do.

As we began the sweep we were hit by a barrage of 82mm. mortars, which resulted in 10 casualties, and a large volume of sniper fire t our direct front.

Our number having already been depleted, Captain Vargas ordered the company to fall back to a more secure position where cover and concealment could be had. From this position we took a quick count of ammunition. Realizing the company was quite low, Captain Vargas ordered a quick emergency resupply of ammunition and we set in a small but tight perimeter for the night.

Almost immediately the artillery FO began a large volume of rounds upon the ville that we had just pulled back to the southeast corner of. At the same time, Captain Vargas instructed the 1/4 to request a flare ship on station for the evening.

Another company, Company B 1/3, swept up relatively near to our position when their company commander was hit and had to be med-evaced. The next senior man was supposed to leave his company in position that night, and together we were to make a two company sweep at first light the next morning. However, the new commander of Company B was quite scared and wanted to pull his company back. Captain Vargas, using his coolness and tact talked to the frightened Company Commander and told him he had nothing to worry about although Captain Vargas knew quite well that there was a large force still in the ville of Dai Do and that we could very well have been counterattacked that night. Company B pulled back and Company G was relatively cut off from friendly support. Captain Vargas was at his best the remainder of the evening. He constantly encouraged the platoon commanders while at the same time kept a 100% watch all evening as flares landed as close as 100 meters away.

Captain Vargas had a quieting effect on Company G. He was respected to the highest degree in all of his words and deeds.

I might add that while the company was pulling back to set up its perimeter, Captain Vargas exposed himself to intense sniper fire by positioning himself with the forward most elements. He was dangerously close to Chi Com grenades and the accurate sniper fire.

Regardless of his own personal safety, the best place to get the close up view of a dangerously tense situation was on the front line and that's where Captain Vargas had a habit of positioning himself in order to encourage the men of his company. He was terribly dedicated and endangered his life on any number of occasions to search out the most tactically successful move for his company. I am honored to have served under him and feel certain he will provide the Marine Corps with many years of dedicated and devoted service."

/S/ 1st Lieutenant Frederick A. Morgan

"On the second of May, while under heavy small-arms fire, Captain Vargas pulled the company back to safety and while doing so, he helped the Battalion Commander back who was also wounded. Then when he had the men back to safety, he risked his life by going back and helping more of the wounded back to safety."

/S/ Corporal Kenneth L. Emery

"On 2 May 1968, Captain Vargas, while under direct fire, maneuvered approximately 25 meters to help clear a jammed M-16 rifle and immediately thereafter, advanced another 50 meters to resupply badly needed M-79 rounds to a grenadier who had completely exhausted his own rounds and was left completely unarmed."

/S/ Corporal Charles R. Pless

"On 1 May 1968, after Golf Company had made their initial entry into the village of Dai Do which was at the time, in the hands of NVA troops, I witnessed an act of the Commanding Officer of Golf Company, Captain Vargas, which definitely rallied the men of Golf Company and organized them effectively enough to stop a counterattack, which threatened to roll right over our position. This attack came directly after Captain Vargas personally assured that all WIA's and KIA's had been taken care of. Captain Vargas stuck with his men, keeping them organized and still combat effective, while calling in close artillery support, resupply, and evacuation of newly wounded Marines."

/S/ Lance Corporal Alan S. Horvath

"On May 2nd 1968, Golf Company, under the direction and Command of Captain Vargas started sweeping through the village of Dai Do. Captain Vargas was personally directing the forward movement of the company. In doing so he was always up front under direct fire. He was traveling from platoon to platoon making sure they moved together. It was not necessary for Captain Vargas to be up front, but he was, which showed the men he wasn't afraid to move forward which gave the men enough confidence to do the same. If Captain Vargas had not been up front personally directing the company's movement I am sure things would not have turned out as well as they did. Nor do I believe the company would have moved as well or done as good a job. I think he also saved a number of lives by being there."

/S/ Corporal Gregory J. Scott

On the second of May, the Captain helped Colonel Weise to the Battalion perimeter after he had been wounded. He then returned to the ville to try to get the other wounded out and had to fight his way back in by throwing grenades and shooting his way in. By my knowledge, with what I saw he was helping wounded out of the ville and when I was med-evaced, I saw him go in the ville for the third time. Without any doubt, I recommend Captain Vargas for the nation's highest medal, the Medal of Honor."

/S/ Pfc. John Costanzo

"Concerning the extraordinary bravery and outstanding leadership of Captain Vargas on the days of 2 May and 3 May, 1968, in the harsh battle of Dai Do, Vietnam. During the time that I was in the Village, I quite a few times saw Captain Vargas going back and forth, helping his wounded troops and at the same time, getting wounded himself. He, even while doing this, managed to keep our company moving and organized. His leadership was outstanding. He risked his own life to save the lives of his troops and also, to keep his company as a superior fighting force."

/S/ Pfc. Dickson L. Stoker IV

"On the second of May at the village of Dai Do, Captain Vargas was not only doing his job as Commanding Officer of Golf Company, he was doing anything and everything that anyone could do to save the lives of his men. It is hard to tell about any one thing that he did, because he did so much. If it hadn't been for Captain Vargas and his fast thinking, Colonel Weise might have died right there in the ville with the other men that never knew what happened that day. I think that Captain Vargas should receive the Medal of Honor for doing a job that I think no other man could have done."

Chapter 3: Vietnam

/S/ Pfc. Ronald E. Koffman

"On 30 April 1968, as a member of Golf Company 2/4, under the command of Captain Vargas, we were given an order to return to Camp Big John, our main perimeter. During the time of our evacuation from Lam Xaun West, we were under heavy enemy artillery barrages. Captain Vargas kept the entire company intact and made a strategic move towards Jones Creek to where the company moved swiftly out of the danger area. Captain Vargas kept in constant contact with the front and the rear of the movement and made sure that any casualties that were sustained, were well taken care of and in a safe area at all tames. During the night after returning to Big John, he received orders for the next days action. We moved by Mike Boats to an area near the ville of Dai Do, where we disembarked and moved to an area where Bravo Company 1/3 was located. After reaching the area, we were given the order to move across a vast open area toward the ville of Dai Do. Under Captain Vargas command, only a small number of Golf Company was able to reach the western end of the ville. Due to heavy sniper and automatic fire, the left flank was unable to reach their commander. As nightfall set in, the small party of 40 some men, including Captain Vargas, we received a vicious counterattack which made them move back to another area and set up a small perimeter. During the night, the might of the NVA, made several attempts to overrun the perimeter. Captain Vargas, realizing the dangerous situation they were in, his men being low on ammunition, exercised extreme caution with small-arms fire, allowing his men to shoot only at definite targets, which there were many of that night. Captain Vargas also used extremely close artillery protection to conserve ammunition. Not receiving a single casualty that night, the morning came with Echo Company moving across the rice paddies to join Golf Company in the ville and sweep the rest of the area, which was done. After securing the small ville by Golf and Echo Company, Golf Company was given the order to move and set up a blocking force for Fox Company who was sweeping west towards Dai Do. Fox Company received heavy casualties and was unable to complete the sweep, so Golf Company was ordered to begin sweeping through Dai Do. Still under the command of Captain Vargas, Golf Company began the sweep. We immediately started receiving heavy mortar, sniper, recoilless rifle and automatic fire. We continued to move through the ville until or flanks started trailing. Realizing this fact, Captain Vargas held for a moment for the flanks to catch up. The NVA apparently realizing the halt, immediately started a counterattack. Captain Vargas held his position in the front until we had received such heavy casualties and we were unable to sustain the huge force no longer. He was unable to organize a tactical retreat and would not leave the area until all wounded were moved to a secure area. Captain Vargas sustained several shrapnel wounds during this period but would not leave due to respect for his company and dedication to his men. He is a man of great intelligence and has a militaristic mind for making strategic maneuvers at the important times. For the extreme care he takes of his men and his attitude over this three day period and of the time I spent with the company, I recommend this man for the Medal of Honor."

/S/ Hospitalman Third Class Larry G. Martin

On 2 May 1968, Company G was reduced to a size of approximately 48 Marines while fighting a strong force in Dai Do. Sometime around the late afternoon, Golf Company along with the Battalion CP continued the attack into Dinh To. The company had a platoon (10 men approximately) on the left, a platoon (13 men) on the right and a reserve unit back. The Company CP was with the assault units and the Battalion CP behind them. I was assigned as the Battalion Commander's body guard.

As we swept through the ville of Dinh To, we received sporadic small-arms fire, but no serious resistance. About 75-100 meters further into the ville, the left flank came under intense small-arms and automatic weapons fire, sustaining several casualties and became pinned down. The reserve platoon, approximately 9 men, was brought up along the left flank to depress the enemy fire. During this engagement, we began to take small-arms, automatic weapons fire, RPG's and Chi Com grenades from our direct front and right.

Foxtrot Company, in reserve behind Company G, began to pull around to the right to attack the enemy from their flank. As soon as Company F moved into the rice paddies adjoining the ville, they were cut in half by several enemy machine-guns. Part of Fox remained in the ville behind

Company G, as the rest of Fox tried to their numerous wounded inside the ville to a place of relatively safe cover.

The enemy fire on the left flank momentarily depressed and Company G brought their wounded to a trench a few meters behind their point of advancement.

The enemy fire once again began, from the enemy counterattack, but more severe than the first engagement. Machine-gun rounds, RPG's, and grenades were exploding everywhere. The number of casualties increased tremendously, plus many KIA's.

At the same time, a machine-gun opened up on the right flank and swept through both command groups positions at this time. One company radioman was killed instantly and 2 seriously wounded. At this time, Captain Vargas cut off his radioman's radio and called in artillery to our front into the assaulting NVA forces. Captain Vargas threw his wounded radioman over the edge of the trench and told him to crawl towards the rear.

The Chi Com grenades and the RPG's increased in their number, and this time more on target. Numerous grenades landed along and in the trenchline we were in, although several failed to explode.

The action on the left flank increased, and approximately 12 NVA ran into the open. Captain Vargas turned instantly and stopped their advance with a full magazine from his M-16 on automatic. The majority of the advancing enemy went down wounded, and a few dispersed into the hedge line.

During this action the Battalion CO was wounded by a small-arms round. Captain Vargas dragged and threw the Battalion CO over an edge behind the trench, returned and continued to fire upon the advancing enemy. The Sergeant Major, realizing the left and right flanks were already moving back and the strength of the enemy's counterattack, yelled for Captain Vargas to pull back. Seconds later, a tremendous explosion in the trenchline wounded Captain Vargas and killed the Sergeant Major.

Captain Vargas, although seriously wounded, assisted the Battalion CO to a position of safety as he continued to fire into four advancing enemy at close range. During this same time I was dragging Sergeant Ballenger, the Battalion NCO radioman. The Battalion CO was aided further to the rear by the AO, Lieutenant Hilton and his radioman.

Captain Vargas returned into the advancing NVA continuing to fire his M-16, and aided remaining wounded survivors to the rear.

The NVA continued their counterattack another 80 meters, and then halted. A small force of NVA continued to fight our rear elements all the way to our earlier secured area.

I would have submitted a statement earlier to support his recommendation, although during the time statements were being collected I was not asked due to the fact I was reported as a KIA."

/S/ Corporal Gregg R. Kraus

The President of the United States takes pleasure in presenting the MEDAL OF HONOR to:

MAJOR MANUEL S. VARGAS
UNITED STATES MARINE CORPS

for action as set forth in the following citation:

"For conspicuous gallantry and intrepidity at the risk of his life above and beyond the call of duty while serving as commanding officer, Company G, in action against enemy forces from April 30, to May 2, 1968. On May 1, 1968, though suffering from wounds he had incurred while relocating his unit under heavy enemy fire the preceding day, Maj. Vargas combined Company G with two other companies and led his men in an attack on the fortified village of Dai Do. Exercising expert leadership, he maneuvered his marines across 700 meters of open rice paddy while under intense enemy mortar, rocket and artillery fire and obtained a foothold in two hedgerows on the enemy perimeter, only to have elements of his company become pinned down by the intense enemy fire. Leading his reserve platoon to the aid of his beleaguered men, Maj. Vargas inspired his men to renew their relentless advance, while destroying a number of enemy bunkers. Again wounded by grenade frag-

ments, he refused aid as he moved about the hazardous area reorganizing his unit into a strong defense perimeter at the edge of the village. Shortly after the objective was secured the enemy commenced a series of counterattacks and probes which lasted throughout the night but were unsuccessful as the gallant defenders of Company G stood firm in their hard-won enclave. Reinforced the following morning, the marines launched a renewed assault through Dai Do on the village of Dinh To, to which the enemy retaliated with a massive counterattack resulting in hand-to-hand combat. Maj. Vargas remained in the open, encouraging and rendering assistance to his marines when he was hit for the third time in the three day battle. Observing his battalion commander sustain a serious wound, he disregarded his excruciating pain, crossed the fire-swept area and carried his commander to a covered position, then resumed supervising and encouraging his men while simultaneously assisting in organizing the battalion's perimeter defense. His gallant actions uphold the highest traditions of the Marine Corps and the U.S. Naval Service."

The president of the United States takes pleasure in presenting the SILVER STAR MEDAL to:

CAPTAIN MANUEL S. VARGAS, JR.
UNITED STATES MARINE CORPS

for service as set forth in the following citation:

"For conspicuous gallantry and intrepidity in action while serving as Commanding Officer of Company G, Second Battalion, Fourth Marines, Ninth Marine Amphibious Brigade in connection with operations against the enemy in the Republic of Vietnam. On 18 March 1968, Captain Vargas' company was participating in a battalion assault against elements of three North Vietnamese Army battal-

ions in the heavily fortified village of Vinh Quan Thuong in Quang Tri Province. While two of the Marine rifle companies advanced on the objective from the east, Captain Vargas led his company, mounted on tanks and amphibian tractors, from the north to an assault position. As the column moved across more than a mile of rice paddies and sand dunes, it came under increasingly intense rocket, artillery and small-arms fire and three of the seven tracked vehicles stalled. Quickly directing his men to dismount, Captain Vargas led them on foot through heavy enemy fire to join the remaining elements of his company which had commenced the assault. Aggressively leading his men through intense fire, he penetrated the enemy's defensive lines, personally killing one hostile soldier as his unit advanced and engaged the North Vietnamese in close combat, often hand-to-hand fighting. As a result of his daring and heroic actions, the battalion seized the objective, killing 127 North Vietnamese soldiers and capturing four of the enemy. By his inspiring leadership, dauntless courage and unfaltering devotion to duty, Captain Vargas was instrumental in the accomplishment of his unit's mission and upheld the highest traditions of the Marine Corps and the United States Naval Service."

For the President,
/S/ V. H. KRULAK
Commanding General, Fleet Marine Force, Pacific

• • •

Name: Major General Ray Louis Smith, USMC.

Biography: Revised September 27, 1994.
Major General Ray L. Smith is the Assistant Chief of Staff, CJ-5, Combined Forces Command, United States Forces Korea.

Chapter 3: Vietnam

General Smith was born on March 13, 1946, in Shidler, Oklahoma. In December 1965 he enlisted in the Marine Corps and reported to the Marine Corps Recruit Depot, Dan Diego, California, in January 1966. He completed Officer Candidate School in March 1967 and The Basic School in August 1967.

Ordered to Vietnam upon completion of school, he served as a rifle platoon commander in Company A, 1st Battalion, 1st Marines, 1st Marine Division. Taking command of the company in Hue during the Tet Offensive in 1968, he commanded the company for the remaining nine months of his tour, seeing combat action in Hue, Khe Sanh, the Rockpile, Con Thien, and Dodge City south of DaNang. While overseas, he was promoted to First Lieutenant in April 1968.

Returning from overseas, he reported to Camp Pendleton, California, for duty as a platoon and company commander and as Aide de Camp in the 5th Division, before receiving orders to Vietnamese Language School. He was promoted to Captain in December 1970 and returned to Vietnam as an advisor with the Vietnamese Marine Corps from beginning to end of the Easter Offensive and counter offensive in 1972.

General Smith returned to Quantico in 1973 to attend the Amphibious Warfare School, then served as a Tactics Instructor at The Basic School. Ordered to Chicago, Illinois, in 1976, he served for two years as the Secretary of the General Staff at the U.S. Military Enlistment Processing Command. During this tour, he was promoted to Major in August 1977. He returned to Oklahoma State University to complete his B.A. degree in Asian studies (1979).

Completing the Armed Forces Staff College in 1980, he reported to the 2d Marine Division, Camp Lejeune, North Carolina. He served as Executive Officer, 2d Battalion, 8th Marines; S-3 and Executive Officer, 8th Marines; G-3 Operations of the Division; and Commanding Officer of the 2d Battalion, 8th Marines, and Battalion Landing Team 2/8. While commanding BLT 2/8, he led the BLT during operation Urgent Fury on Grenada, and on to Beirut, being the last BLT to leave Beirut airfield in February 1984. He was promoted to Lieutenant Colonel in October 1982.

From 1984 to 1985, he was a student at the Naval War College, Newport, Rhode Island. While there, he completed the requirements for a master's degree for International Relations. Following graduation, he reported to Headquarters Marine Corps, Washington, D.C., where he served for three years in Training and Operations assignments.

In May 1988, he assumed command of the 8th Marine Regiment and was promoted to Colonel in November 1988. Upon completion of his command in June 1990, he was ordered to the Joint Staff at the Pentagon where he served as Chief, Southeast Asia Branch, J5. While serving in this capacity, he was selected in December 1991 for promotion to Brigadier General. He was advanced to that grade on June 23, 1992, and assigned duty as Deputy Commanding General, Marine Corps Bases, Japan on July 24, 1992. On July 16, 1993, he was assigned as Commanding General of the Third Marine Division in Okinawa, Japan.

Selected in December 1993 for promotion to Major General, he advanced to that grade in June 1994 and assumed his current duties as Assistant Chief of Staff for plans and policy, U.S. Forces Korea and Combined Forces Command Korea.

His personal decorations include: the Navy Cross; Silver Star Medal with Gold Star; Legion of Merit with Gold Star; Bronze Star Medal; Purple Heart with two Gold Stars; the Defense Meritorious Service Medal with Oak Leaf Cluster; Navy Commendation Medal with Combat "V"; and the Combat Action Ribbon with two Gold Stars.

Major General Smith is married to the former Colleen Hendry of Silver Springs, Maryland. They have three sons: T.J., Ray, and Kevin and a daughter-in-law, Susan Marie, who is married to T.J.

USMC

The following are General Smith's Navy Cross and two Silver Star citations:

The President of the United States takes pleasure in presenting the NAVY CROSS to:

CAPTAIN RAY L. SMITH
UNITED STATES MARINE CORPS

for service as set forth in the following citation:

286

"For extraordinary heroism while serving as an advisor to a Vietnamese Command group numbering approximately 250 Vietnamese Marines located on a small hilltop outpost in the Republic of Vietnam during the period 30 March to 1 April 1972. With the Command Group repulsing several savage enemy assaults, and subjected to a continuing hail of fire from an attacking force estimated to be of two-battalion strength, Captain Smith repeatedly exposed himself to the heavy fire while directing friendly air support. When adverse weather conditions precluded further close air support, he attempted to lead the group, now reduced to only 28 Vietnamese Marines, to the safety of friendly lines. An enemy soldier opened fire on the Marines at the precise moment that they balked when encountering an outer defensive ring of barbed wire. Captain Smith returned accurate fire, disposing of the attacker, and then threw himself backwards on top of the booby-trap-infested wire barrier. Swiftly, the remaining Marines moved over the crushed wire, stepping on Captain Smith's prostrate body, until all had passed safely through the barrier. Although suffering several cuts and bruises, Captain Smith succeeded in leading the Marines to the safety of friendly lines. His great personal valor and unrelenting devotion to duty reflect the highest credit upon himself, the Marine Corps and the United States Naval Service."

/S/ SECRETARY OF THE NAVY

The President of the United States takes pleasure in presenting the SILVER STAR MEDAL to:

SECOND LIEUTENANT RAY LOUIS SMITH
UNITED STATES MARINE CORPS

for service as set forth in the following citation:

"For conspicuous gallantry and intrepidity in action while serving as Commanding Officer of Company A, First Battalion, First Marines, First Marine Division in connection with operations against the enemy in the Republic of Vietnam. On 4 February 1968, while participating in Operation Hue City, Second Lieutenant Smith's unit was assigned the mission of attacking and seizing a school complex occupied by an estimated battalion of North Vietnamese Regulars. As his company advanced toward its objective, the Marine came under intense automatic weapons, small-arms and B-40 rocket fire, pinning down the lead platoon. Reacting instantly, he aggressively maneuvered his remaining platoons forward and directed a heavy volume of fire against the entrenched enemy, suppressing the hostile fire sufficiently to allow his lead platoon to maneuver out of the hazardous area. Concerned with maintaining the momentum of the attack, he repeatedly exposed himself to the enemy fire to better direct the efforts and movements of his forces. Knocked to the ground on numerous occasions by the concussions from nearby explosions, he quickly regained his footing and continued to lead his most heavily engaged units. When it appeared that the assault was faltering, he skillfully employed a recoilless rifle team in addition to a demolition unit against the well-entrenched enemy, enabling his unit to move from one building to another in its relentless attack. His bold leadership and aggressive actions were an inspiration to all who observed him and contributed significantly to the accomplishment of his unit's mission. By his courage, steadfast determination and unwavering devotion to duty in the face of extreme personal danger, Second Lieutenant Smith upheld the highest traditions of the Marine Corps and of the United States Naval Service."

/S/ *V. H. KRULAK*
Commanding General, Fleet Marine Force, Pacific

Chapter 3: Vietnam

The President of the United States takes pleasure in presenting a GOLD STAR in lieu of a second SILVER STAR MEDAL to:

FIRST LIEUTENANT RAY L. SMITH
UNITED STATES MARINE CORPS

for service as set forth in the following citation:

"For conspicuous gallantry and intrepidity in action while serving as Commanding Officer of Company A, First Battalion, First Marines, First marine Division in connection with operations against the enemy in the Republic of Vietnam. On the night of 7 July 1968, Company A was assigned to assist in repulsing two North Vietnamese Army companies that had penetrated the battalion defensive perimeter on Hill 689 near the Khe Sanh Combat Base. Observing the intense enemy mortar and antitank rocket fire and realizing the seriousness of the situation, First Lieutenant Smith unhesitatingly led his men across 100 meters of fire-swept terrain to the beleaguered unit's positions. Ignoring the hostile rounds impacting near him, he skillfully deployed his platoons on line behind the containing forces and commenced his attack against the enemy. Although painfully wounded, First Lieutenant Smith fearlessly moved about the hazardous area shouting words of encouragement to his men and skillfully directing their fire against the North Vietnamese soldiers. With complete disregard for his own safety, he calmly coordinated the evacuation of casualties while resolutely leading his Marines in driving the enemy from the perimeter and subsequently reestablishing the battalion's defensive integrity. His bold initiative and heroic actions inspired all who served with him and were instrumental in the accomplishment of the dangerous mission. By his courage, aggressive leadership and steadfast devotion to duty in the face of great personal danger, First Lieutenant Smith upheld the highest tradi-

tions of the Marine Corps and of the United States Naval Service."

/S/ H. W. BUSE, JR.
Commanding General, Fleet Marine Force, Pacific

APPENDIX

SUMMARY

These thirty-eight men received, (not counting Air Medals, Presidential Citations, Battle Ribbons, Unit Citations etc., and medals from foreign governments), the amazing total of:

MEDAL OF HONOR	22
NAVY CROSS	40
SILVER STAR	34
LEGION OF MERIT	28
DFC	10
BRONZE STAR	17
PURPLE HEART	44
TOTAL	**195 MEDALS**

MILITARY MEDALS

MEDAL OF HONOR: The President may award, and present in the name of Congress, a Medal of Honor to a person who, while a member of the

Armed Forces, distinguished him self conspicuously by gallantry and intrepidity at the risk of his life above and beyond the call of duty.

NAVY CROSS: Second only to the Medal of Honor for Navy personnel, is awarded to Navy and Marine Corps and those attached to such units who distinguish themselves by extraordinary heroism in military operations against an armed enemy.

DISTINGUISHED SERVICE CROSS: Army award (see above).

DISTINGUISHED SERVICE MEDAL: Awarded to any person who, while serving in the Armed Forces in any capacity, shall have distinguished themselves by exceptionally meritorious service to the government in a duty of great responsibility. It may be awarded for combat or noncombat service.

SILVER STAR MEDAL: Awarded to any member of the Armed Forces for gallantry in action, not warranting the Medal of Honor or Navy Cross.

LEGION OF MERIT: Awarded to any member of the Armed Forces who have distinguished themselves by exceptionally meritorious conduct in the performance of outstanding services. If the award is for combat service it is shown by the wearing of a combat "V."

DISTINGUISHED FLYING CROSS: Awarded to any member of the Armed Forces who have distinguished themselves by heroism or extraordinary achievement while participating in an aerial flight.

BRONZE STAR MEDAL: Awarded a person in any branch of the military service who, while serving in any capacity with the Armed Forces of the United States, shall have distinguished themselves by heroic or meritorious achievement or service in connections with military operations against an armed enemy. If the award is for combat service it is shown by the wearing of a combat "V."

Appendix

PURPLE HEART: Awarded to any person wounded or next of kin to any person killed in action while serving with the Armed Forces of the United States. The Purple Heart is awarded for combat action only.

NAME INDEX

Also from the Publisher

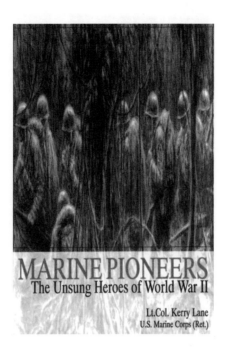

MARINE PIONEERS
The Unsung Heroes of World War II
Lt.Col. Kerry Lane (U.S. Marine Corps, Ret.)

Marine Pioneers: The Unsung Heroes of World War II is a personal history of a young Marine during World War II. This book tells a powerful story that has never been told before and documents a rare look into a "Pioneer Unit", integrated with an infantry unit in the First Marine Division. Kerry Lane, tells the riveting true story of his experiences as a Sergeant while serving with a Marine Pioneer Battalion during the Battle of Guadalcanal and the swamp battle known as "Suicide Creek" in the jungles of Cape Gloucester, New Britain. Assisted by the Marine Historical Canter and other Pioneers, Kerry Lane has gathered numerous battlefield stories, anecdotes, and experiences told by those who were there and who lived them. With his own battlefield experience providing an understanding of men in war, he has crafted an interesting book that tells those stories of marine pioneers in battle. Weaving these stories and vignettes together into the framework of the overall battle, this book honors the many marine pioneers, their companies and battalion, that contributed greatly to the victory that changed the course of the Pacific war.

Size: 6" x 9", over 100 b/w photographs, maps
272 pages, hard cover
ISBN: 0-7643-0227-2
$29.95

THE ADVISOR
The Phoenix Program in Vietnam
Lt.Col. John L. Cook (USA, Ret.)

From his arrival in war-torn Vietnam in 1968 to his reluctant departure twenty-five months later, John Cook served as an advisor in the district of Di An and took part in the systematic operations of the Phoenix Program to destroy the Infrastructure, the political organization of the Viet Cong and North Vietnamese forces. *The Advisor* is the story of those twenty-five months of fighting and laughing and hoping, and of the people who shared them – Major Chau, a man who so tremendously symbolized dedication to the destruction of the Infrastructure, that the Viet Cong made several attempts on his life; Lieutenant Hau, Cook's Vietnamese counterpart and close friend; Colonel Andersen and Major Allen, two of Di An's senior advisors; and other American and Vietnamese colleagues who – fighting a war at its "rice roots," rather than viewing it through myriad news analyses and peace demonstration demands – found it impossible to remain objective about such a conflict. More than the story of bombings, sweep operations, enemy confrontations, and hamlet pillages, *The Advisor* tells how one man came to see the Vietnam War as *his* war, how he became involved in the district villagers' struggle for their freedom from terrorism, and how he learned the true costs of that freedom.

Size: 6" x 9", 70 color and b/w photographs, 3 maps
352 pages, hard cover
ISBN: 0-7643-0137-3
$35.00

YEAR OF THE HORSE: VIETNAM
1st Air Cavalry in the Highlands 1965-1967
Colonel Kenneth D. Mertel (USA, Ret.)

This book is the day-by-day story of the Jumping Mustangs – 1st Battalion, Airborne, 8th Cavalry, of the 1st Air Cavalry Division, written by the man who knows them best, 1st Air Cav Lieutenant Colonel Kenneth Mertel. On 1 July 1965, at Fort Benning, Georgia, the 1st Air Cavalry Division was activated to employ newly developed techniques and tactics, providing the utmost in combat effectiveness and flexibility. After telling of the excitement at Benning over the formation of this revolutionary airmobile division, Colonel Mertel gives a vivid picture of the building of his own Jumping Mustang Battalion, the rigorous training of officers and men and, finally, the long voyage across the Pacific to Vietnam. Now the test. Would the new concept of airmobility, so painstakingly worked out stateside, produce the hoped-for results? The answer came quickly and dramatically in a rapid succession of search and destroy operations. Ia Drang . . . An Khe South . . . Plei Mei . . . the Cambodian border . . . Bong Son . . . Tarzan . . . In precipitous mountains, dense jungles, mud and water-filled rice paddies and expanses of view-obstructing elephant grass, the Jumping Mustangs sought out the enemy, engaging him in combat and stopping him in his tracks. Airmobility more than passed the test. Colonel Mertel pays tribute to the many acts of heroism of his men, who lived, worked and fought together in some of the world's most inhospitable conditions. He also writes movingly of those who never came back. In 1967 the President, at a White House ceremony, recognized the Division's success and valor by awarding it the Presidential Unit Citation for the action at Plei Mei. According to the Chinese calendar, 1966 was the "Year of the Horse." It was the "Year of the Horse" for the Jumping Mustangs in Vietnam.

Size: 6" x 9", 59 color photographs, 9 maps
384 pages, hard cover
ISBN: 0-7643-0138-1
$35.00

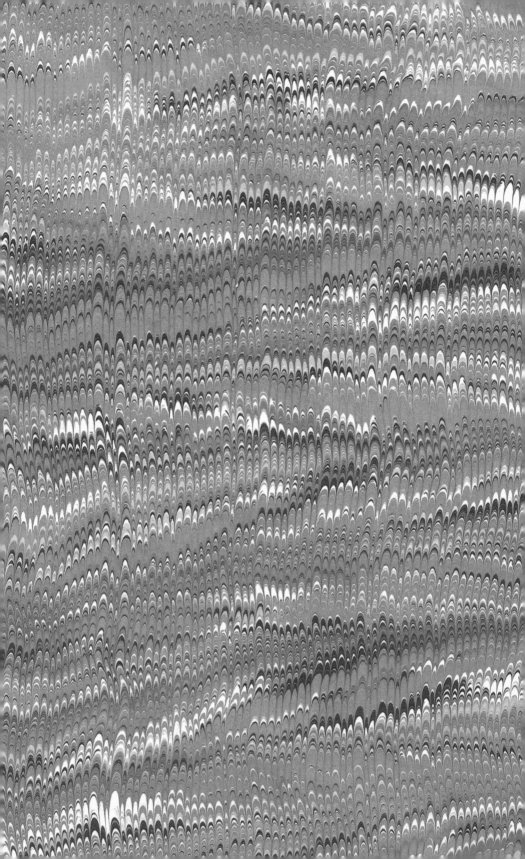